£ 11.16 0 T/ subs.pr.
(2 60S)

JOHN WARD · A SYSTEM OF ORATORY

Anglistica & Americana

A Series of Reprints Selected by
Bernhard Fabian, Edgar Mertner,
Karl Schneider and Marvin Spevack

24

1969

GEORG OLMS VERLAG
HILDESHEIM · NEW YORK

JOHN WARD

A System of Oratory

Delivered in a Course of Lectures Publicly read at Gresham College, London

(1759)

Vol. I

1969

GEORG OLMS VERLAG

HILDESHEIM · NEW YORK

Note

The present facsimile is reproduced from a copy
in the possession of the Library of the University
of Göttingen.
Shelfmark: 8 Ling. VIII 4755.

Certain imperfections in the reproduction (Vol. I,
pages 38, 149 and vol. II, page 44) are due to in-
sufficient inking in the original.

E. M.

Reprografischer Nachdruck der Ausgabe London 1759
Printed in Germany
Herstellung: Druckerei Lokay, 6101 Reinheim / Odw.
Best.-Nr. 5102 066

A

SYSTEM of ORATORY,

Delivered in a

COURSE of LECTURES

Publicly read at

GRESHAM COLLEGE,

L O N D O N.

In TWO VOLUMES.

A
SYSTEM of ORATORY,

Delivered in a

COURSE of LECTURES

Publicly read at

GRESHAM COLLEGE,
LONDON:

To which is prefixed

An INAUGURAL ORATION,
Spoken in Latin, before the Commencement
of the LECTURES, according to the usual
Custom.

By *JOHN WARD*, D.LL. P.R.G.C.
F.R. and A.SS. and T.B.M.

VOL. I.

LONDON:
Printed for JOHN WARD, in *Cornhill*, opposite
to the *Royal Exchange*.
M.DCC.LIX.

ADVERTISEMENT.

THE character of the author of this work, fo well known by his other learned and elaborate writings, would have been fufficient to have recommended it to the public, if he had thought proper to have printed it during his own life; which could not conveniently be done, as he was in the conftant ufe of it in his lectures. It will therefore be neceffary, for the fatisfaction of the reader, to take notice here, that it was the intention of the author, declared to feveral of his friends, and evident from the manufcript itfelf, to be feen at the bookfeller's, that thefe lectures fhould be publifhed : For which purpofe he caufed a fair copy of them to be tranfcribed, after he had from time to time revifed them with his ufual accuracy, during the fpace of thirty eight years, in which he moft punctually difcharged the duties of his Profefforfhip at Grefham College, having been elected into it on the 1ft of September 1720, and dying on the 17th of October 1758.

ADVERTISEMENT

THE
CONTENTS.

XV.

CONTENTS.

ORATIO,

O R A T I O,

Quam in COLLEGIO GRESHAMENSI, cum rhetorices praelegendae provinciam illic fufcepit, publice habuit

IOHANNES WARDVS,

v. kal. Nov. MDCCXX.

De Ufu et Praeftantia Artis Dicendi.

CUM mecum ipfe reputo, quo in loco, quantofque viros, qui hoc munus ante me peregerunt, fubfecutus, verba apud vos, AUDITORES DOCTISSIMI atque HUMANISSIMI, fum facturus, fine metu & tremore in confpectum veftrum prodire nequeo. Nam, ut in celeberrimo hoc et venerando Mufarum domicilio nihil proferre convenit, quod non fit cogitatione eximium, doctrinaque politum et elaboratum; ita, quam fim ab hujufmodi tam naturae, quam artis praefidiis imparatus, haud ignoro. Veruntamen, cum collegii hujufce curatores digniffimi hanc provinciam rhetorices praecepta tradendi mihi demandare dignati fint, duae res funt, quas

A   merito

merito a me expectari sentio : in primis, ut iis gratias agam, per quos in hunc locum devenerim; deinde ut, quod deest ingenio, cura et diligentia pro viribus compensare studeam : ne tantum beneficium in hominem vel ingratum, vel alio quovis modo eo prorsus indignum, collocatum fuisse unquam videatur. Atque ut harum alteram vere et ex animo meo jam facio, cujus gratissima memoria tam altis radicibus menti infixa adhaeret, quae nulla unquam temporis longinquitate evelli possit; sic alteram, quantum in me situm est, omni opera semper contendam.

In praesentia autem pauca de *usu* et *praestantia* rhetorices dicere constitui; unde et occasio sese offeret praecipuis conviciis et contumeliis, quibus injuste a quibusdam ars haec praestantissima petita fuerit, breviter respondendi. Nec aliud sane argumentum, quo praelectiones auspicarer, aut mihi, aut vobis magis convenire existimavi : nam, ut artem aliquam profitenti, eam nec inutilem, nec ignobilem esse, ostendere omnino congruit; ita dignam esse, cui operam et studium impendant, ex re auditorum est moneri. Caeterum, quo commodius id praestari possit, hanc veniam oro, ut benigne et attente me dicentem, ut facitis, audiatis.

ARTIS

ARTIS igitur *ufus*, ut ab illo incipiam, ex commoditatibus, quas homines exinde percipiant, praecipue aeftimari debet; quae fi et jucunditatem quoque fecum afferat, ita ut poetae illud *utile dulci*[1] ei recte tribuatur, nihil defiderari poteft, quo amorem et gratiam apud omnes conciliet; horum autem utrumque ars, de qua loquimur, merito fibi vindicare poteft. Etenim, cum viam rationemque tradat, qua quis apte, compofite, ornate, et copiofe de unaquaque re dicat, non, ut in aliis quibufdam artibus ac difciplinis res fe habet, ufus ejus certis locis et temporibus terminatur, fed femper fere et ubique prodeft ac delectat; quippe quae omni aetati et conditioni hominum conveniat, juventuti ac fenectae, foro et curiae, aulae et caftris pariter fe accommodans. Imo in quovis hominum coetu, communique vitae confuetudine, compto et eleganti orationis genere nihil gratius aut acceptius effe poteft. Res nimis longa et operofa effet fingula artis dicendi commoda enumerare, pauca igitur ex innumeris fere tetigiffe contenti erimus. Vis debitis laudibus virtutem efferre, aut vitii turpitudinem depingere ac vituperare? vis fummorum virorum gefta praeclara celebrare, aliifque ad imitandum exponere; contra vero nequam et impro-

[1] Horat. *De Art. Poet.v.*35.

borum

borum hominum perniciosa facinora in o-
dium et contemptum omnium adducere?
hanc artem cole. Vis alicui ad ea, quae
sibi, vel aliis sint utilia, persuadere; aut ab
iis, quae perniciem et ruinam afferant, de-
hortari? vis patriae de rebus seu belli, seu
pacis deliberanti opem ferre, et saluberrima
consilia ita proponere, ut alios in sententiam
tuam pertrahas? haec ars rationem praebe-
bit. Vis innocentem tueri, ac periculum a
capite ejus depellere; aut de scelerato ut
debita, et communi rei necessaria, sumatur
poena dicendo efficere? ex hac arte adju-
menta petas. In summa, omnia, quae ac-
commodata sunt ad id, quod volumus, per-
suadendum atque obtinendum, haec ars tradit et suppeditat. Quid, quod Protei ritu in
varias formas docta et artificiosa oratio se
convertit, quo, quod sibi velit, assequatur?
Alias enim ut rivulus parum profundus hu-
mili ac demisso sermonis genere humi repit;
alias pleni ac lenissimi fluminis more aequa-
bili cursu fertur ac dilabitur; alias vero quasi
torrens, magno aquarum confluxu turges-
cens, amplissima sententiarum gravitate, et
majestate verborum grandiloqua insurgit.
Jam in longas et circumductas periodos sese
profundit, mox incise et membratim rem
peragere instituit. Nunc docet, nunc quae-
rit;

rit; nunc reticet, nunc exclamat; nunc irritat, nunc demulcet; nunc orat, nunc minatur; quoquoverſum ſeſe commovens, quo in pectus eorum, quibuſcum agit, ſe inſinuet, et in partes ſuas perducat. Porro, ut homines bruta animantia duobus praecipue praeſtant, ratione nimirum et oratione, Cicero, artis hujus optimus aeſtimator, affirmare non dubitavit, *Eloqui copioſe, modo prudenter, melius eſſe, quam vel acutiſſime ſine eloquentia cogitare* [1]. Cujus rei illam quoque rationem ſubjungit: *Quod cogitatio in ſe ipſa vertitur; eloquentia complectitur eos, quibuſcum communitate juncti ſumus.* Qui in id igitur ſolum incumbit, ut mentis perceptiones accurate perpendat, et inter ſe comparet, unde rerum cognitionem obtineat, ſibi tantum ſapit; dum is, qui ſenſa animi clara et concinna oratione efferre ſtudeat, et ad utilitatem et delectationem hominum intelligentiam ſuam confert. Ideoque ad multa vitae officia homines aptos reddit dicendi peritia, ad quae alii prorſus ſunt inepti.

BENEFICIA ex hac arte percepta ſi exemplis eorum, qui ea claruerunt, oſtendere ſuſciperem, pene infinitus eſſem. Par illud celebratiſſimi nominis oratorum, Demoſthenem dico et Ciceronem, ut inſtitutum vitae, fortunam, et mortem quoque haud admo-

[1] *De Off. Lib.* i. *c.* 44.

dum

dum diffimilem habuerunt; fic illud gloriae
utrique convenit, quod non femel patriam
fuam in fummo periculo conftitutam dicendi facultate liberarunt. Quoties ille
aftutiam et fraudes Philippi, quibus liber-
tati Athenienfium infidiatus, eos in ditio-
nem fibi redigere conatus eft, indagavit,
patefecit, elufit? Pari arte et ingenio hic
omnes Catilinae machinationes, ad rem-
publicam Romanam evertendam deftinatas,
detexit, vim atque audaciam fregit, omnia-
que illius ac fociorum nefaria confilia in
auctorum perniciem convertit. Nec minori poftea laude infanas Antonii moli-
tiones diu coercuit et repreffit; donec tandem perfidia eorum, de quibus optime me-
ritus erat, in poteftatem ejus infidiofe tra-
deretur. At nequeo me continere, quin
illud de clariffimo hoc viro memorem, quo
et amicum de caufa capitali poftulatum li-
beravit, et vis fumma eloquentiae, fi alias
unquam, vel maxime enituit. Bello civili
inter Caefarem et Pompeium finito, fum-
maque rerum jam in Caefarem devoluta,
Quintus Ligarius accufatur a Q. Tuberone,
quod Caefaris partibus in Africa hoftis
fuiffet. Ligarii defenfionem Cicero fufci-
pit. Quod cum Caefar intellexit, Quidni,
inquit, Ciceronem orantem audiamus? reus

enim,

enim, cujus caufam agit, pro certo homo
improbus et hoftis eft. Sed cum Cicero
dicere ingreffus eft, oratio tam affectibus
varia et venuftate admirabilis videbatur,
ut Caefaris animum mirifice affecerit, quod
primum incerto vultu, crebraque coloris
mutatione oftendit; poftea vero tantis per-
turbationibus incitatus eft, ut toto corpore
contremefcens libellos quofdam e manu
dimiferit. Caufam igitur obtinuit Cicero,
ac Ligarius crimine liberatus eft [1]. Ita
tot gentium domitor vi eloquentiae fupe-
ratur; et qui per totum fere terrarum orbem victricia arma circumtulerat, armis
potentioribus ipfe tandem devincitur. Mi-
randa fane victoria! in qua togae arma
ceffiffe veriffime Cicero gloriari poffit. Cum
arte igitur militari dicendi facultatem nonnulli conferentes, cui potiffimum palma
tribui debeat, in dubio reliquerunt. Sin
autem caetera pares habeantur, in illis certe
haud parum inter fe difcrepant; quod haec
fine vulnere aut laefione aliqua victoriam
reportat, illa non fine caede et fanguine;
haec volentes captivos ducit et retinet, illa
invitos; haec animos, illa corpora tantum
devincit.

Ex iis autem, quae de ufu rhetorices
hactenus dicta funt, cum et *praeftantia* ejus

[1] Plut. *in vit. Cicer.*

A 4   magna

magna ex parte intelligi poſſit, pauciora de illa dicere opus eſſe videtur. Si rem autem recte perpendamus, quid pulchrius eſſe poteſt, quam ea in re alios excellere, qua homines praecipuo quodam modo bruta animalia excellunt? Quid praeclarius, quam de re quacunque ita dicendo valere, ut non modo auditorum aures demulceas, ſed animos etiam ſumma voluptate perfundas? Quid laudabilius, quam in rebus arduis et difficilibus ſaluberrima conſilia ita proponere, ut ad ea amplectenda homines facile adduci poſſint? Etenim eam vim animis noſtris inſevit natura, ut non modo apta et concinna oratione delectemur, ſed etiam variis exinde motibus concitati huc illuc pro voluntate dicentis ſaepe impellamur. Quanti igitur aeſtimari debet, regnare quodammodo ac dominari in aliorum animis; flectere eos linguae gubernaculo, quo velis; et quid probent, quid rejiciant, quaſi pro imperio ac poteſtate praeſcribere? Egregia ſane res, et digna, quam omni ſtudio et animi contentione confectemur! Itaque non ſine cauſa *flexanimam, atque omnium reginam rerum*, orationem vetus poeta appellavit [1].

At dicet forſan aliquis, homines vi ac pondere rationum, non affectuum impulſu

et

[1] Cic. *De Orat.* Lib. ii. c. 44. *Pacuvio tribuit* Nonius.

et concitatione ad aliquid vel amplexandum vel fugiendum moveri oportere. Bene profecto cum rebus humanis ageretur, fi ita revera effet. Sed quis non quotidiana experientia edoctus plane fentit, plerofque homines aut rationum momenta faepiffime non percipere ; aut fi percipiant, nefcio qua mentis pertinacia et obftinatione ad agendum, prout res poftulent, nullo modo induci poffe, donec affectuum motu incitentur ? Conftet igitur arti praeftantiffimae laus fua et dignitas, ad humani generis imbecillitati opitulandum natae, quae in eo, quo jam res funt ftatu, non modo utilis, fed omnino neceffaria effe manifefto apparet.

Cum tot igitur tantaeque fint artis dicendi virtutes, non mirum eft eam plerofque homines omni aetate in amorem fui et admirationem rapuiffe. Sed ita natura comparatum eft, ut pro variis ac diverfis hominum ingeniis alia aliis placeant, et delectent. Non defuerunt igitur, qui ex artium choro rhetoricen excludere voluerint, ufum modo et exercitationem artis expertem effe dicentes. In hunc autem errorem ex Platonis fententia male intellecta nonnulli olim inciderunt. Nam quae fummus ille philofophus contra fophiftas dixerat,

4

dixerat, qui fictam tantum et fimulatam artis fpeciem adhibebant; illos in artem ipfam perperam detorfiffe oftendit Fabius [1]. Ariftoteles etiam, Platonis difcipulus, in veftibulo operis fui *De arte dicendi,* quae arti fint propria rhetoricae ac dialecticae ex aequo convenire demonftrat. Et profecto quid in fe continet dialectica, cujus caufa artis nomen fibi affumat, quod rhetoricae quoque haud pari jure conveniat? Inveniendi locos, unde quid cuique argumento proprium fit et congruens petantur, docet? Idem facit et rhetorica. Difponendi etiam quae inventa fint, regulas tradit? Tradit et rhetorica. Syllogifmos et inductiones ad fidem faciendam adhibet? Enthymematis et exemplis, nec minori arte, nec felicitate, contendit rhetorica. Pari igitur paffu, ut videmus, hactenus incedunt. In eo autem differunt, quod illa nudis et apertis vocibus, quae ad rem explicandam fufficiant, tantummodo utitur; haec autem pro varia argumenti natura nunc hoc, nunc illud dicendi genus, omnibus verborum luminibus adjunctis, fuo jure adfcifcit. Non infacete igitur Zeno dialecticam *manui claufae,* rhetoricam vero *expanfae* et *dilatatae* comparaffe dicitur [2]. Ni quis forfan illam corporis alicujus offibus inter fe compagibus

[1] *Inft. orat. Lib.* ii. *c.* 15.

[2] Cic. *De fin. Lib.* ii. *c.* 6.

pagibus vinctis et colligatis ; hanc vero eidem corpori carne vestito, nervis instructo, succo et sanguine pleno, quo et aspectu sit gratius, vitaeque functionibus accommodatius, conferre malit. Sed de hac re pluribus dicendi locus alias dabitur.

CAETERUM levis haec videri possit accusatio prae alia quorundam criminatione, qui rhetoricen non modo non esse utilem, sed etiam perniciosam et pestiferam affirmare non dubitarunt. Et hanc etiam infamiam arti suae conflaverunt sophistae, dum inepte satis & arroganter se docere jactarent, quo modo causa inferior dicendo superior posset evadere ; quod non minus ridicule, quam invidiose, ipsi Socrati affingere studuit Aristophanes [1]. Sed istam reprehensionem acutissime refutat Aristoteles, quae mala vulgo ex ea fluere putarentur, illa non arti adscribenda, sed eorum improbitati, qui re per se bona & utilissima ad homines decipiendos abuterentur, docens [2]. Nam quod multa incommoda afferre possit, qui injuste utatur hac dicendi facultate, id in omnibus bonorum generibus, virtute sola excepta, commune esse ostendit; et in iis potissimum bonis, quae maximas habent utilitates, ut in robore, sanitate, divitiis, scientia militari. Quis autem

[1] *In Nub.*

[2] *Rhet. Lib.* i. *c.* 1.

autem fanus divitias unquam contempfit,
feu comparare noluit, quod non pauci vel
ad luxum, vel injuftam dominationem iis
fint abufi? Aut quis militarem artem ne-
gligendam ftatuit, quod illo propofito nonnulli ea fe exercuerint, quo alios facilius
aggrederentur, et in poteftatem fuam redi-
gerent? Ex contrario certe, quo magis ars
aliqua in ufum et commodum humani generis excogitata, nefariorum hominum vitio
in peftem et ruinam illorum traducitur, eo
diligentius ab aliis excoli oportet, quo le-
viori negotio fceleftis eorum confiliis ob-
fiftere poffint. Nec melius faepe aliquis fe
defendere poteft, quam eodem armorum
genere, quo ab alio petitur.

QUANTA igitur fit artis dicendi utilitas,
quanta praeftantia, paucis explicui; pro argumenti quidem dignitate breviter nimis
et angufte fateor, ut noftrum tamen tulit
ingenium. Nec in alia re magis fumma
vis ac facultas eloquendi requiritur, quam
fi de ipfa eloquentia quis dicere inftituat.
Praeterea aliud eft artis praeceptiones tra-
dere, aliud ufu et confuetudine cum laude
exercere. Nam et architectus effe poteft,
qui non aedificat; neque eos ipfa fecat.
Quin et egenus, licet opibus ipfe carens, ad
argenti et auri divites venas alios dirigere
poteft,

poteſt, rationemque docere, qua pretioſum metallum effodiant. Muneri igitur noſtro ſatis me faċturum credam, ſi eas rationes indicem, et quaſi digitum ad fontes intendam, quibus facillime ad eloquentiam perveniri poſſe arbitror. Nulla autem rhetorum pracepta ſine aſſidua et conſtanti exercitatione ad ſolidam, et accuratam dicendi facultatem comparandam ſufficere poſſunt. Non enim ex inani verborum copia, figuratis locutionibus, et periodis apte ac numeroſe cadentibus, ea tota conficitur, ut perperam nonnulli exiſtimaſſe videntur; ſed rerum quoque multarum perceptionem, ſententiarumque gravitatem deſiderat. Omnium itaque diſciplinarum cognitionem Craſſus in oratore requirit [1]. Item oratorum principi *eloquentia nihil aliud eſt, quam copioſe loquens ſapientia* [2]. Et profeċto is ingenuarum artium eſt conſenſus, ut vinculo quodam inter ſe connexae ſint, et mutuo operas praeſtent; nulla vero ea, de qua agimus, potiori jure ex aliis, quae ſibi ſint uſui, deſumit, utpote qua reliquae omnes viciſſim adornatae, et pulchriores et jucundiores fiant.

QUAE cum ita ſint, clariſſimi hujus collegii fundatoris, equeſtris dignitatis viri, Thomae Greſham, prudentiſſimum conſilium

[1] Cic. *De Orat. Lib.* i. *c.* 16.
[2] *Orat. Partit. c.* 23.

huıo omnes bonarum literarum amatores
fine dubio magnopere approbabunt; cui inter caeteras liberales artes et fcientias, quas
hic doceri voluit, etiam rhetorice locum
conftitui placuit. Is enim, ut vir fuit optimus, bonique publici ftudiofiffimus, nihil
antiquius habuiffe videtur; quam ut opes et
divitiae, quibus adeo abundabat, in civium
fuorum commodum impendi poffent. Ideoque cum longo rerum ufu, ac multarum
regionum peragratione bene intelligeret,
quanti res fit momenti honeftas artes publice doceri, quibus hominum mentes ad
virtutem ac debita inter fe officia praeftanda
effingi poffint; in iftum finem ampliffimas
has aedes, quas ipfe habitaverat, Mufis di-
cari juffit. Et hoc quidem egregio confilio
fecit, cum nec ille habuerit, a quibus fibi
fuceedi magis conveniret, nec hae, cui melius fuccederent. In commerciis autem
hominum, et affidua inter fe confuetudine,
cum ars dicendi tanti fit ufus, certe in hac
nobiliffima, et frequentiffima civitate haud
injuria inter caeteras forores ejus locum fibi
vindicare potuit. Igitur hunc ei denegare
noluit vir ille ornatiffimus, fed inter reliquas
accepit; quo nimirum cives vel cum exte-
ris, qui ad hoc per totum terrarum orbem
celeberrimum emporium perpetuo conflu-
unt;

unt; vel inter se de quocunque negotiorum
genere promptius et accuratius differere pos-
sent. Neque hac profecto in re a veterum
sapientia decessit, qui eundem Mercurium
et eloquentiae et mercaturae deum esse
finxerunt; seu, quod eloquentia ad opes ac-
quirendas viam paret, in quem finem et
mercatura praecipue instituitur, unde et
deus quoque divitiarum Mercurius habeba-
tur [1]; seu quod opulentis hominibus, ut
cultus et apparatus, ita et sermonis genus
elegantius, quam aliis conveniat; seu deni-
que, quod fluens et expedita oratio ad con-
tractus et negotia expedienda plurimum
conferat. Sed ut fabulas mittamus, ita usu
evenisse comperimus, ut bene institutae ci-
vitates parem fere sermonis ac morum ex-
colendi curam plerumque habuerint.

 AMPLISSIMUS hic in viri illustrissimi
laudes excurrendi campus sese aperit, qui
de utraque re civibus suis tam sapienter
prospexerit; sed neque ratio, neque limites
instituti nostri, id jam suscipere permittunt.
De argumento enim tam nobili et copioso
prorsus silere quam leviter tangere, omnino
consultius esse duximus. Interim tamen
posteritatem tanta beneficia, et tam eximium in rem literariam munificentiae ex-
emplum, perpetuo gratissima memoria pro-
secuturam

[1] Phurnut.
*De nat.
deor.*
c. 16.

secuturam nequaquam dubitare licet. Is enim in omnium mentibus, qui ulla bonarum artium cura tanguntur, monumentum quovis aere perennius pro certo sibi conftituit.

Ad vos igitur, AUDITORES CANDIDISSIMI, se convertit oratio, qui tanta patientia me audire dignati estis. Praecipue autem vobis, curatores digniffimi, doctiffimique profeffores, maximae grates sunt habendae, quod praesentia vestra me cohoneftare voluiftis. Caeterum, quod omnes tam faciles aures mihi praebuiftis, veftrae potius benevolentiae, quam noftrae dicendi facultati tribuerim. Sed in laetum omen accipiam, quae in posterum de ipsa dicendi arte traditurus sim, vos pari favore accepturos, quo nihil aut dulcius, aut exoptatius, mihi poterit accidere. DIXI

A

A
SYSTEM of ORATORY

READ AT

GRESHAM COLLEGE.

LECTURE I.
Of the Rise and Progress of Oratory.

WE commonly find, that persons L E C T. I. of an ingenuous temper are very desirous to know their benefactors. And certainly those, who have imployed their time to invent or cultivate any part of useful knowledge, ought to be esteemed as such, and remembred with honor and gratitude. For which reason, having indeavoured to shew the *use and excellence* of oratory [1], I shall enter upon these lectures by inquiring into its *rise and gradual improvements* in different ages; from whence it will appear, to whom we are cheifly indebted for the many and great advantages arising from this art. And

[1] In the *inaugural oration.*

in doing this I shall confine myself to rhetoricians, that is, those who either taught
the art, or at least have writen upon it.
Nor will it be necessary, I should mention
all of them; but such only, who have been
most celebrated on either of these accounts.
And as to orators, or those who practised
this art, they, who are desirous to be acquainted with their history, may peruse
Cicero's treatise *Of famous orators*; and the
Dialogue concerning the causes of corrupt elo-
quence, which some ascribe to Tacitus, and
others to Quintilian.

THE invention of oratory is by the Egyp-
tians, and fables of the poets, ascribed to
Mercury. And it is well known, that the
Greeks made their deities the authors likewise of other arts, and supposed that they
presided over them. Hence they gave
Mercury the titles of Λόγι⊙ and Ἑρμῆς,
both which names come from words that
signify to speak. And Aristides calls eloquence *the gift of Mercury* [1]. And for the
same reason antiently the tongue was con-
secrated to him [2]. He was likewise said to
be the interpreter or messenger of the gods;
which office very well suited him, as he
excelled in eloquence. Hence we read in
the Sacred Writings, that when the people

[1] *Platonica secunda.*

[2] Athe-
naeus, *l.* 1.
c. 14.
Phurnutus
De nat.
deorum,
c. 16.

of

of Lyſtra took Barnabas and Paul for gods in human ſhape, becauſe of that ſudden and ſurprizing cure, which was wrought upon the lame man, they called Barnabas *Jupiter,* and Paul *Mercury;* for this reaſon, as the inſpired writer tells us, *becauſe he was the cheif ſpeaker* [1], that is (as the ſpectators then thought) the interpreter or ſpokeſman of Barnabas. [1] *Aᵭs* xiv. 12.

BUT to paſs over theſe fictions of the heathen deities, let us hear what Quintilian ſais of the *origin* of this art; who ſeems to give a very probable account of it in the following paſſage. *The faculty of ſpeech,* ſais he, *we derive from nature, but the art from obſervation. For as in phyſic men by ſeeing that ſome things promote health, and others deſtroy it, formed the art upon thoſe obſervations; in like manner by perceiving that ſome things in diſcourſe are ſaid to advantage, and others not, they accordingly marked thoſe things, in order to imitate the one, and avoid the other. They alſo added ſome things from their own reaſon and judgement, which being confirmed by uſe, they began to teach others, what they knew themſelves* [2]. But no certain account can be given when, or by whom, this method of obſervation firſt began to take place. And [2] *Inſt. Orat. L.* iii. c. 2.

Ariſtotle

Aristotle supposes, not without reason, that the first lineaments of the art were very rude and imperfect ¹. Pausanias indeed in his *Description of Greece* tells us, that Pittheus the uncle of Theseus, taught it at Trezene a city of Peloponnesus, and wrote a book concerning it; which he read himself, as it was published by one of Epidau-

rus ². But as Pittheus lived above a thousand years before Pausanias, who flourished in the time of the emperour Hadrian, some are of opinion he might be imposed upon by the Epidaurian, who published this book under the name of Pittheus. But be that as it will, it is very reasonable to beleive, that the Greeks had the principles of this art so early, as the time of Pittheus. For Theseus his nephew lived not long before the taking of Troy, which, according to Sir Isaac Newton, happened nine hundred and four years before the birth of Christ; at which time Cicero thought it was in much esteem among them. *Homer,* sais he, *would never have given Ulysses and Nestor in the Trojan wars so great commendations on account of their speeches (to one of whom he attributes force, and to the other sweetness of expression) if eloquence had not in those*

times been in great repute ³. And lest any

one

one fhould imagine, that in thofe days they made ufe only of fuch helps, as nature and practice could afford them; the fame poet informs us, that Peleus fent Phenix with his fon Achilles to the Trojan war, to inftruct him not only in the art of war, but likewife of eloquence [1]. But who [1] *Iliad. α.* were the profeffors of this art for fome 443. ages following is not known. For Quintilian fais, that afterwards Empedocles is the firft upon record, who attempted any thing concerning it [2]. And he, by Sir Ifaac [2] *Inft. orat.* Newton's account, flourifhed about five *Lib.* iii. *c.* 1. hundred years after Troy was taken. At which time, as Cicero obferves, men being now fenfible of the powerful charms of oratory, and the influence it had upon the mind, there immediately arofe feveral mafters of it [3]; the cheif of whom are men- [3] *De clar.* tioned by Quintilian, who tells us, that: *orat. c.* 8. *The oldeft writers upon this art are Corax and Tifias, both of Sicily. After them came Gorgias of Leontium in the fame ifland, who is faid to have been the fcholar of Empedocles, and by reafon of his great age (for he lived to be an hundred and nine years old) had many contemporaries. Thrafymachus of Calcedon, Prodicus of Cea, Protagoras of Abdera, Hippias of Elis, and Alcidamus of Elea lived*

B 3 *in*

LECT
I.

*in his time, as likewise Antiphon, who first
wrote orations* [1], *and also upon the art, and
is said to have spoken admirably well in his
own defence; and besides these Polycrates, and
Theodore of Byzantium* [2]. Thus far Quintilian. These persons contributed different
ways towards the improvement of the art.
Corax and Tisias gave rules for methodi-
zing a discourse and adjusting its particular
parts* [3]; as may be conjectured from Cicero's
account of them, who sais : *Tho some had
spoke well before their time, yet none with
order and method* [4]. But Gorgias seems to
have excelled all the rest in fame and reputation; for he was so highly applauded
by all Greece, that a golden statue was
erected to him at Delphos, which was a
distinguishing honour conferred upon him
only [5]. And he is said to have been so
great a master of oratory, that in a public
assembly he would undertake to declaim
immediately upon any subject proposed to
him [6]. He wrote, as Cicero informs us,
in the demonstrative or laudatory way [7];
which requires most of the sublime, and
makes what Diodorus Siculus sais of him
the more probable, that, *He first introduced
the strongest figures, members of periods opposite in sense, of an equal length, or ending
with*

[1] See Voss
De nat.
rhetor.
p. 73.

[2] *Inst. orat.
Lib.* iii.
c. 1.

[3] See Tur-
neb. *ad
dict. Fabii
loc.*

[4] *De clar.
orat. c.*12.

[5] Id. *De
orat. L.*iii.
c 32.

[6] *Ib. lib.* 1.
c. 22.

[7] *De clar.
orat. c.*12.

with a like found, and other ornaments of
that nature [1]. And hence those figures,
which give the greatest force and lustre to
a discourse, were antiently called by his
name [2]. Cicero tells us further, that Thra-
symachus and Gorgias were the first, who
introduced numbers into profe, which Ifocrates afterwards brought to perfection [3].
Quintilian likewife mentions Protagoras,
Gorgias, Prodicus, and Thrafymachus, as
the first, who treated of common places,
and shewed the ufe of them for the invention of arguments [4]. Nor must we omit
Plato, whose elegant dialogue upon this
subject is still extant, which he entitles
Gorgias. For tho he does not lay down
the common rules of the art; yet he very
well explains the nature of it, and main-
tains its true end and ufe against the generality of its profeffors, who had greatly
perverted the original defign of it. Thus
by the study and induftry of fo many in-
genious and great men the art of oratory
was then carried to a confiderable height
among the Grecians. Tho many of thofe,
who profeffed it in thofe times, imployed
their skill rather to promote their own reputation and applaufe, than to ferve the
real interefts of truth and virtue. For *they*

[1] Voff. *De
natura
rhetor.*
p. 70.
[2] Dion.
Halicarn.
*Ep. ad
Pomp.*
[3] *Orat.
c.* 13, 52.

[4]*Inft. orat.
Lib.* iii.
c. 1.

propofed

LECT.
I.
proposed in an arrogant manner (as Cicero

¹ De clar. orat. c. 8.
fais) *to teach how a bad cause might be so managed, as to get the better of a good one* ¹.

That is, they would undertake to charm the ears, and strike the passions of their hearers in so powerful a manner, by sophistical reasonings, turns of wit, and fine language, as to impose falsehood upon them for truth ; than which nothing could be either more disingenuous in itself, or prejudicial to society.

BUT those, who succeded them, seem to have consulted better, both for their own honor, and that of their profession. Isocrates was the most renowned of all Gorgias his scholars, whom Cicero frequently extols with the highest commendations, as the greatest master and teacher of oratory; *Whose school*, as he fais, *like the Trojan horse,*

² De orat. Lib. ii. c. 22.
sent forth abundance of great men ². Aristotle was cheifly induced to ingage in this province from an emulation of his glory ; and would often say in a verse of Sophocles, somewhat varied to his purpose,

> *To be silent it is a shame,*
> *While Isocrates gets such fame* ³.

³ Cic. De orat. L. iii. c. 35. Quint Inst. orat. Lib. iii c. 1. ⁴ Ibidem.
Quintilian fais they both wrote upon the art ⁴, tho there is no system of the former now extant. But that of Aristotle is
esteemed

esteemed the best, and most compleat, of any in the Greek language. In this age the Grecian eloquence appeared in its highest perfection. Demosthenes was an hearer both of Isocrates and Plato, as also of Isaeus (ten of whose orations are yet extant) and by the assistance of a surprizing genius, joined with indefatigable industry, made that advantage of their precepts, that he has been always esteemed by the best judges the prince of Grecian orators. His great adversary and rival Aeschines, after his banishment is said to have gone to Rhodes, and imployed his time there in teaching rhetoric [1]. Theodectes and Theophrastus, both of them scholars of Aristotle, imitated their master in writing upon the art. And from that time the philosophers, especially the stoics and peripatetics, applied themselves to lay down the rules of oratory [2]; which Socrates had before separated from the province of a philosopher. And there is yet preserved a treatise upon this subject, which some have ascribed to Demetrius Phalereus the peripatetic, and scholar of Theophrastus, tho others more probably to Dionysius of Halicarnassus. Quintilian mentions several other famous rhetoricians in

the

[1] Quint. *Inst. orat. Lib* xii. *c* 10. Philostrat. *De Vit. Soph.* in *Aeschin.*

[2] Quint. *Inst. orat. Lib.* iii. *c.* 1.

the following ages, who were likewife writers; as Hermagoras, Athenaeus, Apollonius Molon, Areus Caecilius, Dionyſius of Halicarnaſſus, Apollonius of Pergamus, and Theodore of Gadara [1]. But of theſe nothing now remains upon the ſubject of oratory, except ſome tracts of Dionyſius, who flouriſhed in the reign of Auguſtus Caeſar. Nor have there be wanting ſome eminent writers of this kind among the Greeks ſince the time of Quintilian; two of whom I cannot omit to mention, Hermogenes, and Longinus, the author of the incomparable treatiſe *Of the ſublime,* a book which can ſcarce be too much commended, or too often read.

IT was long before Rome received this art, and not without difficulty at firſt. The reaſon was, becauſe the Romans were for ſeveral ages wholly addicted to military affairs, and to enlarge their territories; ſo that they not only neglected to cultivate learning, but thought the purſuit of it a thing of ill tendency, by diverting the minds of their youth from the cares and toils of war, to a more ſoft and indolent kind of life. Therefore ſo late as the year of their city five hundred ninety two, when by the induſtry of ſome Grecians the liberal

arts

arts began to flourish in Italy, a decree passed the senate, by which all philosophers and rhetoricians were ordered to depart out of Rome [1]. But in a few years after, when Carneades, Critolaus, and Diogenes, who were not only philosophers but orators, came ambassadors from Athens to Rome; the Roman youth were so charmed with the eloquence of their harangues, that they could no longer be stopt from pursuing the study of oratory. And by a further acquaintance with the Greeks it soon gained such esteem, that persons of the first quality imployed their time and pains to acquire it. And a young gentleman, who was ambitious to advance himself in the service of his country, could have little hopes of success, unless he had laid the foundation of his future prospects in that study.

SENECA tells us, that Lucius Plotius, a Gaul, was the first, who taught the art of oratory at Rome in Latin [2]; which Cicero sais, was while he was a boy, and when the most studious persons went to hear him, he lamented that he could not go with them; being prevented by the regard he paid to the opinion of some of his freinds, who thought that greater improvements

[1] Sueton.
*De clar.
rhetor.c.*1.

[2] *Praefat.
ad Lib.* ii.
controv.

12   *A* SYSTEM

provements were made by exercifes in the Greek language under Grecian mafters [1].

[1] See Suet.
De clar.
rhet. c. 2.

Seneca adds, that this profeffion continued for fome time in the hands of freedmen; and that the firft Roman, who ingaged in it, was Blandus of the equeftrian order [2],

[2] Ubi fu-
pra.

who was fucceded by others; fome of whofe lives are yet extant, writen by Suetonius, as many of the Grecians are by Philoftratus and Eunapius. Quintilian likewife gives us the names of thofe among the Romans, who wrote upon the art. *The firft, fais* he, *as far as I can learn, who compofed any thing upon this argument, was M. Cato the Cenfor. After him Anthony the orator began upon the fubject, which is the only work he has left, and that imper-*

[3] See Cic.
De orat.
Lib. 1.
c. 21.

fect [3]. *Then followed fome of lefs note. But he who carried eloquence to its higheft pitch among us, was Cicero; who has likewife by his rules given the beft plan both to practife, and teach the art. After whom modefty would require us to mention no more, had he not told us himfelf, that his Books of rhetoric flipt out of his hands, while he was but a youth* [4]. *And thofe leffer things, which many perfons want, he has purpofely omitted in his Difcourfes of oratory* [5]. *Cornificius wrote largely upon the fame fubject. Stertinius and*

[4] See Cic.
De orat.
Lib. i. c. 2.

[5] See Cic.
Ad fam.
Lib. i.
Ep. 9.

I   *Gallio*

Gallio the father, each of them something.
But Celsus and Lenas were more accurate
than Gallio; and in our times Virginius,
Pliny, and Rutilius. And there are at this
day some celebrated authors of the same kind,
who, if they had taken in every thing, might
have saved my pains [1]. Time has since
deprived us of most of the writers mentioned here by Quintilian. But we have
reason to be more easy under this loss,
since it has preserved to us Cicero's treatises
upon this subject; which we may well
suppose to have been cheifly owing to
their own excellency, and the great esteem
they have always had in the world. Besides his *Two books of invention*, which
Quintilian here calls his *Books of rhetoric*,
there are extant of his *Three books of an*
orator, one *Of famous orators*, and another,
which is called, *The orator*, as also his
Topics, a preface *Concerning the best sort of*
orators, and a treatise *Of the parts of ora-*
tory. Each of which treatises, whether
we regard the justness and delicacy of the
thoughts, the usefulness of the rules, or
the elegance and beauty of the stile, de-
serve to be frequently perused by all who
are lovers of eloquence. For who can be
thought so well qualified to give the rules

of

[1] *Inst. orat. Lib.* iii. c. 1.

of any art, as he who excelled all mankind in the practice of them? But thofe
Four books to Herennius, which are publifhed among Cicero's works, feem with
good reafon to be attributed to Cornificius,
whom Quintilian here mentions. And
Celfus is by fome affirmed to have taught
oratory, whom he alfo places among the
rhetoricians, and whofe *Eight books of medicine* are yet extant, wrote in fo beautiful
a ftile, as plainly fhews him to have been
a mafter of eloquence. But Quintilian
himfelf outdid all, who went before him,
in diligence and accuracy as a writer.
St. Jerom fais, he was the firft who taught
publicly at Rome, and received a falary

[1] *In Chron.
Eufebian.*
from the treafury [1]. But fince he places
this in the eighth year of Domitian, I fear
it will not hold in point of time. For
we are told by Suetonius, that Vefpafian
was the firft, who granted out of the treafury a yearly falary of near eight hundred
pounds fterling to the Latin and Greek

[2] *In vit.
c.* 18.
rhetoricians [2]. A generous act indeed, and
well becoming fo great a prince! But I
return to Quintilian, whofe *Inftitutions* are
fo comprehenfive, and writen with that
great exactnefs and judgement; that they
are generally allowed to be the moft perfect
work

work of this kind. With this excellent L E C T.
author therefore I ſhall finiſh my account   I.
of the Latin rhetoricians.

THERE were indeed ſome others in the
following ages, whoſe works are yet extant; but as they contain nothing of moment, which is not to be found in thoſe
already mentioned, I ſhall forbear to name
them. Much leſs ſhall I deſcend to that
numerous body of writers, who ſince the
revival of learning have treated upon this
ſubject, for the ſame reaſon. And a very
good judge has not long ſince given it as
his opinion; that the method of forming
the beſt ſyſtem of oratory, is to collect it
from the fineſt precepts of Ariſtotle, Cicero,
Quintilian, Longinus, and other celebrated
authors; with proper examples taken from
the choiceſt parts of the pureſt antiquity [1].   [1] A. B. of
This method therefore I ſhall endeavour to   Cambr.
                                             Lett.
purſue in my following diſcourſes.   *p.* 213.

L E C-

L E C T U R E II.

Of the Nature of Oratory.

I N treating upon any art or fcience, it is neceffary in the firft place to explain the nature and defign of it; from whence a judgment may beft be formed of the fitnefs of thofe rules, which are laid down in order to attain it. For this reafon Cicero advifes to begin with a *definition* [1], which gives a general and comprehenfive view of the whole fubject. This method I propofe to take in treating on the art of oratory. And therefore having already confidered the *rife* and *progrefs* of this art, and fhewn the antiquity of it; the fubject of my prefent difcourfe fhall be, firft to define it, and then to explain and illuftrate the feveral parts of the definition, as clearly and breifly as I can.

BUT before I enter upon this, it may not be amifs to obferve, that the terms *rhetoric* and *oratory* having no other difference, but that one is taken from the Greek language, and the other from the Latin, may be ufed promifcuoufly; but the cafe is not the fame with refpect to the

words

[1] *De off.*
Lib. i. *c* 2.

words *rhetorician* and *orator*. For altho the Grecians ufed the former both to ex- prefs thofe, who taught the art, and fuch who practifed it; yet the Romans after- ward, when they took that word into their language, confined it to the teachers of the art, and called the reft *orators*. And there feems to have been a fufficient reafon for this diftinction, fince the art was the fame in both, and might therefore go by either name; but the different province of rhe- toricians and orators made it not improper, they fhould be called by different names. Befides antiently, before rhetoric was made a feparate and diftinct art from philofophy, the fame perfons taught both. And then they were called not only *rhetoricians*, but *fophifts*. But becaufe they often imployed their art rather to vindicate what was falfe and unjuft, than to fupport truth and vir- tue; this difingenuous conduct, by which they frequently impofed upon weak minds, brought a difcredit both upon themfelves and their profeffion. And therefore the name *fophift* or *fophifter* has been more generally ufed in an ill fenfe, to fignify one fkilled rather in the arts of cavilling, than qualified to fpeak well and accurately upon any fubject. I fhall juft mention a remarkable inftance of this kind, as it is related by fome antient writers, and then procede to the principal fubject of my prefent difcourfe. Corax the rhetorician (who is faid firft to have taught the art for money) agreed to inftruct a young man, whofe name was Tifias, upon condition of receiving a certain fumm when he had learnt it. Tifias afterward defering to pay the money, Corax fued him for it. Upon which Tifias, agreably to the method in which he had been taught, afking what was the end of this art, and Corax replying to perfuade, propofed to him this fophifm : If I perfuade the judges I owe you nothing, I will not pay, becaufe I have carried the caufe ; but if I do not perfuade them, I will not pay, becaufe I have not yet learned the art. But Corax, who was too cuning a fophifter to be fo eafily baffled by his fcholar, immediately retorts upon him : Nay, if you do perfuade the judges, you fhall pay, becaufe it is a proof you have learnt the art, and you are bound by your agrement; but if you do not perfuade them, you fhall pay, becaufe they give the caufe againft you. Upon hearing this the judges prefently cried out, *An ill bird hatches an ill egg*; and fo difmiffed them

them without trying the caufe. In the
Greek it is *an ill Corax,* alluding to the
mafter's name, which in that language
fignifies *a raven* [1]. If fuch artifice was
only ufed for mirth and pleafantry, it might
perhaps afford matter of diverfion; but
when it enters into the ferious affairs of
life, and becomes a profeffion, it ought by
all means to be exploded.

[1] Erafm.
Chil.
p. 1420.

BUT I come now to the *definition* of
oratory, which may be thus laid down:
Oratory is the art of fpeaking well upon
any fubject, in order to perfuade.

IT is not neceffary to ufe many words,
to prove that oratory is an *art.* For it is
comprifed under certain rules, agreable to
reafon, delivered in a regular method, and
fuited to attain the end it propofes; which
are characters fufficient to denominate it
an art. Indeed the cafe is the fame here,
as in moft other things, that a good genius
is of itfelf more ferviceable, than the moft
exact acquaintance with all the rules of
art, where that is wanting. But it is
fufficient that art help nature, and carry it
farther, than it can otherwife advance
without it. And he who is defirous to
gain the reputation of a good orator, will
find the affiftance of both very neceffary.

C 2

Some

LECT.
II.

Some perfons have thought, that many of the common fyftems wrote upon the fubject of oratory have been attended with this inconvenience; that by burdening the mind with too great a number of rules about things of lefs importance, they have oftentimes rather difcouraged than promoted the ftudy of eloquence. This undoubtedly is an extreme, which fhould be always carefully avoided. But however, an indifferent guide in a ftrange road is better than none at all. It may be worth while to hear Quintilian's opinion upon this head. *I would not, fais he, have young perfons think they are fufficiently inftru5ted, if they have learned one of thofe compends, which are commonly handed about, and fancy themfelves fafe in the decrees, as it were, of thefe technical writers. The art of fpeaking requires much labour, conftant ftudy, a variety of exercife, many trials, the greateft prudence, and readinefs of thought. But however thefe treatifes are ufeful, when they fet you in a plain and open way, and do not confine you to one narrow tra5t, from which he who thinks it a crime to depart, muft move as flowly as one that walks upon a rope* [1]. We fee he is not for having us confine ourfelves too clofely to fyftems, tho he thinks they are

of

[1] *Inft orat. Lib.* ii. *c.* 13.

of fervice at firft, till ufe and experience
render them lefs neceffary. But I procede.

THE bufinefs of oratory is to teach us
to fpeak well, which, as Cicero explains it,
is to fpeak *juftly*, *methodically*, *floridly*, *and
copioufly* [1].

Now in order to fpeak *juftly*, or perti-
nently, a perfon muft be mafter of his
fubject, that he may be able to fay all that
is proper, and avoid whatever may appear
foreign and trifling. And he muft cloath
his thoughts with fuch words and expreffions, as are moft fuited to the nature
of the argument, and will give it the
greateft force and evidence.

[1] *De In-
vent.Lib.*i.
c. 5.
*De orat.
Lib.*i.*c.*11.

AND as it teaches to fpeak juftly, fo
likewife *methodically*. This requires, that
all the parts of a difcourfe be placed in
their proper order, and with that juft
connexion, as to reflect a light upon each
other, and thereby to render the whole
both clear in itfelf, and eafy to be retained.
But the fame method is not proper for all
difcourfes. And very frequently a different manner is convenient in handling
the fame fubject. For it is plain, that
art, as well as nature, loves variety; and
it difcovers the fpeaker's judgement, when
the difpofition of his difcourfe is fo framed,

C 3

as

LECT. as to appear eafy and natural, rather than
II. the effect of induftry and labour.

To fpeak *floridly* is fo peculiar a property
of this art, that fome have wholly confined it to the pomp and ornaments of
language. But that it extends farther, and
refpects things as well as words, I fhall
have occafion to fhew hereafter, when I
come to treat of the feveral parts of which
it is compofed. It contains indeed the
whole fubject of elocution, but does not
wholly confift in it. True and folid eloquence requires not only the beauties and
flowers of language; but likewife the beft
fenfe and cleareft reafoning. Befides rhetoric gives rules for the feveral forts of ftile,
and directs the ufe of them agreably to the
nature of the fubject. To make this more
evident, I fhall a little confider the difference
between *grammar* and *rhetoric*, that by
fixing the bounds of the former, the extent
of the latter may the more eafily be perceived. *Grammar* then is the art of fpeaking correctly. And he fpeaks *correctly*,
who makes choice of proper words, applies
them in their ufual fenfe, and joins them
together in conftruction agreably to the ufe
and idiom of the language, in which he
difcourfes. Nor does grammar, ftrictly confidered,

fidered, procede any farther. Wherefore
the fubject of ftile, with the different properties, by which the feveral forms of it
are diftinguifhed from each other, belong
to another art, which muft be rhetoric.
For tho rhetoric is faid to be the art of
fpeaking well, and grammar the art of
fpeaking correctly; yet fince the rules for
fpeaking and writing are the fame, under
fpeaking we are to include writing, and
each art is to be confidered as treating of
both. And tho the word *ftile,* in its proper
fenfe, refpects only what is writen ; yet it
is applied to fpeech, and fo I fhall fometimes ufe it. Now there are ufually reckoned three forts of ftile, called the low, middle, and fublime. Should any one therefore, in treating upon a familiar and common fubject, fwell it with florid and pompous language ; or on the contrary, in
handling a lofty and magnificent argument,
fhould he fall into a low and vulgar manner
of expreffion ; what was faid might be all
good grammar, but it would certainly be
very bad oratory. But the orator often
makes ufe of all thefe forts of ftile in the
fame difcourfe, and varies his language according to the different nature of each
part of his fubject, and his particular view

C 4   at

LECT
II.
at that time in speaking. Tho the use of this art is not wholly confined to an orator, or one who speaks in public ; but, as Plato observes [1], does in some measure extend to all occasions of discourse.

[1] *In Phae-dro.*

BUT the force of oratory appears in nothing more, than a *copiousness of expression*, or a proper manner of inlargement, suited to the nature of the subject, which is of great use in persuasion, and makes the last property, required by Cicero, of speaking well. A short and concise account of things is often attended with obscurity, from an omission of some necessary circumstances relating to them. Or however, where that is not the case, yet for want of proper embelishments to inliven the discourse, and thereby to excite and fix the hearers attention, it is apt to slip thro their minds without leaving any impression. But where the images of things are drawn in their full proportion, painted in their proper colours, set in a clear light, and represented in different views, with all the strength and beauties of eloquence, they captivate the minds of the audience with the highest pleasure, ingage their attention, and by an irresistible force move and bend them to the design of the speaker.

THE

THE *subject* of oratory, as I have said in the definition, is *every thing*. For there is nothing, but what is capable of receiving much advantage and ornament from this art. Indeed the subject of *logic* is equally extensive; but the difference both in its short and concise way of reasoning from the fluency and copiousness of oratory; and the end it proposes, which is only the knowledge of truth, while the other carries us to action, render it intirely a distinct art. So a statuary and a mason are conversant in the same matter, that is stone; but as the one uses it in buildings, and the other in forming images, these are arts plainly different. And both physics and medicine are imployed about the human body; but as the former only contemplates its nature and properties, while the latter gives prescriptions to cure its disorders, no one esteems them the same art. However, it is not necessary, that an orator should be acquainted with all arts; because there is none, upon which he may not have occasion to discourse. But since some have formerly been of that opinion, as we learn from Quintilian, I shall give you his answer to it, who has very fully expressed himself upon this head. *Some,*

LECT.
II.
ſais he, *have aſſerted, that an orator muſt be ſkilled in all arts, if he is to ſpeak upon all.*
I might here reply in the words of Cicero, in whom I find this expreſſion : In my opinion no one can be an excellent orator, who has not acquired the knowledge of all the great and laudable arts [1].   *But it is ſufficient for me, if the orator be not unacquainted with the ſubject, about which he is to diſcourſe. He is not indeed acquainted with all cauſes, and yet he ſhould be able to talk upon all. Upon which then ſhall he ſpeak? Upon thoſe which he has learnt. The ſame is to be ſaid of arts. Thoſe, of which he is to ſpeak, let him firſt learn ; and of thoſe which he has learned, let him ſpeak. But will not a work-man talk better about his own art? or a muſician of muſic? Yes certainly, if the orator be wholly ignorant of the ſubject.   For even a peaſant, or an illiterate perſon, will repre-ſent his own cauſe to better advantage than an orator, who is intirely unacquainted with it ; but being once inſtructed by the muſician, workman, or peaſant, he will diſcourſe better upon thoſe ſubjects, than he who taught him [2].*
By this paſſage it appears, that Quintilian thought much leſs furniture neceſſary for an orator, than Cicero had done, who re-quired a knowledge of all the *great arts* ;
by

[1] See *De orat.* Lib. i. c. 6.

[2] *Inſt. orat.* Lib. ii. c. 21.

by which he feems to have meant all
thofe, which at that time were efteemed
liberal arts among the Romans. And yet
what Cicero thought requifite, was greatly
fhort of fome others, who had infifted
upon a fkill in *all arts*; which, if at all
practicable, could doubtlefs be attained but
by very few.

THE principal *end* and defign of oratory
is to *perfuade*. For which reafon it is
frequently called *the art of perfuafion*. Indeed the orator has often other fubordinate
views: as when he endeavours either to
delight his hearers, with what is pleafant
and agreable; or to conciliate their good
opinion, by a fmooth and artful addrefs:
but ftill both thefe are in order to perfuade and excite them to action. Some
have objected to this, that perfuafion is
not peculiar to oratory, and other things
are found to have as much influence to
that end. So money, authority, and intereft perfuade; and fometimes the very
afpect, and a forrowful countenance, fhall
fway the mind as much, or more, than
words. Thus when Anthony the orator
in defending M. Aquilius produced his
garment, and expofed the holes, thro
which he had received feveral wounds in
defence of his country; it is thought,
that

that the Roman populace were principally moved by that fight to clear him from his accufation. And we are told by Cato, that Servius Galba had the like good fortune merely by raifing the compaffion of the people, when he produced not only his own helpleſs children, but likewiſe carried about the fon of Gallus Sulpitius in his own arms [1]. No one will deny, that the ſeveral things here mentioned are ſuited to perſuade, by influencing the paſſions ; but this is no juſt exception, why perſuaſion may not properly be ſaid to be the end of oratory ; ſince it is of a different kind, and means only ſo far, as that end can be attained by ſpeaking. Nor can this be with any greater reaſon denied, becauſe the orator does not always gain his point ; than curing the diſeaſes of human bodies can be denied to be the end of the art of medicine, becauſe the phyſician may not always prove ſucceſsful.

[1] Quint. *Inſt. orat. Lib.* ii. *c.* 16.

UPON the whole therefore, as the orator has always this in view ; while he imploys his art in purſuing only thoſe ends, for which it was at firſt deſigned, the perſuading men to good and virtuous actions, and diſſuading them from every thing that is ill and vicious ; nothing can be more commendable in itſelf, or uſeful to human ſocieties.

LECTURE III.

Of the Division of Oratory.

HAVING in my laſt diſcourſe treated upon the *nature* of oratory, I now procede to conſider the *diviſion* of it. This will give us a more diſtinct view of the art, by repreſenting the ſeveral parts of which it conſiſts, and afford us a plan for our future diſcourſes, that we may procede regularly in the explication of them. And every one muſt be ſenſible of the advantages, that attend method and order, as they render things more clear and conſpicuous, and very much help the memory to retain them.

LECT. III.

Now oratory conſiſts of theſe four parts; *Invention, Diſpoſition, Elocution,* and *Pronunciation.* This will appear by conſidering the nature of each of them, and what it contributes in forming an orator. Every one who aims to ſpeak well and accurately upon any ſubject, does naturally in the firſt place inquire after and purſue ſuch thoughts, as may ſeem moſt proper to explain and illuſtrate the thing, upon which he deſigns to diſcourſe. And if the nature

of

of it requires, that he fhould bring reafons to confirm what he fais, he not only feeks the ftrongeft, and fuch as are like to be beft received; but alfo prepares to anfwer any thing, which may be offered to the contrary. This is *Invention*. After this he deliberates with himfelf in what method to difpofe of thofe things, which have occured to his mind, that they may appear in the plaineft light, and not lofe their force by diforder and confufion. This is the bufinefs of *Difpofition*. His next concern is to give his thoughts an agreable drefs, by making choice of the fiteft words, cleareft expreffions, fmooth and harmonious periods, with other ornaments of ftile, as may beft fuit the nature of his fubject, brighten his difcourfe, and render it moft entertaining to his hearers. And this is called *Elocution*. The laft thing he attends to, is to deliver what he has thus compofed, with a juft and agreable *Pronunciation*. And daily experience convinces us, how much this contributes both to ingage the attention, and imprefs what is fpoken upon the mind. This then is the method to which nature directs, in order to qualify ourfelves for difcourfing to the beft advantage. Tho by cuftom and habit

thefe

thefe things become fo familiar to us, that we do not always attend to them feparately in their natural order. However it is the bufinefs of art to follow nature, and to treat of things in that manner, which fhe dictates.

INDEED fome have excluded both *invention* and *difpofition* from the art of oratory, fuppofing they more properly belong to logic ; but, I think, without any juft reafon. For, as was fhewn in my laft difcourfe, two arts may be converfant about the fame fubject, without interfering, provided they have not the fame end, and their manner of treating it be likewife different. Thus both logic and rhetoric teach us to reafon from the fame principles, as from the caufe, effects, circumftances, and many others, whence arguments are ufually taken. But befides thefe, rhetoric directs us to other confiderations, more peculiarly adapted to conciliate the mind, and affect the paffions, with which the other art has no concernment. For logic contents itfelf with fuch principles of reafoning, which arifing from the nature of things, and their relations to each other, may fuffice to difcover truth from falfehood, and fatisfy thinking and confiderate

LECT
III.
siderate perfons. Nor does it propofe any
thing more than affent, upon a juft view
of things fairly reprefented to the mind.
But rhetoric not only directs to thofe arguments, which are proper to convince the
mind; but alfo confiders the various paffions and interefts of mankind, with the
bias they receive from temper, education,
converfe, or other circumftances of life;
and teaches how to fetch fuch reafons
from each of thefe, as are of the greateft
force in perfuafion. It is plain therefore
that rhetoric not only fupplies us with
more heads of *invention* than logic, but
that they very much differ from each
other in the ufe and defign of them; the
one imploying them only as principles of
knowledge, but the other cheifly as motives to action.

Nor is their manner of treating them
lefs different, which refpects *difpofition*.
The logician fo places the feveral propofitions of a fyllogifm in a certain prefcribed
method, that the relation between the
terms may be evident, and the conclufion
appear to be fairly drawn from the premifes. And if either of the premifes feems
weak, or the truth of it not fufficiently
clear, he fupports it by a frefh argument;

and

and fo procedes in one fuccinct and uniform chain of reafoning, till he has made
out the proof of what he at firft propofed.
But the orator is not thus tied down to
mode and figure; or to perfect fyllogifms,
which he feldom ufes: but reafons in the
manner he thinks moft convenient; begins
with either of the premifes, and fometimes
with the conclufion itfelf; confirms one
part with proper reafons, and enlarges
upon it for greater evidence and variety,
before he procedes to another; and drops
any part, which he thinks fufficiently clear
of itfelf, and may be fupplied by the attentive hearer. And thus by a diverfity
of method, and an agreable variety, he
confults the pleafure and entertainment of
his hearers, as well as their inftruction.
Befides, he confiders the frame and ftructure of his whole difcourfe, and as his
view is not every where the fame, he divides it into certain parts, and fo difpofes
each of them, as may beft anfwer his intention. From all which it appears, that
Difpofition, confidered as a part of oratory,
is widely different from that, which is
taught by logic.

THE third part of oratory before mentioned is *Elocution*. In what this confifts

has been hinted already. All acknowledge
it belongs to this art, tho many seem to
mistake the true nature and extent of it.
For nothing is more common, than to suppose that only to be oratory, which is delivered in a florid and pompous stile.
Whereas *Elocution* comprehends all characters of stile, and shews how each of
them is to be applied ; and directs as well
to a choice of words, and propriety of expression, as to the ornaments of tropes and
figures. Indeed as the florid and sublime
characters more especially relate to the
orator's province, who has the greatest occasion for them ; the name of *Eloquence*
has been more peculiarly appropriated to
those characters. But to suppose from
hence, that the art of oratory is wholly
confined to these, or that the orator acts
out of his sphere, when he does not use
them, is equally to mistake in both cases.

In Aristotle's time rhetoricians had
treated only of the three parts already
mentioned. And accordingly he himself
sais : *There are three things to be treated
of in rhetoric : the first respects the invention
of arguments, the second elocution, and the
third the right placing the several parts of
a discourse* [1]. And if we consider the art

¹ *De rhe-
tor Lib.* iii.
c. 1.

in

in itfelf, without regard to the principal LECT.
ufe and application of it ; nothing further III.
feems to be neceffary. For as architecture
confifts in three things ; materials proper
for building, the putting together thofe
materials, and beautifying the whole ftructure ; fo here, the invention of arguments,
placing every thing in its juft order, and
giving it a fuitable and proper drefs, feems
to contain the whole of this art. And
where difcourfes are only publifhed in
order to be read, nothing can be done
further. But the cheif end of oratory,
which is perfuafion, is often much better
attained by fpeaking, than writing. The
orator's province is to be the mouth of
an affembly, to addrefs to others in perfon,
to advife them to their good, diffuade
them from things prejudicial, and excite
them by all proper motives to fall in with,
and purfue their true intereft. He is to
appear upon all occafions as a patron of
truth and virtue, and to oppofe every thing,
which has a tendency to fubvert them.
And he, who ingages in this province,
will find it neceffary to be mafter not only
of a ready invention ; an eafy method of
difpofing his thoughts ; and a happy elocution ; but likewife of all the arts of ad-

D 2   drefs,

drefs, and advantages of a good delivery. This fhews the neceffity of the fourth part of oratory, which is called *Pronunciation*, and fometimes *Action*. For as this does not only comprehend the juft management of the voice, but likewife of the countenance and gefture, that each of them may fuit the nature of the argument, and manner of expreffion; from the former of thefe it has been called *Pronunciation*, and from the latter *Action*, both being generally underftood by the antients under either name [r]. It feems highly probable, that orators took this firft from the ftage. Whence the Greeks call it ὑπόκρισις, which is a word borrowed from the theatre, and fignifies the perfonating of another, as actors do on the ftage, by their manner of fpeech and behaviour fuited to the perfons of thofe, whom they reprefent. And Ariftotle tells us, that in his time fome rules had been writen for the pronunciation of actors [z]. But however the name might take its origin from the theatre, yet the pronunciation of an orator is very different from that of actors. For his manner of expreffion has not that rapture and extafy, which we fometimes find in tragedy; nor do the ludicrous motions and geftures of the ftage

fuit

[r] See Cic. *De invent.* *Lib.* i. *c.* 7.

[z] *Ubi fupra.*

fuit the gravity of his character. His de- LECT.
fign is not barely to amufe or terrify, but III.
fo far to affect the paffions, as thereby to
ingage the mind to a more ready compliance with what is offered. Ariftotle
faw, that the want of this was a defect in
the rules of oratory; and therefore, tho
he mentions but three parts of the art, he
has notwithftanding given fome few pre-
cepts concerning it [1]. And it is plain, [1] *Ubi fu-*
that Demofthenes was then very fenfible *pra.*
of its influence, and laid the greateft ftrefs
upon it; who, as we are told in Cicero,
*being afked, what was the principal thing in
oratory, is faid to have given the firft, fecond, and third place to action, as if the
whole art confifted in it* [2]. But tho it was [2] *De orat.*
not introduced into the fchools fo early, *Lib.* iii.
as the other parts of this art; yet many *c. 56.*
fince Ariftotle have writen upon it more
largely; nor is any fyftem efteemed perfect, in which this is wanting.

BUT many writers add a fifth part of
oratory to the four already mentioned, and
that is *Memory*. And this opinion is fupported by great authorities. For Cicero
more than once divides the art into five
parts [3]; and fo does Quintilian, who fais: [3] *De In-*
The whole of oratory confifts, as the moft and *vent.Lib.*i.
c. 7. &
beft alibi.

C 3

beſt authors reckon, of five parts ; *Invention,* *Method, Elocution, Memory, Pronunciation or Action* [1]. But if we conſider the uſe of this faculty, it is very evident, that it is not peculiar to oratory, but common to all arts and ſciences; for which reaſon it ought not to be eſteemed as a part of this art, diſtinct from all others. Tho ſince none have more occaſion for its aſſiſtance than the orator, and there ſeems to be no other art, to which it can ſo properly be refered (unleſs it be made a diſtinct art of itſelf) I ſhall hereafter ſpeak more of it, in treating upon *Pronunciation,* to which it ſeems moſt properly to relate.

WHAT has been hitherto ſaid of the nature and uſe of the ſeveral parts of oratory, may, I preſume, be ſufficient to ſhew, that the diviſion here made is adequate to the ſubject, and comprehenſive of the whole art. A fuller and more diſtinct explication of each of them, in the order now laid down, will be the buſineſs of our following diſcourſes. At preſent it may not be amiſs to reduce the ſeveral things, about which it treats, to a few general heads, which may be of ſervice hereafter to ſhew the different uſe of ſome of its parts in each of them.

[1] *Inſt. orat. Lib.* iii. *c.* 3.

ALL

ALL difcourfe then confifts of *things* or ideas, and *words* the figns of thofe ideas, by which they are expreffed to others. And therefore fome have reduced the four parts of oratory already mentioned to two, *Invention*, and *Elocution*; the former of which they attribute to things, and the latter to words [1]. But as they bring *Dif-pofition* under *Invention*, and *Pronunciation* under *Elocution*, there is no real difference between this divifion of the art, and the former. I fhall procede therefore with the divifion of its fubject. And what relates purely to *words*, I fhall refer to its proper place, which is *Elocution*. But the *things* it treats of are differently divided, accor-ding to their different nature, or the feveral ways of confidering them.

[1] See Voff. *De rhe-tor. nat. & conftit. c.* 17.

AND firft, they are either *fimple* or *com-plex:* that is fingle, individual things; or fuch as are connected in propofitions. Thus for inftance: If *Virtue* was made the fub-ject of a difcourfe, and any one fhould fpeak in the praife of it, fhew the excel-lency of its nature, the pleafure that at-tends the practice of it, and its happy effects to human fociety; this would be a fimple theme. But fhould it be inquired: *Whether virtue is to be fought for itfelf?*

the

the fubject would be complex. For here are two things mentioned, *virtue* and *fought for itfelf*; and the relation thefe ftand in to each other, or whether they are fo connected, that one may juftly be affirmed of the other, is the matter which comes under confideration.

AGAIN, the argument of a difcourfe may be either a *general*, or a *particular propofition*. A general propofition is that, which is expreffed in general terms, divefted of all circumftances, fuch as perfons, time, place, and the like. And a particular propofition is limited by fome or other of thefe circumftances, which the former wants. So if the queftion be put : *Whether it be lawful for a man to kill himfelf?* the inquiry is general. But if it be afked : *Whether Cato did well in fo doing ?* this is particular.

BUT the principal diftribution of the fubject of oratory is made, by dividing it into three kinds of difcourfe, called by the antients *demonftrative*, *deliberative*, and *judicial*. The *firft* of thefe comprehends all fuch difcourfes, as relate to the praife or difpraife of perfons, or things. This is a very extenfive feild, and contains in it whatever in nature or art, on the account

2   of

of any good or bad qualities, excellences or defects, is fit to be made the subject of a difcourfe. By this virtue is applauded, and vice cenfured; good examples recommended to the imitation of others, and bad ones expofed to their abhorrence. All panegyric and invective are its proper themes. So that the cheif defign of thefe difcourfes is to infpire men with generous fentiments of honor and virtue, and to give them a diftafte to every thing, that is bafe and vitious, by examples of each, which are the moft powerful means of inftruction. Tho, as has been faid already, they are not wholly confined to perfons. To the *deliberative* kind belongs whatever may become a fubject of debate, confultation, or advice. Of this fort are all fpeeches made in public affemblies, which refpect the common good and benefit of mankind, their lives, liberties, and eftates; whatever is advifed to, or diffuaded from, upon the foot of any valuable intereft, which is the end propofed in thefe difcourfes, fo far as it is confiftent with honor and juftice. The laft head contains all *judicial fubjects*; by this property is fecured, innocence protected, juftice maintained, and crimes punifhed. All

matters

matters canvaſſed at the bar are of this ſort. And it is doubtleſs a very valuable and uſeful end in ſpeaking, to vindicate juſtice and equity in oppoſition to fraud or violence. Ariſtotle is ſaid to have been the author of this diviſion [1], which ſeems to be very juſt; ſince perhaps there is no ſubject of oratory, whether ſacred or civil, but may be refered to one or other of theſe heads. And not only the view and intention of the ſpeaker (as we have ſeen already) is different in each of them, which would be ſufficient to diſtinguiſh them from one another; but they require likewiſe a different ſtile and way of management, as will be ſhewn hereafter, when I come to treat of each of them in particular.

[1] See Quint. *Inſt. orat.* *Lib.* iii. *c.* 4.

L E C-

L E C T U R E IV.

Of Invention in general, and particularly of Common Places.

A FINE and ſtately building affords an agreable proſpect, tho ſeen at a diſtance ; but the beauty and elegancy of its parts, their proportion and order, with the united harmony and ſplendor reſulting from the whole, which diſcover themſelves at a nearer view, give a much greater pleaſure to a curious and judicious eye. In like manner, tho the account already given of the *nature* of oratory, its importance, and the great ends it is deſigned to anſwer, may excite a regard for it in ſtudious and inquiſitive minds ; yet a more diſtinct explication of the ſeveral parts, whereof it conſiſts, and the fitneſs of its precepts to attain their reſpective ends, will doubtleſs very much contribute to highten its juſt value and eſteem. I now propoſe therefore to enter upon this ſubject, and in the proſecution of it, I ſhall follow the method before laid down in my laſt diſcourſe on the *diviſion* of oratory. And as I there obſerved the ſimilitude between the arts of ſpeaking and building, in both

of

LECT. of which the artift firft collects his mate-
IV. rials, then adjufts them in proper order,
and afterwards gives them fuch ornaments
as fuit his defign ; I fhall accordingly begin
with *Invention*, which furnifhes the orator
with materials. For invention, confidered
in general, is the difcovery of fuch things,
as are proper to perfuade [1]. And in order
to attain this end, the orator propofes to
himfelf three things; to prove or illuftrate
the fubject upon which he treats, to conciliate the minds of his hearers, and to
ingage their paffions in his favor. And
as thefe require different kinds of arguments or motives, invention furnifhes him
with a fupply for each of them, as will be
fhewn in their order.

[1] Voff.
Part.orat.
*Lib.*1. *c.*2.
§. 1.

I SHALL firft confider that part of *Invention*, which directs to *arguments proper
for the proof of a thing*; which, as Cicero
tells us, is, *The difcovery of fuch things, as
are really true, or that feem to be fo, and
make the thing, for which they are produced,
appear probable* [2]. And the things, which
are thus difcovered, are called *Arguments*.
For, *an Argument*, as defined by him, *is a
reafon, which induces us to beleive, what before we doubted of* [3]. If we reflect upon
thofe things, which relate to the common
affairs

[2] *De in-*
*vent.Lib.*i.
c. 7.

[3] *Topic.*
c. 2.

affairs of life, and the numerous tranf-
actions between mankind, we fhall find
that moſt of them are of a dubious nature,
and liable to various conſtructions, as they
are taken in different views; from whence
a diverſity of opinions is formed concerning them.   And where the nature of the
thing does not admit of certainty, every
conſiderate and prudent perſon will give
into that ſide of the queſtion, which carries
in it the greater degree of probability.
And as theſe are the ſubjects, with which
the antient orators were principally concerned, we find by Cicero's definition, that
all he requires of ſuch arguments, as they
commonly made uſe of, is to render a thing
probable.   Indeed there are ſome things,
which do not ſo much require reaſoning,
as a proper and ſuitable manner of repreſenting them, to make them credible;
and becauſe the ſeveral ways of illuſtrating
theſe are alſo taught by the precepts of
this art, they are likewiſe in a large ſenſe
of the word called *arguments*.

BUT as different kinds of diſcourſes require different *arguments*, rhetoricians have
conſidered them two ways; in general,
under certain heads, as a common fund
for all ſubjects; and in a more particular
manner,

LECT.
IV.
manner, as they are fuited to *demonſtra-tive*, *deliberative*, or *judicial* difcourſes. At preſent I ſhall treat only upon the former of theſe. And now, that one thing may receive proof and confirmation from another, it is neceſſary that there be ſome relation between them; for all things are not equally adapted to prove one another. And that we may the better conceive this, I ſhall make uſe of a plain and familiar inſtance. In meaſuring the quantity of two things, which we would ſhew to be either equal or unequal, if they are of ſuch a nature, that one cannot be applied to the other, then we take a third thing, which may be applied to them both; and that muſt be equal at leaſt to one of the two, which if applied to the other, and found equal to that alſo, we preſently conclude, that thoſe two things are equal; but if it be unequal to the other, we ſay, that thoſe two things are unequal. Becauſe it is the certain and known property of all quantities, that whatſoever two things are equal to a third, are equal to one another; and where one of any two things is equal to a third, and the other unequal, thoſe two things are unequal to one another. What has been ſaid of quantities, will hold

2   true

true in all other cafes, that fo far as any
two things or ideas agree to a third, fo far
they agree to one another. And by agre-
ing I underftand this, that the one may be
affirmed of the other. So likewife on the
contrary, as far as one of any two things
or ideas does agree to a third, and the
other does not, fo far they difagree with
one another, in which refpect one of them
cannot be truly affirmed of the other.
Since therefore in every propofition one
thing is fpoken of another, if we would
find out whether the two ideas agree to
each other or not, where this is not evident of itfelf, we muft find out fome third
thing, the idea of which agrees to one of
them; and then that being applied to the
other, as it does agree or difagree with it,
fo we may conclude, that the two things
propofed do agree or difagree with one
another. This will be made more clear
by an example or two. Should it be inquired, *Whether virtue is to be loved?*
the agreement between virtue and love
might be found by comparing them feparately with happinefs, as a common meafure to both. For fince the idea of happinefs agrees to that of love, and the idea
of virtue to that of happinefs; it follows,

that

that the ideas of virtue and love agree to one another; and therefore it may be affirmed, *That virtue is to be loved.* But on the contrary, becaufe the idea of mifery difagrees with that of love, but the idea of vice agrees to that of mifery, the two ideas of vice and love muft confequently difagree with one another; and therefore it would be falfe to affert, *That vice is to be loved.* Now this third thing logicians call the *Medium* or *middle Term*, becaufe it does as it were connect two extremes, that is, both parts of a propofition. But rhetoricians call it an *Argument*, becaufe it is fo applied to what was before propofed, as to become the inftrument of procuring our affent to it. I have mentioned thefe plain examples only for illuftration, by which we may in fome meafure perceive the nature and ufe of arguments.

BUT from whence, and by what methods they are to be fought, I fhall now explain.

A LIVELY imagination and readinefs of thought are undoubtedly a very great help to invention. Some perfons are naturally endued with that quicknefs of fancy, and penetration of mind, that they are feldom at a lofs for arguments either to defend

their

their own opinions, or to attack their adverfaries. However thefe things being the gift of nature, and not to be gained by art, do not properly fall under our prefent confideration.

BUT, I fuppofe, it will be readily granted, that great learning and extenfive knowledge are a noble fund for invention. Indeed Craffus, the Roman orator, carries this matter much farther, when he fais : *I think, that no one ought to be accounted an orator, who is not thoroughly accomplifhed with all thofe arts, which are fit for a gentleman to learn. For tho in an oration we do not make ufe of them, yet whether we have learnt them, or not, will appear very eafily, and cannot be hid. As in fculpture, tho the artift doth not directly make ufe of the art of painting, yet it is not difficult to difcover whether he underftand painting or not. In like manner in difcourfes at the bar, in the forum, or fenate, tho other arts are not made ufe of, yet it prefently appears, whether the perfon fpeaking be only acquainted with the method of declaming, or comes to it qualified with all the liberal arts* [1]. It may be hard to deny the name of orator to all fuch, who fall fhort of the qualifications here mentioned ; and Quintilian, as I have

[1] *Cic. De orat. Lib.i. c. 16.*

fhewn

shewn in a former discourse [1], is for making considerable abatements; but yet it must be owned, that the greater furniture any one has acquired of useful learning, he will by that means be better prepared to speak in public upon all occasions. An orator therefore should be furnished with a stock of important truths, solid maxims of reason, and a variety of knowledge, collected and treasured up both from observation, and a large acquaintance with the liberal arts; that he may not only be qualified to express himself in the most agreable manner, but likewise to support what he sais with the strongest and clearest arguments.

BUT the greatest help to invention is, for a person to consider well before hand the subject, upon which he is to speak, and not to venture to affirm any thing concerning it, which he has not first a clear notion of himself. The better any one understands a thing himself, the better is he able to explain it to others. For tho the same arguments do not strike the minds of all persons with equal force, either because they do not come equally prepared to attend to what is said; or from a different way of thinking, to which they have been

I   ac-

accuſtomed: yet there is no method, by which any one can more reaſonably hope to bring others to his opinion, than by laying before them thoſe very arguments, by which upon a cloſe conſideration of the thing he was himſelf induced to beleive it. And the more thoroughly he is himſelf perſuaded of the truth of what he ſais, he will be qualified to impreſs it with greater ſtrength and clearneſs upon the minds of thoſe, to whom he ſpeaks.

But becauſe all are not born with a like happy genius, and have not the ſame opportunity to cultivate their minds with learning and knowledge; and becauſe nothing is more difficult than to dwell long upon the conſideration of one thing, in order to find out the ſtrongeſt arguments, which may be offered for and againſt it; upon theſe accounts art has preſcribed a method to leſſen in ſome meaſure theſe difficulties, and help every one to a ſupply of arguments upon any ſubject. And this is done by the contrivance of *common places,* which Cicero calls the *ſeats* or *heads of arguments,* and by a Greek name *topics* [1]. They are of two ſorts, *internal* and *external.* As to the former, tho things with regard to their nature and properties are

[1] *Topic. c. 1, 2.*

E 2　　　　　ex-

LECT. exceding various, yet they have certain
IV. common relations, by means whereof the
truth of what is either affirmed or denied
concerning them in any refpect may be
evinced. The antient Greek rhetoricians
therefore reduced thefe relations to fome
general heads; which are termed *common
places*, becaufe the reafons or arguments
fuited to prove any propofition are repofited
in them, as a common fund or receptacle.
And they are called *internal heads*, becaufe
they arife from the fubject, upon which
the orator treats; and are therefore diftinguifhed from others named *external*, which
he fetches from without, and applies to
his prefent purpofe, as will be fhewn here-
[1] *Lect.* V. after [1]. Cicero and Quintilian make them
fixteen; three of which comprehend the
whole thing they are brought to prove;
namely, *Definition*, *Enumeration*, and *Notation*; and of the remaining thirteen fome
contain a part of it, and the reft its various
properties and circumftances, with other
confiderations relating to it; and thefe are
*Genus, Species, Antecedents, Confequents, Ad-
juncts, Conjugates, Caufe, Effect, Contraries,
Oppofites, Similitude, Diffimilitude*, and *Comparifon*. I fhall give a breif account of each
of thefe, in the order now mentioned.

DE-

DEFINITION explains the nature of the
thing defined, and fhews what it is.   And
to whatfoever the definition agrees, the
thing defined does fo likewife.   If therefore Socrates be a rational creature, he is
a man; becaufe it is the definition of a
man, that he is a rational creature.

ENUMERATION takes in all the parts
of a thing.   And from this we prove,
that what agrees to all the parts, agrees
to the whole; and what does not agree
to any one or more parts, does not agree
to the whole.   As when Cicero proves to
Pifo, that all the Roman ftate hated him;
by enumerating the feveral ranks and or-
ders of Roman citizens, who all did fo [1].   [1] *In Pifon.*

NOTATION or etymology explains the *c. 27.*
meaning or fignification of a word.   From
which we reafon thus: If he cannot pay
his debts, he is infolvent: For that is the
meaning of the word infolvent.

GENUS is what contains under it two
or more forts of things, differing in nature.
From this head logicians reafon thus:
Becaufe every animal is mortal, and man
is an animal, therefore man is mortal.
But orators make a further ufe of this argument, which they call afcending from
the hypothefis to the thefis, that is, from a

par-

LECT.
IV.
particular to a general. As should a person, when speaking in praise of justice, take occasion from thence to commend and shew the excellency of virtue in general, with a view to render that particular virtue more amiable. For since every species contains in it the whole nature of the genus, to which it relates, besides what is peculiar to itself, whereby it is distinguished from it; what is affirmed of the genus, must of necessity be applicable to the species.

SPECIES is that, which comprehends under it all the individuals of the same nature. From hence we may argue: He is a man, therefore he has a rational soul. And orators sometimes take occasion from this head to descend from the thesis to the hypothesis; that is, in treating upon what is more general to introduce some particular contained under it, for the greater illustration of the general.

ANTECEDENTS are such things, as being once allowed, others necessarily, or very probably follow. From this head an inseparable property is proved from its subject: as, It is material, and therefore corruptible.

CONSEQUENTS are such things, as being allowed, necessarily, or very probably infer
their

their antecedents. Hence the subject is
proved from an inseparable property, in
this manner: It is corruptible, and therefore material.

ADJUNCTS are separable properties of
things, or circumstances that attend them.
These are very numerous, and afford a
great variety of arguments, some of which
usually occur in every discourse. They do
not necessarily infer their subject, but if
fitly chosen render a thing credible, and
are a sufficient ground for assent. The
way of reasoning from them we shall shew
presently.

CONJUGATES are words deduced from
the same origin with that of our subject.
By these the habit is proved from its acts :
as, He who does justly, is just. He does
not act wisely, therefore he is not wise.
But this inference will not hold, unless
the actions appear continued and constant.

A CAUSE is that, by the force of which
a thing does exist. There are four kinds
of causes, matter, form, efficient and end,
which afford a great variety of arguments.
The way of reasoning from them is to
infer the effect from the cause : as, Man is
endued with reason, therefore he is capable
of knowledge.

E 4 AN

A S Y S T E M

AN EFFECT is that, which arifes from a caufe, therefore the caufe is proved by it; as, He is endued with knowledge, therefore with reafon.

CONTRARIES are things, which under the fame genus are at the utmoft diftance from each other. So that what we grant to the one, we utterly deny the other : as, Virtue ought to be embraced, therefore vice fhould be avoided.

OPPOSITES are fuch things, which, tho repugnant to each other, yet are not directly contradictory : as, to love and to injure, to hate and to commend. They differ from contraries in this, that they do not abfolutely exclude one another. An argument is drawn from things repugnant thus : He will do a man a mifcheif, therefore he does not love him. He loves a man, therefore he will not reproach him.

SIMILITUDE is an agreement of things in quality. Thus Cicero proves, that pernicious citizens ought to be taken out of the ftate; by the likenefs they bear to corrupted members, which are cut off to prevent further damage to the body [1].

[1] *Philipp.* viii. *c. 5.*

DISSIMILITUDE is a difagreement of things in quality. From this head Cicero fhews the preference of his own exile to

Pifo's

Piſo's government of Macedonia; by the difference between their conduct, and the people's eſteem of them [1].

COMPARISON is made three ways. For either a thing is compared with a greater, with a leſs, or with its equal. This place therefore differs from that of ſimilitude on this account, that the quality was conſidered in that, but here the quantity. An argument from the greater is thus drawn: If five legions could not conquer the enemy, much leſs will two. And by this the manner of the reſt may be eaſily conceived.

I SHALL juſt give one example ſomewhat larger, than I have hitherto done, of the manner of reaſoning from theſe heads, whereby the uſe of them may further appear. If any one therefore ſhould have indeavoured to perſuade Cicero not to accept of his life upon the condition offered him by Antony; that he would burn his Philippic orations, which had been ſpoken againſt him; he might be ſuppoſed to uſe ſuch arguments as theſe; partly taken from the adjuncts of Cicero, partly from thoſe of Antony, and partly from the thing itſelf. And firſt with re-

4   gard

gard to Cicero it might be said: That so great a man ought not to purchase his life at so dear a price, as the loss of that immortal honor, which by so great pains and labor he had acquired. And this might be confirmed by another argument. That now he was grown old, and could not expect to live much longer. And from the character of Antony he might argue thus: That he was very crafty and deceitful, and only designed by giving him hopes of life, to have the Philippics first burnt, which otherwise he knew would transmit to posterity an eternal brand of infamy upon him; and then he would take off the author. And this might be shewn by comparison. For since he would not spare others, who had not so highly exasperated him, and from whom he had not so much to fear; certainly he would not forgive Cicero, since he knew well enough, that so long as he lived, he himself could never be in safety. And lastly an argument might also be fetched from the nature of the thing itself in the following manner. That Cicero by this action would shamefully betray the state, and the cause of liberty, which he had thro his whole life most

cou-

couragiously defended, with so great honor to himself, and advantage to the
public [1]. Upon such an account a person
might have used these, or the like arguments with Cicero, which arise from the
forementioned heads.

FROM this account of *Common Places* it
is easy to conceive, what a large feild of
discourse they open to the mind upon
every subject. These different considerations furnish out a great number and variety of arguments, sufficient to supply the
most barren invention. He can never be
at a loss for matter, who considers well
the nature of his subject, the parts of which
it consists, the circumstances which attend
it, the causes from whence it springs, the
effects it produces, its agreement, disagree-
ment, or repugnancy to other things, and
in like manner carries it thro all the remaining heads. But altho this method
will assist us very much to inlarge upon
a subject, and place it in different views;
yet a prudent man is not so desirous to say
a great deal, as to speak to the purpose,
and therefore will make choice of proper
arguments, and such only, which have a
direct tendency to confirm or illustrate his
subject.

LECT.
IV.

ſubject.   And for this end, it is neceſſary for him to gain firſt a thorough knowledge of his ſubject, and then arguments will naturally ſpring up in his mind proper to ſupport it ; and if he be ſtill at a loſs, and find occaſion to have recourſe to theſe heads, he will readily perceive from whence to take thoſe, which are beſt ſuited to his purpoſe.

LEC-

LECTURE V.

Of external Topics.

THE nature and defign of *Common* Places have been fhewn already; and a particular account of thofe, which, becaufe they are taken from the fubject matter of a difcourfe, are therefore called *internal*, has likewife been given. But the orator fometimes reafons from fuch topics, as do not arife from his fubject, but from things of a different nature, and for that reafon are called *external*. And becaufe the former are more properly invented by him, and the effect of his art, Ariftotle calls them *artificial Topics*, and the latter *inartificial* [1]. But as they both require fkill in the management, Quintilian very much blames thofe, who take no notice of thefe latter, but exclude them from the art of rhetoric [2]. I propofe therefore to make them the fubject of my prefent difcourfe, and fhew the methods of reafoning from them. They are all taken from authorities, and are by one general name called *Teftimonies*.

[1] *De rhetor. Lib.* i. *c.* 2. See alfo Quint. *Inft. orat. Lib.* v. *c.* 1.

[2] *Ibid.*

Now

LECT.
V.
Now a *Teſtimony* may be expreſſed by writing, ſpeech, or any other ſign proper to declare a perſon's mind. And all *teſtimonies* may be diſtinguiſhed into two ſorts, *divine* and *human.* A *divine Teſtimony,* when certainly known to be ſuch, is inconteſtable, and admits of no debate, but ſhould be acquieſced in without heſitation. Indeed the antient Greeks and Romans eſteemed the pretended oracles of their deities, the anſwers of their augurs, and the like fallacies, divine teſtimonies. But with us no one can be ignorant of their true notion, tho they do not ſo directly come under our preſent conſideration. *Human Teſtimonies* are of various kinds, but as they furniſh the orator with arguments (in which view I am now to conſider them) they may be reduced to three heads; *Writings, Witneſſes,* and *Contracts.*

By *Writings* here are to be underſtood writen laws, wills, or other legal inſtruments, expreſſed and conveyed in that manner. And it is not ſo much the force and validity of ſuch teſtimonies, conſidered in themſelves, that is here intended; as the occaſion of diſpute, which may at any time ariſe concerning their true deſign and import, when produced in proof upon
either

either fide of a controverfy. And thefe
are five; *Ambiguity, Difagreement between*
the words and intention, Contrariety, Rea-
foning, and *Interpretation* [1]. I fhall fpeak
to each of thefe in their order.

A WRITING is then faid to be *ambi-*
guous, when it is capable of two or more
fenfes, which makes the writer's defign
uncertain. Now ambiguity may arife either
from fingle words, or the conftruction of
fentences. From fingle words; as when
either the fenfe of a word, or the application of it is doubtful. As: *fhould it be*
queftioned, whether ready money ought to be
included under the appellation of chattels left
by a will. Or: *if a teftator bequeath a*
certain legacy to his nephew Thomas, and he
has two nephews of that name. But ambiguity is alfo fometimes occafioned from
the conftruction of a fentence; as when
feveral things, or perfons having been already mentioned, it is doubtful to which
of them, that which follows ought to be
refered. For example: a perfon writes
thus in his will: *Let my heir give as a*
legacy to Titius, an horfe out of my ftable,
which he pleafe [2]. Here it may be queftioned whether the word *he* refers to the
heir, or to Titius; and confequently, whether

[1] Cic. *De Invent. Lib.* ii. *c.* 40.

[2] See Quint. *Inft. orat. Lib.* vii. *c.* 9. Et Cic. *De Invent. Lib.* ii. *c.* 40.

ther the heir be allowed to give Titius which horſe he pleaſe, or Titius may chooſe which he likes beſt. Now as to controverſies of this kind, in the firſt caſe above mentioned, the party, who claims the chattels, may plead, that all moveable goods come under that name, and therefore that he has a right to the money. This he will endeavour to prove from ſome inſtances, where the word has been ſo uſed. The buſineſs of the oppoſite party is to refute this, by ſhewing that money is not there included. And if either ſide produce precedents in his favor, the other may indeavour to ſhew the caſes are not parallel. As to the ſecond caſe, ariſing from an ambiguity in the name, if any other words or expreſſions in the will ſeem to countenance either of the claimants, he will not fail to interpret them to his advantage. So likewiſe if any thing ſaid by the teſtator, in his life time, or any regard ſhewn to either of theſe nephews more than the other, may help to determine, which of them was intended ; a proper uſe may be made of it. And the ſame may be ſaid with regard to the third caſe. In which the legatee may reaſon likewiſe from the common uſe of language, and ſhew,

shew, that in such expressions it is usual
to make the reference to the last or next
antecedent; and from thence plead, that
it was the design of the testator to give
him the option. But in answer to this it
may be said, that allowing it to be very
often so; yet in this instance it seems
more easy and natural, to repeat the verb
give after *please*, and so to supply the sentence, *which he please to give him*, refering
it to the heir; than to bring in the verb
choose, which was not in the sentence before, and so by supplying the sense, *which
he please to choose*, to give the option to
Titius. But where controversies of this
kind arise from a law, recourse may be
had to other laws, where the same thing
has been expressed with greater clearness,
which may help to determine the sense of
the passage in dispute.

A SECOND controversy from *Writings*
is, when one party adheres to the *words*,
and the other to what he asserts was the
writer's *intention*. Now he who opposes
the literal sense, either contends, that what
he himself offers is the simple and plain
meaning of the writing; or that it must
be so understood in the particular case in
debate. An instance of the former is this,

VOL. I.   F   as

as we find it in Cicero. A perſon who died without children, but left a widow, had made this proviſion in his will: *If I have a ſon born to me, he ſhall be my heir.* And a little after: *If my ſon die, before he comes of age, let Curius be my heir* [1]. There is no ſon born, Curius therefore ſues for the eſtate, and pleads the intention of the teſtator, who deſigned him for his heir, if he ſhould have no ſon, who arrived at age; and ſais, there can be no reaſon to ſuppoſe, he did not intend the ſame perſon for his heir, if he had no ſon, as if he ſhould have one, who afterwards died in his minority. But the heir at law inſiſts upon the words of the will, which, as he ſais, require, that firſt a ſon ſhould be born, and afterwards die under age, before Curius can ſuccede to the inheritance. And there being no ſon, a ſubſtituted heir, as Curius was, can have no claim, where the firſt heir does not exiſt, from whom he derives his pretention, and was to ſuccede by the appointment of the will. Of the latter caſe rhetoricians give this example: *It was forbiden by a law to open the city gates in the night. A certain perſon notwithſtanding in time of war did open them in the night, and let*

[1] See Cic.
De orat.
Lib. ii.
c. 32.
De invent.
Lib. ii.
c. 42.

in

in some auxiliary troops, to prevent their being cut off by the enemy, who was posted near the town. Afterwards, when the war was over, this person is arraigned, and tried for his life, on the account of this action [1]. Now in such a case the prosecutor founds his charge upon the express words of the law; and pleads, that no sufficient reason can be assigned for going contrary to the letter of it, which would be to make a new law, and not to execute one already made. The defendant on the other hand alleges, that the fact, he is charged with, cannot however come within the intention of the law; since he either could not, or ought not to have complied with the letter of it in that particular case, which must therefore necessarily be supposed to have been excepted in the design of that law, when it was made. But to this the prosecutor may reply; that all such exceptions, as are intended by any law, are usually expressed in it: and instances may be brought of particular exceptions expressed in some laws; and if there be any such exception in the law under debate, it should especially be mentioned. He may further add; that to admit of exceptions not expressed in the

[1] Hermog. *De stat.* §. 11.

law

L E C T. law itſelf, is to enervate the force of all
  V.   laws by explaining them away, and in
effect to render them uſeleſs. And this
he may further corroborate, by comparing
the law under debate with others, and
conſidering its nature, and importance, and
how far the public intereſt of the ſtate is
concerned in the due and regular execution
of it; from whence he may infer, that
ſhould exceptions be admited in other
laws of leſs conſequence, yet however they
ought not in this. Laſtly, he may conſider the reaſon alleged by the defendant,
on which he founds his plea, and ſhew,
there was not that neceſſity of violating
the law in the preſent caſe, as is pretended.
And this is often the more requiſite, becauſe the party, who diſputes againſt the
words of the law, always endeavours to
ſupport his allegations from the equity of
the caſe. If therefore this plea can be
enervated, the main ſupport of the defendant's cauſe is removed. For as the former arguments are deſigned to prevail with
the judge to determine the matter on this
ſide the queſtion, from the nature of the
caſe; ſo the intention of this argument is
to induce him to it, from the weakneſs of
the defenſe made by the oppoſite party.
                                            But

But the defendant will on the contrary
ufe fuch arguments, as may beft demonftrate the equity of his caufe, and endeavour to vindicate the fact from his
good defign, and intention in doing it.
He will fay, that the laws have alloted
punifhments for the commiffion of fuch
facts, as are evil in themfelves, or prejudicial to others; neither of which can be
charged upon the action, for which he is
accufed: that no law can be rightly executed, if more regard be had to the words
and fyllables of the writing, than to the
intention of the legiflator. To which purpofe he may allege that direction of the
law itfelf, which fais: *The law ought not
to be too rigoroufly interpreted, nor the words
of it ftrained; but the true intention and
defign of each part of it duly confidered* [1].
As alfo that faying of Cicero : *What law
may not be weakened and deftroyed, if we
bend the fenfe to the words, and do not regard the defign and view of the legiflator* [2] ?
Hence he may take occafion to complain
of the hardfhip of fuch a procedure, that
no difference fhould be made between an
audacious and wilful crime, and an honeft
or neceffary action, which might happen
to difagree with the letter of the law, tho

[1] *L.* 19.
bibend.

[2] *Pro Cae-
cin. c.* 18.

F 3   not

LECT.
V.
not with the intent of it. And as it was obferved before to be of confiderable fervice to the accufer, if he could remove the defendant's plea of equity; fo it will be of equal advantage to the defendant, if he can fix upon any words in the law, which may in the leaft feem to countenance his cafe, fince this will take off the main force of the charge.

THE third controverfy of this kind is, when two writings happen to *clafh* with each other, or at leaft feem to do fo. Of this Hermogenes gives the following inftance. One law injoins: *He, who continues alone in a fhip during a tempeft, fhall have the property of the fhip.* Another law fais: *A difinherited fon fhall injoy no part of* **¹Hermog.** *his father's eftate* ¹. Now a fon, who had **De Stat.** **§. 12.** been difinherited by his father, happens to be in his father's fhip in a tempeft, and continues there alone, when every one elfe had deferted it. He claims the fhip by the former of thefe laws, and his brother tries his right with him by the latter. In fuch cafes therefore it may firft be confidered, whether the two laws can be reconciled. And if that cannot be done, then which of them appears more equitable. Alfo whether one be pofitive, and

I

the

the other negative; becaufe prohibitions
are a fort of exceptions to pofitive injunc-
tions. Or if one be a general law; and
the other more particular, and come nearer
to the matter in queftion. Likewife which
was laft made: fince former laws are often
abrogated, either wholly or in part, by
fubfequent laws; or at leaft were defigned
to be fo. Laftly, it may be obferved,
whether one of the laws be not plain and
exprefs, and the other more dubious, or
has any ambiguity in it. All or any of
which things that party will not omit to
improve for his advantage, whofe intereft
is concerned in it.

THE fourth controverfy is *Reafoning*. As
when fomething not exprefsly provided for
by a law, is infered by fimilitude, or
parity of reafon, from what is contained
in it. Quintilian mentions this inftance
of it: *There was a law made at Tarentum
to prohibit the exportation of wool, but a
certain perfon exports fheep* [1]. In this cafe
the profecutor may firft compare the thing,
which occafions the charge, with the words
of the law, and fhew their agreement, and
how unneceffary it was, that particular
thing fhould have been exprefsly mentioned in the law, fince it is plainly con-

[1] *Inft. orat.
Lib.* vii.
c. 8.

F 4   tained

tained in it, or at leaft an evident confequence from it. He may then plead that
many things of a like nature are omited
in other laws for the fame reafon. And
laftly, he may urge the reafonablenefs and
equity of the procedure. The defendant
on the other hand will endeavour to fhew
the deficiency of the reafoning, and the
difference between the two cafes. He will
infift upon the plain and exprefs words of
the law, and fet forth the ill tendency of
fuch inferences, and conclufions drawn from
fimilitudes, and comparifons; fince there is
fcarce any thing, but in fome refpect may
bear a refemblance to another.

THE laft controverfy under this head is
Interpretation, in which the difpute turns
upon the true meaning and explication of
the law, in reference to that particular
cafe. We have the following inftance of
this in the Pandects: *A man who had two
fons, both under age, fubftitutes Titius as heir
to him, who fhould die laft, provided both of
them died in their minority. They both perifh
together at fea, before they came to age.
Here arifes a doubt, whether the fubftitution
can take place, or the inheritance devolves to
the heir at law* [1]. The latter pleads, that
as neither of them can be faid to have died
laft,

[1] *L.* 9 *ff.*
de rebus
dub.

I

laſt, the ſubſtitution cannot take place, which was ſuſpended upon the condition, that one died after the other. But to this it may be ſaid, it was the intention of the teſtator, that if both died in their nonage, Titius ſhould ſuccede to the inheritance ; and therefore it makes no difference whether they died together, or one after the other ; and ſo the law determines it.

THE ſecond head of external arguments are *Witneſſes*. Theſe may either give their evidence, when abſent, in writing ſubſcribed with their name; or preſent, by word of mouth [1]. And what both of them teſtify, may either be from hear-ſay ; or what they ſaw themſelves, and were preſent at the time it was done. As the weight of the evidence may be thought greater or leſs on each of theſe accounts, either party will make ſuch uſe of it, as he finds for his advantage. The characters of the witneſſes are alſo to be conſidered ; and if any thing be found in their lives, or behaviour, that is juſtly exceptionable, to invalidate their evidence, it ought not to be omited. And how they are affected to the contending parties, or either of them, may deſerve conſideration ; for ſome allowances may be judged reaſonable in caſe of freindſhip,

[1] See Quint. *Inſt. orat.* Lib. v. c. 7.

LECT. V. ſhip, or enmity, where there is no room for any other exception. But regard ſhould cheiſly be had to what they teſtify, and how far the cauſe is affected by it. Cicero is very large upon moſt of theſe heads in his defenſe of Marcus Fonteius, with a deſign to weaken the evidence of the Gauls againſt

[1] *Cap.* 6. &c.

him [1]. And where witneſſes are produced on one ſide only, as orators ſometimes attempt to leſſen the credit of this kind of proof, by pleading that witneſſes are liable to be corrupted, or biaſſed by ſome prevailing intereſt or paſſion, to which arguments taken from the nature and circumſtances of things are not ſubject; it may be anſwered on the other hand, that ſophiſtical arguments, and falſe colourings are not expoſed to infamy or puniſhment, whereas witneſſes are reſtrained by ſhame and penalties, nor would the law require them, if they were not neceſſary.

THE third and laſt head of external arguments are *Contracts*, which may be either public or private. By public are meant the tranſactions between different ſtates, as leagues, alliances, and the like; which depend on the laws of nations, and come more properly under deliberative diſcourſes, to

[2] See *Lect.* IX.

which I ſhall refer them [2]. Thoſe are called

pri-

private, which relate to leſſer bodies, or ſocieties of men, and ſingle perſons ; and
may be either writen, or verbal. And it
is not ſo much the true meaning and pur-
port of them, that is here conſidered, as
their force and obligation. And, as the
Roman law declares, *Nothing can be more
agreable to human faith, than that perſons
ſhould ſtand to their agreements* [1]. Therefore in controverſies of this kind, the party,
whoſe intereſt it is, that the contract ſhould
be maintained, will plead, that ſuch cove-
nants have the force of private laws, and
ought religiouſly to be obſerved, ſince the
common affairs of mankind are tranſacted
in that manner ; and therefore to violate
them, is to deſtroy all commerce and ſo-
ciety among men. On the other ſide it
may be ſaid, that juſtice and equity are
cheifly to be regarded, which are immu-
table. And beſides, that the public laws
are the common rule to determine ſuch
differences, which are deſigned to redreſs
thoſe, who are aggreived. And indeed
where a compact has been obtained by force
or fraud, it is in itſelf void, and has no
effect either in law or reaſon. But on the
other hand, the Roman lawyers ſeem to
have very rightly determined, that all ſuch

ob-

[1] *L.* 1. *pr.
ff. de poet.*

LECT.
V.
obligations, as are founded in natural equity, tho not binding by national laws, and
are therefore called *nuda pacta*, ought however in honor and confcience to be performed [1].

[1] Pauli
Recept.
Sent.
Lib. ii.
t. 14. *de*
ufur. §. 1.
& ibi
Schulting.

THUS I have gon thro the common
heads of invention, both internal and external, which may be of fervice to an orator, when his view is to inform his hearers,
and prove the truth of what he afferts.
But the particular application of them to
the feveral forts of difcourfes, he may have
occafion to treat upon, I fhall explain in
fome following lectures.

LEC-

LECTURE VI.

Of the State of a Controversy.

IN my two laſt diſcourſes I conſidered the nature of *Common Places*, with the method of reaſoning from them ; and ſhould now procede in a more particular manner to ſhew the uſe of them in the ſeveral kinds of diſcourſes; but there is one thing, which muſt be firſt inquired into, and that is, what rhetoricians call, *The State of a Cauſe* or *Controverſy*. For the antients obſerving, that the principal queſtion, or point of diſpute, in all controverſies might be refered to ſome particular head, reduced thoſe heads to a certain number; that both the nature of the queſtion might by that means be better known, and the arguments ſuited to it be diſcovered with greater eaſe. And theſe heads they call *States*.

BY the *State of a Controverſy* then we are to underſtand, the principal point in diſpute between contending parties, upon the proof of which the whole cauſe or controverſy depends. We find it expreſſed by ſeveral other names in antient writers:

as,

LECT.
VI.

[1] Quint.
Inft orat.
Lib. iii.
c. 6.
Juven.
Sat. 6.

as, *the conftitution of the caufe, the general head, and the cheif queftion* [1]. And as this is the principal thing to be attended to in every fuch difcourfe; fo it is what firft requires the confideration of the fpeaker, and fhould be well fixed and digefted in his mind, before he procedes to look for arguments proper to fupport it. Thus Antony, the Roman orator, fpeaking of his own method in his pleadings, fais: *When I underftand the nature of the caufe, and begin to confider it, the firft thing I endeavour to do is, to fettle with myfelf what that is, to which all my difcourfe relating to the matter in difpute ought to be refered: then I diligently attend to thofe other two things, how to recommend myfelf, or thofe for whom I plead, to the good efteem of my hearers; and how to influence their minds,*

[2] De orat.
Lib. ii.
c. 27.

as may beft fuit my defign [2]. This way of proceding appears very agreable to reafon and prudence. For what can be more abfurd, than for a perfon to attempt the proof of any thing, before he has well fettled in his own mind a clear and diftinct notion, what the thing is, which he would endeavour to prove? Quintilian defcribes

[3] Inft. orat.
Lib. iii.
c. 6.

it to be, *That kind of queftion, which arifes from the firft conflict of caufes* [3]. In judi-

cial

cial cases it immediately follows upon the charge of the plaintif, and plea of the defendant. Our common law expresses it by one word, namely, the *Issue.* Which interpreters explain, by describing it to be, *That point of matter depending in suit, whereupon the parties join, and put their cause to the trial* [1]. Examples will further help to illustrate this, and render it more evident. In the cause of Milo, the charge of the Clodian party is, *Milo killed Clodius.* Milo's plea or defense, *I killed him, but justly.* From hence arises this grand question, or state of the cause : *Whether it was lawful for Milo to kill Clodius?* And that Clodius was lawfully killed by Milo, is what Cicero in his defense of Milo principally endeavours to prove. This is the main subject of that fine and beautiful oration. The whole of his discourse is to be considered as centering at last in this one point. Whatever different matters are occasionally mentioned, will, if closely attended to, be found to have been introduced some way or other, the better to support and carry on this design. Now in such cases, where the fact is not denied, but something is offered in its defense, the state of the cause is taken from the

[1] Manley *in voc.* Issue.

de-

LECT.
VI.

defendant's plea, who is obliged to make it good. As in the inftance here given, the cheif point in difpute was the lawfulnefs of Milo's action, which it was Cicero's bufinefs to demonftrate. But when the defendant denies the fact, the ftate of the caufe arifes from the accufation; the proof of which then lies upon the plaintif, and not, as in the former cafe, upon the defendant. So in the caufe of Rofcius, the charge made againft him is, *That he killed his father.* But he denies the fact. The grand queftion therefore to be argued is: *Whether or not he killed his father?* The proof of this lay upon his accufers. And Cicero's defign in his defenfe of him is to fhew, that they had not made good their charge. But it fometimes happens, that the defendant neither abfolutely denies the fact, nor attempts to juftify it; but only endeavours to qualify it, by denying that it is a crime of that nature, or deferves that name, by which it is expreffed in the charge. We have an example of this propofed by Cicero: *A perfon is accufed of facrilege, for taking a thing, that was facred, out of a private houfe. He owns the fact, but denies it to be facrilege; fince it was committed in a private houfe, and not*

in

in a temple. Hence this queſtion ariſes :
Whether to take a ſacred thing out of a
private houſe is to be deemed ſacrilege, or
only ſimple theft [1] ? It lies upon the ac- [1] *De In-vent. Lib.* ii. *c.* 18.
cuſer to prove, what the other denies ; and
therefore the ſtate of the cauſe is here
alſo, as well as in the preceding caſe, taken See alſo Quint.
from the inditement. *Inſt. orat. Lib.* vii.

BUT beſides the principal queſtion, there *c.* 3.
are other ſubordinate queſtions, which follow upon it in the courſe of a diſpute,
and ſhould be carefully diſtinguiſhed from
it. Particularly that, which ariſes from
the reaſon or argument, which is brought
in proof of the principal queſtion. For
the principal queſtion itſelf proves nothing,
but is the thing to be proved, and becomes
at laſt the concluſion of the diſcourſe.
Thus in the cauſe of Milo, his argument
is : *I killed Clodius juſtly, becauſe he aſſaſſinated me.* Unleſs the Clodian party be
ſuppoſed to deny this, they give up their
cauſe. From hence therefore this ſubordinate queſtion follows : *Whether Clodius
aſſaſſinated Milo ?* Now Cicero ſpends much
time in the proof of this, as the hinge, on
which the firſt queſtion, and conſequently
the whole cauſe depended. For if this
was once made to appear, the lawfulneſs

of

LECT.
VI.
of Milo's killing Clodius, which was the grand queſtion or thing to be proved, might be infered, as an allowed conſequence from it. This will be evident, by throwing Milo's argument, as uſed by Cicero, into the form of a ſyllogiſm.

> *An aſſaſſinator is lawfully killed:*
> *Clodius was an aſſaſſinator :*
> *Therefore he was lawfully killed by Milo,*
>   *whom he aſſaſſinated.*

If the minor propoſition of this ſyllogiſm was granted, no one would deny the concluſion. For the Roman law allowed of ſelf defenſe. But as Cicero was very ſenſible this would not be admited, ſo he takes much pains to bring the court into the beleif of it. Now where the argument brought in defenſe of the ſecond queſtion is conteſted, or the orator ſuppoſes that it may be ſo, and therefore ſupports that with another argument, this occaſions a third queſtion conſequent upon the former ; and in like manner he may procede to a fourth. But be they more or fewer, they are to be conſidered but as one chain of ſubordinate queſtions, dependent upon the firſt. And tho each of them has its particular ſtate, yet none of theſe is, what rhetoricians call *The State*

I

of

of the Caufe, which is to be underftood only of the principal queftion. And if, as it frequently happens, the firft or principal queftion is itfelf directly proved from more than one argument; this makes no other difference, but that each of thefe arguments, fo far as they are followed by others to fupport them, become a diftinct feries of fubordinate queftions, all dependent upon the firft. As when Cicero endeavours to prove, that Rofcius did not kill his father, from two reafons or arguments : *Becaufe he had neither any caufe to move him to fuch a barbarous action, nor any opportunity for it* [1].

[1] *Pro Rofc. Amer. c.* 14.

MOREOVER, befides thefe fubordinate queftions, there are alfo incidental ones often introduced, which have fome reference to the principal queftion, and contribute towards the proof of it, tho they are not neceffarily connected with it, or dependent upon it. And each of thefe alfo has its *State*, tho different from that of the *Caufe*. For every queftion, or point of controverfy, muft be ftated, before it can be made the fubject of difputation. And it is for this reafon, that every new argument advanced by an orator is called a queftion, becaufe it is confidered as a

frefh

fresh matter of controversy. In Cicero's
defense of Milo, we meet with several of
this sort of questions, occasioned by some
aspersions, which had been thrown out by
the Clodian party to the prejudice of Milo.
As, *That he was unworthy to see the light,*
who owned he had killed a man. For Milo
before his trial had openly confessed, he
killed Clodius. So likewise, *That the se-*
nate had declared the killing of Clodius was
an illegal action. And further, *That Pom-*
pey, by making a new law to settle the man-
ner of Milo's trial, had given his judgement
against Milo. Now to each of these Cicero replies, before he procedes to the
principal question. And therefore, tho
the question, in which the state of a controversy consists, is said by Quintilian to
arise from, *the first conflict of causes,* yet we
find by this instance of Cicero, that it is
not always the first question in order, upon
which the orator treats.

BUT it sometimes happens, that the
same cause or controversy contains in it
more than one state. Thus in judicial
causes, every distinct charge occasions a
new state. All Cicero's orations against
Verres relate to one cause, founded upon
a law of the Romans against unjust ex-
actions,

actions, made by their governors of provinces upon the inhabitants; but as that
profecution is made up of as many charges,
as there are orations, every charge, or inditement, has its different ftate. So likewife his oration in defenfe of Coelius has
two ftates, in anfwer to a double charge
made againft him by his adverfaries: one,
*for borrowing money of Clodia, in order to
bribe certain flaves to kill a foreign ambaf-
fador*; and the other, *for an attempt afterward to poifon Clodia herfelf.* Befides
which there were alfo feveral other matters of a lefs heinous nature, which had
been thrown upon him by his accufers,
with a defign, very likely, to render the
two principal charges more credible; to
which Cicero firft replies, in the fame
manner, as in his defenfe of Milo.

THo all the examples, we have hitherto
brought to illuftrate this fubject, have been
taken from judicial cafes; yet not only
thefe, but very frequently difcourfes of the
deliberative kind, and fometimes thofe of
the demonftrative, are managed in a con-
troverfial way. And all controverfies have
their *State.* And therefore Quintilian very
juftly obferves, that *ftates belong both to
general and particular queftions; and to all*

G 3 *forts;*

sorts of causes demonstrative, deliberative, *and judicial* [1]. In Cicero's oration for the Manilian law, this is the main point in dispute between him, and those who opposed that law : *Whether Pompey was the fittest person to be intrusted with the management of the war against Mithridates?* This is a subject of the deliberative kind. And of the same nature was that debate in the senate, concerning the demolition of Carthage. For the matter in dispute between Cato, who argued for it, and those who were of the contrary opinion, seems to have been this : *Whether it was for the interest of the Romans to demolish Carthage* [2]? And so likewise in those two fine orations of Cato and Caesar, given us by Sallust, relating to the conspirators with Catiline, who were then in custody, the controversy turns upon this : *Whether those prisoners should be punished with death, or perpetual imprisonment?* Examples of the demonstrative kind are not so common; but, I think, Cicero's oration concerning the *Answers of the soothsayers*, may afford us an instance of it. Several prodigies had lately happened at Rome, upon which the soothsayers being consulted, assigned this as the reason of them ; because some places con-
secrated

[1] *Inst. orat.*
Lib. iii.
c. 6.
See also
Cic. *De*
orat.
Lib. ii.
c. 42.

[2] See *Flor.*
Lib. ii.
c. 15. &c.

fecrated to the gods, had been afterwards converted to civil ufes. Clodius charged this upon Cicero, whofe houfe was rebuilt at the public expenfe, after it had been demolifhed by Clodius, and the ground confecrated to the goddefs Liberty. Cicero in this oration retorts the charge, and fhews, that the prodigies did not refpect him, but Clodius. So that the queftion in difpute was: *To which of the two thofe prodigies related.* This oration does not appear to have been fpoken in a judicial way, and muft therefore belong to the demonftrative kind. His invective againft Pifo is likewife much of the fame nature, wherein he compares his own behaviour and conduct with that of Pifo.

As to the number of thefe *States,* both Cicero and Quintilian reduce them to three. I fhall recite Quintilian's reafon, which he gives for this opinion. *We muft, fais he, agree with thofe, whofe authority Cicero follows, who tell us, that three things may be inquired into in all difputes; whether a thing is, what it is, and how it is. And this is the method, which nature prefcribes. For in the firft place it is neceffary the thing fhould exift, about which the difpute is: becaufe no judgement can be made*

G 4 *cither*

LECT.
VI.

either of its nature, or quality, till its ex-
istence be manifest; which is therefore the.
first question. But tho it be manifest, that
a thing is, it does not presently appear what
it is ; and when this is known, the quality
yet remains : and after these three are setled,
no further inquiry is necessary [1]. Thus far
Quintilian. Now the first of these three
states is called the *conjectural* state ; as if
it be inquired : *Whether one person killed*
another ? This always follows upon the
denial of a fact, by one of the parties, as
was the case of Roscius. And it receives
its name from hence, that the judge is
left, as it were, to conjecture, whether the
fact was really commited, or not, from
the evidence produced on the other side.
The second is called the *definitive* state,
when the fact is not denied ; but the dispute turns upon the nature of it, and what
name is proper to give it; as in that example of Cicero : *Whether to take a sacred*
thing out of a private house be theft, or
sacrilege? For in this case it is necessary
to settle the distinct notion of those two
crimes, and shew their difference. The
third is called the state of *quality*, when
the contending parties are agreed both as
to the fact, and the nature of it ; but the

dis-

[1] *Inst. orat.*
Lib. iii.
c. 6.

difpute is : *Whether it be juft or unjuft, profitable or unprofitable, and the like :* as in the caufe of Milo. Aristotle [1], and from him Voffius [2], add a fourth ftate, namely of *quantity,* As : *Whether an injury be fo great, as it is faid to be.* But Quintilian thinks this may be refered to fome or other of the preceding ftates ; fince it depends upon the circumftances of the fact, as the intention, time, place, or the like [3].

[1] *De rhetor.Lib.*iii. *c.* 26.
[2] *Inft.orat. Lib.*1. *c.*6. § 7.
[3] *Inft. orat. Lib.* iii. *c.* 6.

FROM what has been faid upon this fubject, the ufe of it may in a good meafure appear. For whoever ingages in a controverfy, ought in the firft place to confider with himfelf the main queftion in difpute, to fix it well in his mind, and keep it conftantly in his view ; without which he will be very liable to ramble from the point, and bewilder both himfelf, and his hearers. And it is no lefs the bufinefs of the hearers principally to attend to this ; by which means they will be helped to diftinguifh and feparate from the principal queftion, what is only incidental, and to obferve how far the principal queftion is affected by it ; to perceive what is offered in proof, and what is only brought in for illuftration ; not to be mifled

4   by

by digreſſions, but to diſcern when the ſpeaker goes off from his ſubject, and when he returns to it again; and, in a word, to accompany him thro the whole diſcourſe, and carry with them the principal chain of reaſoning, upon which the cauſe depends, ſo as to judge upon the whole, whether he has made out his point, and the concluſion follows from the premiſes. The neceſſity of this is generally the greater, in proportion to the length of a diſcourſe, however exact and artful the compoſition may be. They, who have read Cicero's orations with care, cannot but know, that altho they are formed in the moſt beautiful manner, and wrought up with the greateſt ſkill; yet the matter of them is often ſo copious, the arguments ſo numerous, the incidents either to conciliate or move his audience ſo frequent, and the digreſſions ſo agreable; that without the cloſeſt attention it is many times no eaſy matter to keep his main deſign in view. A conſtant and fixed regard therefore to the ſtate of the cauſe, and principal point in diſpute, is highly neceſſary to this end. But tho rhetoricians treat of theſe ſtates only as they relate to controverſies, and become the ſubject matter of diſpute between differing parties;

parties; yet every difcourfe has one or more principal heads, which the fpeaker cheifly propofes to prove or illuftrate. And therefore what has been faid upon this fubject, may likewife be confidered, as proper to be attended to in all difcourfes.

I HAVE only to add, that hitherto I have treated of the nature and ufe of the three ftates fo far, as relates to them in general; a more particular account of them, with the arguments, which are properly fuited to each ftate, will be given hereafter in their due place [1].

[1] See *Lect.* IX.

LEC-

L E C T U R E VII.

Of Arguments suited to Demonstrative Discourses.

THE general method of deducing *Arguments* from *Common Places*, has been already explained. But more fully to shew the use of this subject, and the assistance it affords the orator, it may not be improper separately to consider the particular heads, which are more especially suited to the several kinds of discourses. These are subordinate to the former, and spring from them, like branches from the same stock, or rivulets from a common fountain; as will evidently appear, when we come to explain them.

THIS is what I propose to enter upon at present, and shall begin with those, which relate to *demonstrative* discourses. And as these consist either in praise or dispraise, agreably to the nature of all contraries, one of them will serve to illustrate the other. Thus he, who knows, what *Arguments* are proper to prove the excellency of virtue, and commend it to our esteem; cannot be much at a loss for such, as will shew

the

the odious nature of vice, and expose it to every one's abhorrence; since they are all taken from the same heads, and directly the reverse of each other. In treating therefore upon the topics, suited to this kind of discourses, I need only mention those, which are requisite for praise; from whence such, as are proper for dispraise, will easily enough be discovered.

Now we praise either *persons* or *things:* under which division all beings with their properties and circumstances may be comprehended, so as to take in whatever belongs either to nature or art. But in each part of the division I shall confine my discourse principally to those subjects, relating to social life, in which oratory is more usually conversant. And under the former head, which respects persons or intelligent beings, I shall only speak of men. The antient sophists among the Greeks in their laudatory speeches seem rather to have studied, how to display their own eloquence, than to make them serve any valuable purposes in life; for their characters were so hightened, like poetical images, as suited them more to excite wonder and surprise, than to become the proper subjects of imitation. And for this reason Aristotle excludes

LECT.
VII.

¹ Quint.
Inst. orat.
Lib. iii.
c. 7.

cludes them from the number of civil difcourfes, or fuch as relate to the affairs of
fociety ¹. Tho if we confider their nature, rather than the abufe of them, they
appear to be very proper fubjects for an
orator, and to come within the main defign
of his province, which is perfuafion. For
to what purpofe can eloquence be better
employed, than to celebrate virtuous perfons, or actions, in fuch a manner, as to
excite mankind to their imitation, which
is the proper end of fuch difcourfes. And
indeed the panegyrics of the Greeks, which
were pronounced in the general affemblies
of their feveral ftates, feem to have been
defigned to recommend virtue by fo public
a teftimony, as appears by that of Ifocrates
in praife of the Athenians. For as to the
invectives of Demofthenes againft king Philip, they are rather of the *deliberative* kind,
and fo do not come under our prefent confideration; fince the orator's principal view
in thofe difcourfes is to animate the Athenians in a defenfe of their liberties, by a
vigorous profecution of the war againft
king Philip; to which end he likewife
propofes the fiteft methods for carrying it
on with fuccefs. And moft of Cicero's invectives againft Mark Antony may be refered

fered to the same kind of discourses. But as it is evident from common observation, that men are more influenced by examples, than precepts; so the celebrating virtue, and exposing vice, from particular instances in human life, as patterns to others in what they ought to pursue, and what to avoid, has by wise men been generally esteemed very serviceable to mankind. For which reason likewise the transmiting to posterity the lives of great and eminent men has met with good acceptance, as a useful and laudable design. And therefore the Romans, who were sensible that such discourses were not only suited for entertainment, but might likewise be made very useful to the public, did not confine them to the schools of rhetoricians, and the exercises of young persons. For it was their custom, as Quintilian tells us, to have them pronounced in public assemblies, even by magistrates, and sometimes by an order from the senate [1]. So we read, that a funeral oration was spoken in honor of Junius Brutus by Publicola, his collegue in the consulship [2]. And a like discourse, with a statue and public funeral was decreed by the senate to the honor of M. Juventius [3]. Tho afterwards indeed we

[1] *Inst. orat.
Lib.* iii.
c. 7.

[2] Dion.
Hal.
Lib. v.
c. 17.

[3] Dion.
Cass.
Lib. xlvi.
p. 324.

we generally find this office performed by some relation. In compliance with which custom, as Suetonius relates, Augustus, when but twelve years of age, pronounced a funeral discourse in praise of his grandmother Julia [1]. And Tiberius, when but nine years old, paid the like honor to his deceased father, as the same historian informs us [2]. And Cicero's invective against Piso, with his second against Mark Antony, may be refered to *demonstrative* discourses, as they respect things that were past, and so could not then be subjects for consultation. For all praise or dispraise must either regard what is past, or present. And generally speaking, persons are most affected by present things. Indeed the encomiums of antient heroes, and their famous actions, are very entertaining, and afford an agreable pleasure in the recital; but such examples of virtue, as are still in being, or at least yet fresh in memory, have the greatest influence for imitation.

But in praising or dispraising *persons*, rhetoricians prescribe two methods. One is, to follow the order, in which every thing happened, that is mentioned in the discourse; the other is, to reduce what is said under certain general heads, with-

[1] *In Vit. c.* 9.

[2] *In Vit. c.* 6.

out

out a ſtrict regard to the order of
time.

IN purſuing the former method, the
diſcourſe may be very conveniently divided
into three periods. The firſt of which
will contain, what preceded the perſon's
birth ; the ſecond, the whole courſe of his
life ; and the third, what followed upon
his death.

UNDER the firſt of theſe may be comprehended, what is proper to be ſaid concerning his country or family. And therefore, if theſe were honorable, it may be
ſaid to his advantage, that he no ways
diſgraced them, but acted ſuitably to ſuch
a deſcent. But if they were not ſo, they
may be either wholly omited, or it may
be ſaid, that inſtead of deriving thence any
advantage to his character, he has confered
a laſting honor upon them ; and that it
is not of ſo much moment where, or from
whom a perſon derives his birth, as how
he lives.

IN the ſecond period, which is that of
his life, the qualities both of his mind
and body, with his circumſtances in the
world, may be ſeparately conſidered. Tho
as Quintilian rightly obſerves : *All exter-*
nal advantages are not praiſed for them-

VOL. I.   H   *ſelves,*

LECT. *selves, but according to the use, that is made*
VII. *of them. For riches, and power, and in-*
terest, as they have great influence, and may
be applied either to good or bad purposes,
are a proof of the temper of our minds, and
therefore we are either made better, or worse
¹*Inst. orat.* *by them* [1]. But these things are a just
Lib iii.
c. 7. ground for commendation, when they are
the reward of virtue, or industry. Bodily
indowments are health, strength, beauty,
activity, and the like; which are more or
less commendable, according as they are
imployed. And where these, or any of
them, are wanting, it may be shewn, that
they are abundantly compensated by the
more valuable indowments of the mind.
Nay sometimes a defect in these may give
an advantageous turn to a person's character; for any virtue appears greater, in
proportion to the disadvantages the person
laboured under in exerting it. But the
cheif topics of praise are taken from the
virtues and qualifications of the mind. And
here the orator may consider the disposition, education, learning, and several virtues, which shone thro the whole course
of the person's life. In doing which the
preference should always be given to virtue above knowledge, or any other accom-

3   plishment.

plishment. And in actions, those are most considerable, and will be heard with greatest approbation, which a person either did alone, or first, or wherein he had fewest associates; as likewise those, which exceded expectation, or were done for the advantage of others, rather than his own. And further, as the last scene of a man's life generally commands the greatest regard, if any thing remarkable at that time was either said or done, it ought particularly to be mentioned. Nor should the manner of his death, or cause of it, if accompanied with any commendable circumstances, be omited; as if he died in the service of his country, or in the pursuit of any other laudable design.

THE third and last period relates to what followed after the death of the person. And here the public loss, and public honors confered upon the deceased, are proper to be mentioned. Sepulchers, statues, and other monuments to perpetuate the memory of the dead, at the expence of the public, were in common use both among the Greeks and Romans. But in the earliest times, as these honors were more rare, so they were less costly. For as in one age it was thought a sufficient

H 2 reward

reward for him, who died in the defense of his country, to have his name cut in a marble inscription; with the cause of his death; so in others it was very common to see the statues of gladiators, and persons of the meanest rank, erected in public places. And therefore a judgement is to be formed of these things from the time, custom, and circumstances of different nations; since the frequency of them renders them less honorable, and takes off from their evidence, as the rewards of virtue. But, as Quintilian sais: *Children are an honor to their parents, cities to their founders, laws to those who compiled them, arts to their inventors, and useful customs to the authors of them* [1].

[1] *Inst. orat. Lib.* iii. *c.* 7.

AND this may suffice for the method of praising persons, when we propose to follow the order of time, as Isocrates has done in his *funeral oration* upon Evagoras, king of Salamis, and Pliny in his *panegyric* upon the emperor Trajan. But as this method is very plain and obvious, so it requires the more agreable dress to render it delightful; left otherwise it seem rather like an history, than an oration. For which reason we find, that epic poets, as Homer, Virgil, and others, begin with the

the middle of their ſtory, and afterwards take a proper occaſion to introduce what preceded, to diverſify the ſubject, and give the greater pleaſure and entertainment to their readers.

THE other method above hinted was, to reduce the diſcourſe to certain general heads, without regarding the order of time. As if any one in praiſing the elder Cato ſhould propoſe to do it, by ſhewing, that he was a moſt prudent ſenator, an excellent orator, and moſt valiant general ; all which commendations are given him by Pliny [1]. In like manner the character of a good general may be compriſed under four heads, ſkill in military affairs, courage, authority, and ſucceſs ; from all which Cicero commends Pompey [2]. And agreably to this method Suetonius has writen the lives of the firſt twelve Caeſars.

[1] *Hiſt. Nat. Lib.* vii. *c.* 27.

[2] *Pro leg. Manil. c.* 11.

BUT in praiſing of perſons care ſhould always be taken, to ſay nothing that may ſeem fictitious, or out of character, which may call the orator's judgement, or integrity in queſtion. It was not without cauſe therefore, that Lyſippus the ſtatuary, as Plutarch tells us, blamed Apelles for painting Alexander the Great with thunder in his hand ; which could never ſuit his

cha-

LECT.
VII.
character, as a man, however he might boast of his divine descent; for which reason Lysippus himself made an image of him holding a spear, as the sign of a war-

[1] *De Jf. &
Ofir.*
rior [1]. Light and trivial things in commendations are likewise to be avoided, and nothing mentioned, but what may carry in it the idea of something truly valuable, and which the hearers may be supposed to wish for, and is proper to excite their emulation. These are the principal heads of praise with relation to men. In dispraise, as was hinted before, the heads contrary to these are requisite; which being sufficiently clear from what has been said, need not particularly be insisted on.

I PROCEDE therefore to the other part of the division, which respects *things,* as distinguished from *persons.* By which we are to understand all beings inferior to man, whether animate or inanimate; as likewise the habits and dispositions of men, either good or bad, when considered separately, and apart from their subjects, as arts and sciences, virtues and vices; with whatever else may be a proper subject for praise or dispraise. Some writers indeed have for their own amusement, and the diversion of others, displayed their eloquence in a

jocose

jocofe manner upon fubjects of this kind.
So Lucian has writen in praife of a *fly*,
and Synefius an elegant encomium upon
baldnefs. Others, on the contrary, have
done the like in a fatyrical way. Such is
Seneca's *Apotheofis* or confecration of the
emperor Claudius; and the *Myfopogon* or
beard hater, writen by Julian the emperor. Not to mention feveral modern authors, who have imitated them in fuch
ludicrous compofitions. But as to thefe
things, and all of the like nature, the obfervation of Antony in Cicero feems very
juft: *That it is not neceffary to reduce every
fubject we difcourfe upon to rules of art* [1].   [1] *De orat.*
For many are fo trivial, as not to deferve   *Lib.* ii.
it; and others fo plain and evident of   *c.* 11.
themfelves, as not to require it. But fince
it frequently comes in the way both of
orators and hiftorians to defcribe *countries*,
cities, and *facts*, I fhall breifly mention the
principal heads of invention, proper to illuftrate each of thefe.

COUNTRIES then may be celebrated
from the pleafantnefs of their fituation, the
clemency and wholefomnefs of the air,
and goodnefs of the foil, to which laft
may be refered the fprings, rivers, woods,
plains, mountains, and minerals. And to

H 4.   all

all thefe may be added their extent, cities,
the number and antiquity of the inhabitants, their policy, laws, cuftoms, wealth,
character for cultivating the arts both of
peace and war, their princes, and other
eminent men they have produced. Thus
Pacatus has given us a very elegant defcription of Spain, in his *panegyric upon the em-*
Cap. 4. *peror Theodofius*, who was born there [1].

CITIES are praifed from much the fame
topics, as countries. And here, whatever
contributes either to their defenfe, or ornament, ought particularly to be mentioned;
as the ftrength of the walls and fortifica-
tions, the beauty and fplendor of their
buildings, whether facred or civil, public
or private. We have in Herodotus a very
fine defcription of Babylon, which was once
the ftrongeft, largeft, and moft regular city
[2] *Lib.* i. in the world [2]. And Cicero has accurately
c. 178. defcribed the city Syracufe, in the ifland
[3] *Act.* iv. Sicily, in one of his orations againft Verres [3].
in Verr.
c. 52. BUT *facts* come much oftner under the
cognizance of an orator. And thefe receive their commendation from their honor, juftice, or advantage. But in defcribing them all the circumftances fhould be
related in their proper order, and that in
the moft lively and affecting manner, fuited

2   to

LECT.
VII.

to their different nature. Livy has reprefented the demolition of Alba by the
Roman army, which was fent thither to
deftroy it, thro the whole courfe of that
melancholy fcene, in a ftile fo moving and
pathetic, that one can hardly forbear con-
doling with the inhabitants, upon reading
his account.

Bu t in difcourfes of this kind, whether
of praife or difpraife, the orator fhould (as
he ought indeed upon all occafions) well
confider where, and to whom he fpeaks.
For wife men often think very differently
both of perfons and things from the common people. And we find that learned
and judicious men are frequently divided
in their fentiments, from the feveral ways
of thinking, to which they have been accuftomed. Befides different opinions prevail, and gain the afcendant, at different
times. While the Romans continued a
free nation, love of their country, liberty,
and a public fpirit, were principles in the
higheft efteem among them. And therefore when Cato killed himfelf, that he
might not fall into the hands of Caefar,
and furvive the liberty of his country, it
was thought an inftance of the greateft
heroic virtue; but afterwards, when they
had

LECT.
VII.
had been accuftomed to an arbitrary government, and the fpirit of liberty was now
loft, the poet Martial could venture to fay,

[1] *Lib.* ii.
ep. 80.
Death to avoid 'tis madnefs fure to die [1].

A prudent orator therefore will be cautious
of oppofing any fettled and prevailing notions of thofe, to whom he addreffes; unlefs it be neceffary, and then he will do it
in the fofteft and moft gentle manner.

Now if we look back, and confider the
feveral heads of praife, enumerated under
each of the fubjects above mentioned ; we
fhall find, they are taken from their nature, properties, circumftances, or fome
other general topic ; as was intimated in
the begining of this difcourfe.

L E C-

LECTURE VIII.

Of Arguments suited to Deliberative Discourses.

IN my last discourse I began to treat upon the particular heads of argument, suited to the three kinds of orations, and I went thro those, which properly relate to the *demonstrative* kind. I shall now procede to give a breif account of such, as more peculiarly respect *deliberative* subjects, in which we either advise to a thing, or dissuade from it. And they are taken from the nature and circumstances of the thing itself under consultation.

THIS kind of discourses must certainly have been very antient, since doubtless from the first beginning of mens conversing together, they deliberated upon their common interest, and offered their advice to each other. But neither those of the *laudatory*, nor *judicial* kind, could have been introduced, till mankind was settled in communities, and found it necessary to incourage virtue by public rewards, and bring vice under the restraint of laws. The early practice of *suasory* discourses

appears

LECT. appears from sacred writ, where we find,
VIII. that when Moses was ordered upon an em-
baſſy into Egypt, he would have excuſed
[1] *Exod.* iv. himſelf for want of eloquence [1]. And Ho-
10. mer repreſents the Greeks at the ſeige of
Troy, as flocking like a ſwarm of bees to
[2] *Iliad.* β. hear their generals harangue them [2]. Nor
87. is this part of oratory leſs conſpicuous for
its uſefulneſs to mankind, than its antiquity; being highly beneficial either in
councils, camps, or any ſocieties of men.
How many inſtances have we upon record,
where the fury of an inraged multitude
has been checked and appeaſed by the prudent and artful perſuaſion of ſome particular perſon? The ſtory of Agrippa Mene-
nius, when the commons of Rome with-
drew from the ſenators, and retired out of
the city, is too well known, to need reci-
[3] *Liv.* ting [3]. And how often have armies been
Lib. ii. animated and fired to the moſt dangerous
c. 32. exploits, or recalled to their duty, when
Flor. ready to mutiny, by a moving ſpeech of
Lib. i. *c.* 23. their general? many inſtances of which we
find in hiſtory.

ALL deliberation reſpects ſomething future, for it is in vain to conſult about
what is already paſt. The ſubject matter
of it, are either things public or private,
ſacred

facred or civil; indeed all the valuable concerns of mankind, both prefent and future, come under its regard. And the end propofed by this kind of difcourfes is cheifly profit or intereft. But fince nothing is truly profitable, but what is in fome refpect good ; and every thing, which is good in itfelf, may not in all circumftances be for our advantage ; properly fpeaking, what is both good and profitable, or beneficial good, is the end here defigned. And therefore, as it fometimes happens, that what appears profitable, may feem to interfere with that, which is ftrictly juft and honorable; in fuch cafes it is certainly moft advifeable to determine on the fafer fide of honor and juftice, notwithftanding fome plaufible things may be offered to the contrary. But where the difpute lies apparently between what is truly honeft, and fome external advantage propofed in oppofition to it, all good men cannot but agree in favor of honefty. Such was the cafe of Regulus, who being taken prifoner by the Carthaginians, was permited to go to Rome upon giving his oath, that unlefs he could perfuade the fenate to fet at liberty fome young Carthaginian noblemen, then prifoners at Rome,

in

LECT. VIII. in exchange for him, he fhould return again to Carthage. But Regulus, when he came to Rome, was fo far from endeavouring to prevail with the fenate to comply with the defire of the Carthaginians, that he ufed all his intereft to diffuade them from harkening to the propofal. Nor could the moft earneft intreaties of his neareft relations and freinds, nor any arguments they were able to offer, ingage him to continue at Rome, and not return again to Carthage. He had then plainly in his view on the one fide eafe, fecurity, affluence, honors, and the enjoyment of his freinds; and on the other certain death, attended with cruel torments. However thinking the former not confiftent with truth and juftice, he chofe the latter [1]. And he certainly acted, as became an honeft and brave man, in choofing death, rather than to violate his oath. Tho whether he did prudently in perfuading the fenate not to make the exchange, or they in complying with him, I fhall leave others to determine. Now when it proves to be a matter of debate, whether a thing upon the whole be really beneficial or not; as here arife two parts, advice and diffuafion, they will each require proper heads of argument. But

[1] Florus, *Lib.* ii. *c.* 2.

as

as they are contrary to each other, he who is acquainted with one, cannot well be ignorant of the other. For which reason, as in my laft difcourfe, I recited only the topics fuited for praife, leaving thofe for difpraife to be collected from them; fo here likewife, I fhall cheifly mention thofe proper for advice, from whence fuch as are fuited to diffuade will eafily be perceived. Now the principal heads of this kind are thefe following, which are taken from the nature and properties of the thing itfelf under confideration.

AND firft, *pleafure* often affords a very cogent argument in difcourfes of this nature. Every one knows, what an influence this has upon the generality of mankind. Tho, as Quintilian remarks, pleafure ought not of itfelf to be propofed, as a fit motive for action in ferious difcourfes, but when it is defigned to recommend fomething ufeful, which is the cafe here. So would any one advife another to the purfuit of polite literature. Cicero has furnifhed him with a very ftrong inducement to it, from the pleafure which attends that ftudy, when he fais: *If pleafure only was propofed by thefe ftudies, you would think them an entertainment becoming a man of fenfe,*

*fenfe, and a gentleman. For other purfuits
neither agree with all times, all ages, nor
all places; but thefe ftudies improve youth,
delight old age, adorn profperity, afford a re-
fuge and comfort in adverfity, divert us at
home, are no hindrance abroad, fleep, travel,*

[1] *Pro Ar-
chia, c. 7.* *and retire with us in the country* [1].

A SECOND head is *profit* or advantage,
which has no lefs influence upon many
perfons, than the former; and when it
refpects things truly valuable, is a very juft
and laudable motive. Thus Cicero, when
he fends his *Books of offices* to his fon,
which he wrote in Latin for his ufe, advifes him to make the beft advantage both
of his tutor's inftructions, and the conver-
fation at Athens, where he then was; but
withal to perufe his philofophical treatifes,
which would be doubly ufeful to him,
not only upon account of the fubjects, but
likewife of the language, as they would
enable him to exprefs himfelf upon thofe
arguments in Latin, which before had only
been treated of in Greek.

THE laft head of this kind, which I
fhall mention, is *honor*. And no argument
will fooner prevail with generous minds,
or infpire them with greater ardor. Virgil
has very beautifully defcribed Hector's
ghoft

ghoſt appearing to Aeneas, the night Troy
was taken, and adviſing him to depart,
from this motive of honor.

O goddeſs-born, eſcape by timely flight
The flames, and horrors of this fatal night.
The foes already have poſſeſs'd the wall,
Troy nods from high, and totters to her fall.
Enough is paid to Priam's royal name;
More than enough to duty, and to fame.
If by a mortal hand my father's throne
Cou'd be defended, 'twas by mine alone [1].

[1] *Aen. Lib.* ii. *v.* 289.

The argument here made uſe of, to perſuade Aeneas to leave Troy immediately
is, that he had already done all that could
be expected from him, either as a good
ſubject, or brave ſoldier; both for his king,
and country; which were ſufficient to ſecure his honor; and now there was nothing more to be expected from him, when
the city was falling, and impoſſible to be
ſaved; which could it have been preſerved
by human power, he himſelf had done it.

BUT altho a thing conſidered in itſelf
appear beneficial, if it could be attained,
yet the expediency of undertaking it may
ſtill be queſtionable; in which caſe the
following heads taken from the circumſtances, which attend it, will afford proper
arguments to ingage in it.

VOL. I. I AND

LECT.
VIII.

AND firſt the *poſſibility* of ſucceding may ſometimes be argued, as one motive to this end. So Hannibal endeavoured to convince king Antiochus, that is was poſſible for him to conquer the Romans, if he made Italy the ſeat of the war; by obſerving to him, not only that the Gauls had formerly deſtroyed their city; but that he had himſelf defeated them, in every battle he fought with them in that country [1].

[1] Juſtin,
Lib. xxxi.
c. 5.

BUT the bare poſſibility of a thing is ſeldom a ſufficient motive to undertake it, unleſs on very urgent occaſions. And therefore an argument founded upon *probability* will be much more likely to prevail. For in many affairs of human life, men are determined either to proſecute them or not, as the proſpect of ſucceſs appears more or leſs probable. Hence Cicero after the fatal battle at Pharſalia diſſuades thoſe of Pompey's party, with whom he was engaged, from continuing the war any longer againſt Caeſar; becauſe it was highly improbable after ſuch a defeat, by which their main ſtrength was broken, that they ſhould be able to ſtand their ground, or meet with better ſucceſs, than they had before [2].

[2] *Ad fam.*
Lib. vii.
ep. 3.

I

BUT

BUT further, since probability is not a motive strong enough with many persons to ingage in the prosecution of a thing, which is attended with considerable difficulties, it is often necessary to represent the *facility* of doing it, as a further reason to induce them to it. And therefore Cicero makes use of this argument to incourage the Roman citizens in opposing Mark Antony (who upon the death of Caesar had assumed an arbitrary power) by representing to them, that his circumstances were then desperate, and that he might easily be vanquished [1].

[1] *Philipp. iv. c. 5.*

AGAIN, if the thing advised to can be shewn to be in any respect *necessary*, this will render the motive still much stronger for undertaking it. And therefore Cicero joins this argument with the former, to prevail with the Roman citizens to oppose Antony, by telling them, that, *The consideration before them was not in what circumstances they should live ; but whether they should live at all, or die with ignominy and disgrace* [2]. This way of reasoning will sometimes prevail, when all others prove ineffectual. For some persons are not to be moved, till things are brought to an

[2] *Ibidem.*

I 2   ex-

extremity, and they find themselves reduced to the utmost danger.

To these heads may be added the consideration of the *event*, which in some
cases carries great weight with it.   As
when we advise to the doing of a thing
from this motive, that whether it succede
or not, it will yet be of service to undertake it.   So after the great victory gained
by Themistocles over the Persian fleet, at
the streights of Salamis, Mardonius advised Xerxes to return into Asia himself,
left the report of his defeat should occasion
an insurrection in his absence ; but to leave
behind him an army of three hundred
thousand men under his command ; with
which, if he should conquer Greece, the
cheif glory of the conquest would redound
to Xerxes ; but if the design miscarried, the
disgrace would fall upon his generals [1].

[1] Justin.
Lib. ii.
c. 13.

THESE are the principal heads, which
furnish the orator with proper arguments
in giving advice.   Cicero in his oration
for the Manilian law, where he endeavours
to persuade the Roman people to choose
Pompey for their general in the Mithridatic war, reasons from three of these topics, into which he divides his whole discourse ;

courfe; namely, the neceffity of the war, the greatnefs of it, and the choice of a proper general.   Under the firft of thefe he fhews, that the war was neceffary from four confiderations; the honor of the Roman ftate, the fafety of their allies, their own revenues, and the fortunes of many of their fellow citizens, which were all highly concerned in it, and called upon them to put a ftop to the growing power of king Mithridates, by which they were all greatly indangered.   So that this argument is taken from the head of *neceffity*. The fecond, in which he treats of the greatnefs of the war, is founded upon the topic of *poffibility*.   For tho he fhews the power of Mithridates to be very great, yet not fo formidable, but that he might be fubdued; as was evident from the many advantages, Lucullus had gained over him and his affociates.   In the third head he endeavours to prevail with them to intruft the management of the war in the hands of Pompey, whom he defcribes as a confummate general, for his fkill in military affairs, courage, authority, and fuccefs, in all which qualities he reprefents him as fuperior to any other of their generals, whom they could at that time make choice

I 3   of.

LECT.
VIII.

of. The defign of all which was to perfuade them, they might have very good
reafon to hope for fuccefs, and a happy
event of the war, under his conduct. So
that the whole force of his reafoning under
this head is drawn from *probability*. Thefe
are the three general topics, which make
up that fine difcourfe. Each of which is
indeed fupported by diverfe other arguments and confiderations, which will be
obvious in perufing the oration itfelf, and
therefore need not be here enumerated.
On the contrary, in another oration he endeavours to diffuade the fenate from con-
fenting to a peace with Mark Antony, becaufe it was bafe, dangerous, and impracticable [1].

[1] *Philipp.*
vii. *c.* 3.

BUT no fmall fkill and addrefs are required in giving advice. For fince the tempers and fentiments of mankind, as well
as their circumftances, are very different
and various; it is often neceffary to accommodate the difcourfe to their inclinations and opinions of things. And therefore the weightieft arguments are not always the moft proper, and fiteft to be ufed
on all occafions. Cicero, who was an admirable mafter of this art, and knew per-
fectly well how to fuit what he faid to the

taſte

taſte and reliſh of his hearers, in treating upon this ſubject, diſtinguiſhes mankind into two ſorts; the ignorant and unpoliſhed, who always prefer profit to honor; and ſuch as are more civilized and polite, who prefer honor and reputation to all other things [1]. Wherefore they are to be moved by theſe different views, praiſe, glory, and virtue influence the one; while the other is only to be ingaged by a proſpect of gain, and pleaſure. Beſides it is plain, that the generality of mankind are much more inclined to avoid evils, than to purſue what is good; and to keep clear of ſcandal and diſgrace, than to practiſe what is truly generous and noble. Perſons likewiſe of a different age act from different principles; young men for the moſt part view things in another light, from thoſe who are older, and have had more experience, and conſequently are not to be influenced from the ſame motives. Every nation alſo has its particular cuſtoms, manners, and polity, which give a different turn to the genius of the inhabitants. Hence we find in hiſtory, that what was commendable in one country, was a diſgrace in another. For which reaſon, Cornelius Nepos, in writing the life of that

[1] *Orat. Partit. c. 25, &c.*

I 4   ex-

excellent Theban general, Epaminondas, introduces his account of him by ſaying: *I muſt caution my readers, not to judge of foreign cuſtoms by their own; nor to think, that ſuch things as are diſregarded by them, were equally contemned by others.* For we know that muſic with us is unbecoming the character of a gentleman, and dancing is looked upon as a vice; but theſe things are approved, and in great eſteem among the Greeks. And therefore when Cato, by way of reproach, had called Muraena a dancer; Cicero queſtions the fact, as highly improbable; ſince, as he ſais: *No ſober man would dance even at a modeſt entertain-ment* [1]. I mention this to ſhew, how requiſite it is many times to guard againſt common prejudices, and to ſuit our diſcourſe to the ſentiments of thoſe, to whom we addreſs. And this can never be more neceſſary, than in giving advice. The ſpeech of Alexander, made to his ſoldiers before he ingaged the Perſians, as we have it in Curtius, is finely wrought up in this reſpect. For as his army was compoſed of different nations, the parts of his diſcourſe are admirably well ſuited to their ſeveral views in proſecuting the war. He reminds his countrymen, the Macedonians,

[1] *Pro Mu-raen. c. 6.*

I   of

of their former victories in Europe; and
tells them, that Perfia is not to be the
boundary of their conquests, but they are
to extend them farther than either Her-
cules or Bacchus had done: that Bactra
and the Indies would be theirs, and that
what they faw, was but a fmall part of
what they were to poffefs: that neither the
rocks of Illyrium, nor the mountains of
Thrace, but the fpoils of the whole eaft
were now before them : that the conqueft
would be fo eafy, they would fcarce have
occafion to draw their fwords, but they
might pufh the enemy with their bucklers.
Then he reminds them of their fubduing
the Athenians under his father Philip, and
the late conqueft of Boeotia, the victory at
the river Granicus, and the many cities
and countries now behind them, and under
their fubjection. When he addreffes to
the Greeks, he tells them, they are now
going to ingage with thofe, who had been
the enemies of their country, firft by the
infolence of Darius, and afterwards of
Xerxes, who would have deprived them
even of the neceffaries of life, who deftroyed their temples, demolifhed their
towns, and violated both their facred and
civil rights. And then directing his dif-

courfe

LECT.
VIII.
courfe to the Illyrians and Thracians, who
were accuftomed to live by plunder, he in-
courages them with the profpect of booty,
from the rich armour and furniture of the
Perfians, which they might be mafters of
with the greateft eafe : and tells them, they
would now exchange their barren mountains and fnowy hills, for the fertile coun-
[1] *Lib.* iii.
c. 10.
try and feilds of Perfia [1].

IT feems unneceffary to add more examples for the illuftration of that, which
fo frequently occurs in all good writers,
who give us any difcourfes of this nature.
And therefore I fhall only obferve further,
that not only matters of advice and exhor-
tation, but likewife all confolatory and pe-
titory fpeeches, come under this head of
difcourfes. Befides we often find thofe
things intermixed, which relate to the *laudatory* kind ; as in Cicero's oration for the
Manilian law, a confiderable part of it is
imployed in the praife of Pompey. But
his view in that was only to induce his
hearers, to choofe him for their general, and
a difcourfe ought to receive its name from
the principal defign of the fpeaker.

L E C-

LECTURE IX.

Of Arguments suited to Judicial Discourses.

I COME now to consider the arguments, proper for the third and last sort of discourses, which relates to *judicial* affairs. And in these both the Grecian and Roman youth, who were desirous to gain a reputation for eloquence, used commonly to give the first proofs of their genius and ability. The first of Cicero's orations now extant, is his defence of Publius Quintius, which he spoke in the twenty sixth year of his age [1]. *Deliberative* discourses were not made before a judge, but in larger assemblies, either of the body of the Roman citizens, or the senate. And as they generally related to affairs of great importance, and such as respected the state; they required some authority in the speaker, which he had gained by former proofs of his ability and judgement. The bar therefore (as we call it) was commonly the place, where young orators used first in public to exercise and try their genius. And they took care in a particular manner to prepare themselves for this, by declaiming

LECT.
IX.

[1] *Euseb. in Chron.* See also *Cic. De clar. orat. c. 90, &c.*

LECT.
IX.

claming before hand either in the fchools, or under the inftruction of fome fkilful perfon in private. Nor did the greateft perfons at Rome think it beneath them to affift young gentlemen in this defign [1].

Now in *judicial* controverfies there are two parties, the plaintif or profecutor, and the defendant or perfon charged. The fubject of them is always fomething paft. And the end propofed by them Cicero calls *equity*, or *right and equity* [2]; the former of which arifes from the laws of the country, and the latter from reafon and the nature of things. For at Rome the praetors had a court of equity, and were impowered, in many cafes relating to property, to relax the rigor of the writen laws. But as this fubject is very copious, and caufes may arife from a great variety of things, writers have reduced them to three heads, which they call *States*, to fome one of which all *judicial* procedings may be refered; namely, *whether a thing is, what it is*, or *how it is*. By the *State* of a caufe therefore is meant the principal queftion in difpute, upon which the whole affair depends. Which if it ftops in the firft enquiry, and the defendant denies the fact, the *State* is called *conjectural*; but if the
fact

[1] Cic. *De clar. orat.* c. 89.

[2] *De orat. Lib.* i. c. 31, 38. *Orat. Partit.* c. 37.

fact be acknowledged, and yet denied to
be what the adverfary calls it, it is termed
definitive; but if there is no difpute either
about the fact, or its name, but only the
juftice of it, it is called the *State* of *quality :* as was fhewn more largely before in
a former lecture [1]. But I then confidered [1] See *Lect.* VI.
thefe *States* only in a general view, and
defered the particular heads of argument,
proper for each of them, to this *judicial*
kind of difcourfes; where they moft frequently occur, and from which examples
may eafily be accommodated to other fubjects. And this is what I am now particularly to treat of.

ALL *judicial* caufes are either *private* or
public. They are called *private,* which relate to the right of particular perfons; and
they are likewife called *civil* caufes, as
they are converfant about matters of property. *Public* caufes are thofe, which relate to public juftice, and the government
of the ftate; which are alfo called *criminal,* becaufe by them crimes are profecuted, whether capital, or thofe of a lefs
heinous nature. I fhall take the heads of
the arguments only from this latter kind,
becaufe they are more copious, and eafy to
be illuftrated by examples; from which
fuch

LECT.
IX.

such as agree to the former, namely *civil* causes, will sufficiently appear.

AND I shall begin with the *conjectural* state, which comes first in the order of inquiry. When therefore the accused person denies the fact, there are three things, which the prosecutor has to consider: Whether he *would* have done it, whether he *could*, and whether he *did* it [1]. And hence arise three topics; from the *Will*, the *Power*, and the *Signs*, or circumstances, which attended the action. The affections of the mind discover the *Will*; as, passion, an old grudge, a desire of revenge, a resentment of an injury, and the like. Therefore Cicero argues from Clodius's hatred of Milo, that he designed his death, and from thence infers, that he was the aggressor in the combat between them, wherein Clodius was killed [2]. This is what he principally endeavours to prove, and comes properly under this *State:* for Milo owned that he killed him, but alleged that he did it in his own defence. So that in regard to this point, which of them assaulted the other, the charge was mutual. The prospect of advantage may also be alleged to the same purpose. Hence it is said or L. Cassius, that whenever he sat as judge

in

[1] Quint. *Inst orat. Lib.* vii. *c.* 2.

[2] *Pro Milon. c.* 13.

LECT.
IX.

in a case of murder, he used to advise and move the court, to examine, to whom the advantage arose from the death of the deceased [1]. And Cicero puts this to Antony concerning the death of Caesar. *If any one, sais he, should bring you upon trial, and use that saying of Cassius,* cui bono, *who got by it, look to it, I beseech you, that you are not confounded* [2]. To these arguments may be added, hope of impunity, taken either from the circumstances of the accused person, or of him who suffered the injury. For persons, who have the advantage of interest, freinds, power, or money, are apt to think they may easily escape; as likewise such, who have formerly commited other crimes with impunity. Thus Cicero represents Clodius as hardened in vice, and above all the restraint of laws, from having so often escaped punishment upon commiting the highest crimes [3]. On the contrary, such a confidence is sometimes raised from the condition of the injured party, if he is indigent, obscure, timorous, or destitute of freinds; much more if he has an ill reputation, or is loaded with popular hatred and resentment. It was this presumption of the obscurity of Roscius, who lived in the

[1] Ascon. ad Cicer. orat. pro Milon. See also Cic. pro Rosc. Amer. c. 30.

[2] Philipp. ii. c. 14. Et pro Milon. c. 12.

[3] Pro Mil. c. 14.

the country, and his want of intereſt at Rome, which encouraged his accuſers to charge him with killing his father, as Cicero ſhews in his defenſe of him [1]. Laſtly, the temper of a perſon, his views, and manner of life, are conſiderations of great moment in this matter. For perſons of bad morals, and ſuch who are addicted to vice, are eaſily thought capable of commiting any wickedneſs. Hence Salluſt argues from the evil diſpoſition, and vitious life of Catiline, that he affected to raiſe himſelf upon the ruins of his country [2]. The ſecond head is the *power* of doing a thing; and there are three things which relate to this, the *place*, the *time*, and *opportunity*. As if a crime is ſaid to have been commited in a private place, where no other perſon was preſent; or in the night; or when the injured perſon was unable to provide for his defence. Under this head may likewiſe be brought in the circumſtances of the perſons; as if the accuſed perſon was ſtronger, and ſo able to overpower the other; or more active, and ſo could eaſily make his eſcape. Cicero makes great uſe of this topic in the caſe of Milo, and ſhews, that Clodius had all the advantages of *place*, *time*, and *opportunity*

to

[1] *In perorat.*

[2] *Bell. Cat. c. 5.*

to execute his defign of killing him [1]. The third head are the *Signs* and circumftances, which either preceded, accompanied, or followed the commiffion of the fact. So threats, or the accufed perfon being feen at or near the place before the fact was commited, are circumftances that may probably precede murder; fighting, crying out, bloodfhed, are fuch as accompany it; palenefs, trembling, inconfiftent anfwers, hefitation or faltering of the fpeech, fomething found upon the perfon accufed, which belonged to the deceafed, are fuch as follow. Thus Cicero proves, that Clodius had threatened the death of Milo, and given out that he fhould not live above three days at the fartheft. Thefe arguments, taken from conjectures, are called *prefumptions*, which, tho they do not directly prove, that the accufed perfon commited the fact, with which he is charged; yet, when being laid together they appeared very ftrong, fentence by the Roman law might fometimes be given upon them [2] to convict him.

THESE are the topics, from which the profecutor takes his arguments. Now the bufinefs of the defendant is to invalidate thefe. Therefore fuch as are brought from

[1] *Pro Milon. c.* 19.

[2] *L. ult. de probation.*

LECT.
IX.
the *Will*, he either endeavours to ſhew are not true, or ſo weak as to merit very little regard. And he refutes thoſe taken from the *Power*, by proving, that he wanted either opportunity, or ability: as, if he can ſhew, that neither the place nor time inſiſted on was at all proper; or that he was then in another place. In like manner he will endeavour to confute the *Circumſtances*, if they cannot directly be denied, by ſhewing that they are not ſuch, as do neceſſarily accompany the fact, but might have proceeded from other cauſes, tho nothing of what is alleged had been commited; and it will be of great ſervice to aſſign ſome other probable cauſe. But ſometimes the defendant does not only deny, that he did the fact, but charges it upon another. Thus Cicero in his oration for Roſcius, not only defends him from each of theſe three heads, but likewiſe charges the fact upon his ac-
ſ *Cap.* 28. cuſers [1].

I COME now to the *definitive* ſtate, which is principally concerned in defining and fixing the name proper to the fact. Tho orators ſeldom make uſe of exact definitions, but commonly chooſe larger deſcriptions, taken from various properties of the ſubject, or thing deſcribed.

THE

THE heads of argument in this *State* are much the same to both parties. For each of them defines the fact his own way, and endeavours to refute the other's definition. We may illustrate this by an example from Quintilian: *A person is accused of sacrilege, for stealing money out of a temple, which belonged to a private person* [1]. The fact is owned, but the question is, *Whether it be properly sacrilege?* The prosecutor calls it so, because it was taken out of a temple. But since the money belonged to a private person, the defendant denies it to be sacrilege, and sais it is only simple theft. Now the reason why the defendant uses this plea, and insists upon the distinction, is, because by the Roman law the penalty of theft was only four times the value of what was stolen; whereas sacrilege was punished with death [2]. The prosecutor then forms his definition agreable to his charge, and sais: *To steal any thing out of a sacred place is sacrilege.* But the defendant excepts against this definition, as defective; and urges, that it does not amount to sacrilege, unless the thing stolen was likewise sacred. And this case might once perhaps have been a matter of controversy, since we find it expressly

[1] See *Lect.* VI. *p.* 81.

[2] *Inst.* §. 5. *de oblig. quae ex delicto. L.* 9. *ff. ad legem Jul peculat. &c.*

K 2   de-

LECT
IX.

determined in the Pandects, that, *An action of sacrilege should not lie, but only of theft, against any one, who should steal the goods of private persons deposited in a temple* [1].

[1] *L. 5. ff. ad leg. Jul. pecul. &c.*

THE second thing is the proof brought by each party to support his definition, as in the example given us by Cicero, of one, *who carried his cause by bribery, and was afterwards prosecuted again upon an action of prevarication* [2]. Now if the defendant was cast upon this action, he was by the Roman law subjected to the penalty of the former prosecution [3]. Here the prosecutor defines prevarication to be, *any bribery or corruption in the defendant, with a design to pervert justice.* The defendant therefore, on the other hand, restrains it to, *bribing only the prosecutor.*

[2] *Orat. Partit. c. 36.*

[3] *L. ult. ff. de prae-var.*

AND if this latter sense agree better with the common acceptation of the word, the prosecutor in the third place pleads the intention of the law, which was to comprehend all bribery in judicial matters under the term of prevarication. In answer to which the defendant endeavours to shew, either from the head of contraries, that a real prosecutor and a prevaricator are used as opposite terms in the law; or from the etymology of the word, that a prevaricator denotes

denotes one, who pretends to appear in
the profecution of a caufe, while in reality
he favors the contrary fide [1] ; and confe- [1] Cic.
quently, that money given for this end, *Orat.Part.*
only can, in the fenfe of the law, be called *c. 36. L. 1*
prevarication. *princ. ff. de
praevar.*

LASTLY, the profecutor pleads, it is unreafonable, that he, who does not deny the fact, fhould efcape by a cavil about a word. But the defendant infifts upon his explication, as agreable to the law, and fais, the fact is mifreprefented and blackened, by affixing to it a wrong name.

THE third ftate is that of *quality*, in which the difpute turns upon the juftice of an action. And here the defendant does not deny he did the thing, he is charged with ; but afferts it to be right and equitable, from the circumftances of the cafe, and the motives which induced him to it.

AND firft, he fometimes alleges, the reafon of doing it was in order to prevent fome other thing of worfe confequence, which would otherwife have happened. We have an inftance of this in the life of Epaminondas, who, with two other generals, joined in the command with him, marched the Theban army into Pelopon-

K 3 nefus

LECT.
IX.

nefus againſt the Lacedaemonians; but by the influence of a contrary faction at home, their commiſſions were ſuperſeded, and other generals ſent to command the army. But Epaminondas being ſenſible, that if he obeyed this order at that time, it would be attended with the loſs of the whole army, and conſequently the ruin of the ſtate, refuſed to do it; and having perſuaded the other generals to do the like, they happily finiſhed the war, in which they were engaged; and upon their return home, Epaminondas, taking the whole matter upon himſelf, on his trial was acquited [1]. The arguments proper in this caſe are taken from the juſtice, uſefulneſs, or neceſſity of the action. The accuſer therefore will plead, that the fact was not juſt, profitable, nor neceſſary, conſidered either in itſelf, or comparatively with that, for the ſake of which it is ſaid to have been done. And he will endeavour to ſhew, that what the defendant aſſigns, for the reaſon of what he did, might not have happened, as he pretends. Beſides, he will repreſent of what ill conſequence it muſt be, if ſuch crimes go unpuniſhed. The defendant, on the other hand, will argue from the ſame heads, and endeavour to prove

[1] Nepos
in vit. 7.

prove the fact was juft, ufeful, or neceffary. And he will further urge, that no juft eftimate can be made of any action, but from the circumftances which attend it; as the defign, occafion, and motives for doing it; which he will reprefent in the moft favorable light to his own caufe, and endeavour to fet them in fuch a view, as to induce others to think, they could not but have done the fame, in the like circumftances.

AGAIN, the caufe of an action is fometimes charged by the defendant upon the party, who received the damage, or fome other perfon, who either made it neceffary, or injoined him to do it. The firft of thefe was Milo's plea for killing Clodius, becaufe he affaulted him, with a defign to take away his life. Here the fact is not denied, as in the cafe of Rofcius, above mentioned, under the *conjectural* ftate; but juftified from the reafon of doing it. For that an affaffinator might juftly be killed, Cicero fhews both from law and reafon [1]. [1] *Cap.* 4. The accufer therefore in fuch a cafe will, if there be room for it, deny the truth of this allegation. So the freinds of Clodius affirmed, that Milo was the aggreffor, and not Clodius; which Cicero in his defenfe

K 4   *of*

of Milo principally labours to refute. In the second cafe the profecutor will fay, no one ought to offend, becaufe another has offended firft; which defeats the courfe of public juftice, renders the laws ufelefs, and deftroys the authority of the magiftrate. The defendant, on the other hand, will endeavour to reprefent the danger and neceffity of the cafe, which required an immediate remedy, and in that manner; and urges, that it was vain and impracticable to wait for redrefs in the ordinary way, and therefore no ill confequence can arife to the public. Thus Cicero in defending Sextius, who was profecuted for a riot, in bringing armed men into the forum, fhews that his defign was only to repel force with force; which was then neceffary, there being no other means left for the people to affemble, who were excluded by a mob

[r] *Cap.* 35. of the contrary party [r]. Of the third cafe we have alfo an example in Cicero, who tells us, that, *in making a league between the Romans and Samnites, a certain young nobleman was ordered by the Roman general to hold the fwine (defigned for a facrifice); but the fenate afterwards difapproving the terms, and delivering up their general to the Samnites, it was moved, whether this young man*

man ought not likewise to be given up [1].
Thofe, who were for it, might fay; that
to allege the command of another is not
a fufficient plea for doing an ill action.
And this is what the Roman law now exprefsly declares [2]. But in anfwer to that
it might be replied; that it was his duty
to obey the command of his general, who
was anfwerable for his own orders, and
not thofe, who were obliged to execute
them; and therefore to give up this young
nobleman, would be to punifh one perfon
for the fault of another.

LASTLY, a fact is fometimes rather ex-
cufed, than defended, by pleading that it
was not done defignedly, or with any ill
intent. This is called *conceffion*, and contains two parts, *apology* and *intreaty*. The
former reprefents the matter as the effect
of inadvertency, chance, or neceffity. Ariftotle gives us an example of inadvertency
or imprudence in a woman at Athens, who
gave a young man a love potion, which
killed him; for which fhe was tried, but
acquited [3]. Tho afterwards this was made
criminal by the Roman law [4]. The cafe
of Adraftus, as related by Herodotus, is
an inftance of chance; who being intrufted
by Craefus with the care of his fon, as

they

[1] *De In-
vent.
Lib.* ii.
c. 30.

[2] *L.* 1.
§. 13. *ff.
de vi &
vi armat.*

[3] *Mag. Mo-
ral. Lib.* i.
c. 17.

[4] *L.* 38.
§. 5 *ff. de
poenis.*

they were hunting, killed him accidentally with a javelin, which he threw at a boar [1]. It is neceffity, when a perfon excufes his making a default, from ftrefs of weather, ficknefs, or the like. Thus Cicero pleaded his illnefs, contracted by the fatigue of a long journey, as an excufe for not appearing in the fenate upon the fummons of Mark Antony; who threatened to oblige him to it by pulling his houfe down [2]. But what the defendant here attributes to inadvertency, chance, or neceffity, the oppofite party will attribute to defign, negligence, or fome other culpable reafon; and reprefent it as a matter injurious to the public, to introduce fuch precedents; and alfo produce inftances, if that can be done, where the like excufes have not been admited. On the other hand, the defendant will infift on his innocence, and fhew the hardfhip and feverity of judging mens actions rather by the event, than from the intention: that fuch a procedure makes no difference between the innocent and the guilty; but muft neceffarily involve many honeft men in ruin and deftruction, difcourage all virtuous and generous defigns, and turn greatly to the prejudice of human fociety. He will alfo confider the inftances

[1] *Lib.* i. *c.* 43.

[2] *Philipp.* i. *c.* 5.

3

al-

alleged by the accuſer, and ſhew the dif- ference between them and his own caſe. And laſtly, he will have recourſe to intreaty, or a ſubmiſſive addreſs to the equity and clemency of the court, or party offended, for pardon; as Cicero has done in his oration to Caeſar, in favor of Ligarius.

THESE inſtances are ſufficient to ſhew the nature of the arguments ſuited, to *judicial* diſcourſes, which are deduced from a variety of the general topics.

L E C-

L E C T U R E X.

Of the Character and Address of an Orator.

HAVING in several discourses considered and explained the first part of invention, which furnishes the orator with such arguments, as are necessary for the proof of his subject; I am next to shew what are the proper means to conciliate the minds of his hearers, to gain their affection, and to recommend both himself, and what he sais to their good opinion and esteem. For the parts of invention are commonly thus distinguished; that the first respects the *subject* of the discourse, the second the *speaker*, and the third the *hearers*. Now the second of these, which is what I am at present to explain, is by Quintilian called, a *propriety of manners*. And in order to express this, it is necessary, as he tells us, *that every thing appear easy and natural, and the disposition of the speaker be discovered by his words* [1]. We may form an easy conception of this from the conduct of such persons, who are most nearly concerned in each others welfare. As when

[1] *Inst. orat. Lib.* vi. *c.* 2.

I

re-

relations or freinds converse together upon any affairs of importance, the temper and disposition of the speaker plainly shews itself by his words and manner of addrefs. And what nature here directs to without colouring or disguise, the orator is to endeavour to perform by his art. Tho indeed, if what a person fais, be inconsistent with his usual conduct and behaviour at other times; he cannot expect it should gain much credit, or make any deep impression upon his hearers. Which may be one reason, why the antient rhetoricians make it so necessary a qualification in an orator, that he be a good man; since he should always be consistent with himself, and, as we say, talk in character. And therefore it is highly requisite, that he should not only gain the skill of assuming those qualities, which the nature and circumstances of his discourse require him to express; but likewise, that he should use his utmost endeavours to get the real habits implanted in his mind. For as by this means they will be always expressed with greater ease and facility; so by appearing constantly in the course of his life, they will have more weight and influence upon particular occasions.

Now

LECT.
X.

Now there are four qualities, more efpecially fuited to the character of an orator,
which fhould always appear in his difcourfes, in order to render what he fais acceptable to his hearers; and thefe are, *Wifdom*, *Integrity*, *Benevolence*, and *Modefty*.

WISDOM is neceffary, becaufe we eafily
give into thofe, whom we efteem wifer
and more knowing than ourfelves. Knowledge is very agreable and pleafant to all,
but few make very great improvements in
it, either by reafon they are employed in
other neceffary affairs, and the mind of man
cannot attend to many things at once; or
becaufe the way to knowledge at firft is
hard and difficult, fo that perfons either
do not care to enter upon the purfuit of
it, or if they do, they are many times foon
difcouraged, and drop it, for want of fufficient refolution to furmount its difficulties.
Such therefore, who either cannot, or do
not care to give themfelves the trouble of
examining into things themfelves, muft take
up with the reprefentation of others; and
it is an eafe to them to hear the opinion
of perfons, whom they efteem wifer than
themfelves. No one loves to be deceived,
and fuch who are fearful of being mifled,
are pleafed to meet with a perfon, in whofe
wifdom,

wisdom, as they think, they can safely trust. The character of wisdom therefore is of great service to an orator, since the greater part of mankind are swayed by authority, rather than arguments.

BUT this of itself is not sufficient, unless the opinion of *Integrity* be joined with it. Nay, so far from it, that the greater knowledge and understanding a man is supposed to have, unless he likewise have the character of an honest man, he is often the more suspected. For knowledge without honesty is generally thought to dispose a person, as well as qualify him, to deceive. Quintilian, in treating upon *Narration*, has a very remarkable passage to this purpose, which I shall here transcribe. *I must not omit,* sais he, *how much the authority of the speaker gives credit to what he relates, which is to be gained principally by his life, and partly from his manner of speaking. For the more grave and honest this appears to be, what he affirms must necessarily carry with it the greater weight. In this part therefore especially all suspicion of design is to be avoided, that nothing seem counterfeit, nothing feigned; but all things to flow rather from the nature of the subject, than the art of the speaker. But this we cannot away with,*

LECT. *with, who think our art loft, if it does not*
  X. *appear ; whereas it ceafes to be art, when it*

¹ *Inft. orat.*
Lib. iv.
c. 2.

does appear ¹. And what Quintilian obferves here with refpect to *Narration,* the
beft writers all recommend as neceffary
thro the whole conduct of an orator.

AND to both thefe qualities the appearance of kindnefs and *Benevolence* fhould
likewife be added. For tho a perfon have
the reputation of wifdom and honefty, yet
if we apprehend, he is either not well affected to us, or at leaft regardlefs of our
intereft, we are in many cafes apt to be
jealous of him. Mankind are naturally
fwayed by their affections, and much influenced thro love or freindfhip ; and therefore nothing has a greater tendency to induce perfons to credit what is faid, than in-
timations of affection and kindnefs. Freinds
are mutually concerned for each other's
intereft ; and for that reafon we readily
harken to thofe, who, we think, wifh us
well, becaufe we are perfuaded they fpeak
fincerely. Indeed, in fome cafes, our intereft may happen to be the fame with
his, who, we may apprehend, in other
refpects has no great regard for us ; and
then we may beleive he will do that for
his own fake, which he would not have
done

done for ours. For nothing more closely
unites men to one another, than common interest. The best orators have been always sensible, what great influence the expressions of kindness and benevolence have upon the minds of others, to induce them to beleive the truth of what they say; and therefore they frequently endeavour to impress them with the opinion of it. Thus Demosthenes begins his celebrated oration for Ctesiphon. *It is my hearty prayer*, sais he, *to all the deities, that this my defence may be received by you with the same affection, which I have always expressed for you, and your city.* And it is a very fine image of it, which we have in Cicero, where, in order to influence the judges in favor of Milo, he introduces him speaking thus, as became a brave man, and a patriot, even upon the supposition he should be condemned by them: *I bid my fellow citizens adieu; may they continue flourishing and prosperous; may this famous city be preserved, my most dear country, however it has treated me; may my fellow citizens enjoy peace and tranquillity without me, since I am not to enjoy it with them, tho I have procured it for them; I will withdraw, I will be gone* [1].

[1] *Pro Milon. c.* 34.

Vol. I.   L   The

THE fourth and laft *quality* above mentioned, as neceffary to the character of an
orator, is *Modefty*. And it is certain, that
what is modeftly fpoken, is generally better
received, than what carries in it an air of
boldnefs and confidence. Moft perfons,
tho ignorant of a thing, do not care to be
thought fo, and would have fome deference paid to their underftanding. But
he who delivers himfelf in an arrogant and
affuming way, feems to upbraid his hearers
with ignorance, while he does not leave
them to judge for themfelves, but dictates
to them, and as it were demands their
affent, to what he fais; which is certainly
a very improper method to win upon them.
For not a few, when convinced of an error
in fuch a way, will not own it; but will
rather adhere to their former opinion, than
feem forced to think right, when it gives
another the opportunity of a triumph. For,
as Quintilian rightly obferves: *The mind of*
man has naturally fomething in it that is
fublime, haughty, and impatient of a fuperior.
And therefore men readily help and affift the
conquered, and fuch who fubmit; becaufe in
that they act as fuperiors: for when emula-
tion ceafes, humanity takes place. But he
who extols himfelf, above what he ought, is
looked

looked upon to depress and despise others, and not so much to raise himself, as lessen them; which excites envy [1]. A prudent orator therefore will behave himself with mo- desty, that he may not seem to insult his hearers; and will set things before them in such an ingaging manner, as may re- move all prejudice, either from his per- son, or what he asserts. But at the same time, firmness and resolution is as necessary as modesty, that he may appear to confide in the justice and truth of his cause. For to speak timorously, and with hesitation, destroys the credit of what is offered; and so far as the speaker seems to distrust, what he sais himself, he often induces others to do the like.

BUT, as has been said already, great care is to be taken, that these characters do not appear feigned and counterfeit. For what is fictitious, can seldom be long concealed. And if this be once discovered, it makes all that is said suspected, how specious soever it may otherwise appear. This is very handsomly expressed by Vir- gil, where he introduces Juno thus spea- king to Venus, and pretending a reconci- liation with Aeneas:

[1] *Inst. orat. Lib.* ii. *c.* 2.

L 2

But

But shall celestial discord never cease?
Tis better ended in a lasting peace.
You stand possess'd of all your soul desir'd,
Poor Dido with consuming love is fir'd;
Your Trojan with my Tyrian let us join,
So Dido shall be yours, Aeneas mine,
One common kingdom, one united line.
Eliza shall a Dardan lord obey,
*   And lofty Carthage for a dow'r convey* [1].

[1] *Aen.*
Lib iv.
v. 98.

What could appear more fair and advantageous, than this proposal? But yet it
would not take. Venus does not credit it,
because she perceives the fraud, and, as the
poet adds,

closely smiles
At her vain project, and discover'd wiles.

If men always loved truth for its own excellency, it would be sufficient to propose
it clearly and plainly; nor would the assistance of art be necessary, in order to induce them to embrace it. But it frequently happens, that truth clashes with
what men account their interest, and for
that reason they will not regard it. An
ungrateful truth will either not be heard,
or soon discarded. And many times, where
persons cannot contradict, what is offered;
yet, if that contradict their settled opinions, they will still suppose it may not

be

be true. Nor is it a difficult thing for
perſons to bring themſelves to ſuch a beleif, while they forbear calmly and ſe-
riouſly to conſider the arguments offered
on the other ſide. And ſince matters are
thus, it is often neceſſary for the orator to
have recourſe to art, in order to obtain
that, which otherwiſe he cannot come at.
For this purpoſe therefore, it is very ſer-
viceable to accommodate his diſcourſe to
the temper and inclination of his audience,
that while they willingly attend to what
is pleaſing and agreable to them, they may
at the ſame time likewiſe be induced to
entertain thoſe things, which, propoſed in
another manner, would have been leſs attended to, or heard with prejudice. As
phyſicians ſometimes gild over bitter pills,
to pleaſe the palate, and by that means
benefit the patient. And for this end, it
is further neceſſary, that the orator ſhould
know the world, and be well acquainted
with the different tempers and diſpoſitions
of mankind. Nor indeed can any one
reaſonably hope to ſuccede in this province, without well conſidering the circumſtances of time and place, with the ſentiments and diſpoſitions of thoſe, to whom
he ſpeaks; which, according to Ariſtotle.

L 3   may

may be distinguished four ways, as they discover themselves by the several *affections*, *habits*, *ages*, and *fortunes* of mankind [1]. And each of these require a different conduct and manner of address.

The *affections* denote certain emotions of the mind, which, during their continuance, give a great turn to the disposition. For love prompts to one thing, and hatred to another. The like may be said of anger, lenity, and the rest of them; as I shall shew, when I come to treat of them particularly [2].

Persons differ likewise according to the various *habits* of their mind. So a just man is inclined one way, and an unjust man another; a temperate man to this, and an intemperate man to the contrary.

And as to the several *ages* of men, Aristotle has described them very accurately, and how persons are differently affected in each of them. I shall content myself with the substance of what he sais, to prevent being tedious. He divides the lives of men, considered as hearers, into three stages; youth, middle age, and old age. Young men, he sais, have generally strong passions, and are very eager to obtain, what they desire; but are likewise very

very mutable, so that the same thing does not please them long. They are ambitious of praise, and quick in their resentments. Lavish of their money, as not having experienced the want of it. Frank and open, because they have not often been deceived; and credulous for the same reason. They readily hope the best, because they have not suffered much, and are therefore not so sensible of the uncertainty of human affairs; for which reason they are likewise more easily deceived. They are modest from their little acquaintance with the world. They love company and chearfulness, from the briskness of their spirits; and think well of their freinds. They imagine they know more than they do, and for that reason, are apt to be too positive. In a word, they generally excede in what they do, love violenty, hate violently, and act in the same manner thro the rest of their conduct. The disposition of old men is generally contrary to the former. They are cautious, and enter upon nothing hastily; having in the course of many years been often imposed upon, having often erred, and experienced the prevailing corruption of human affairs; for which reason they are likewise

L 4   suspicious,

LECT. X. ſuſpicious, and moderate in their affections, either of love or hatred. They purſue nothing great and noble, and regard only the neceſſaries of life. They love money, having learnt by experience the difficulty of geting it, and how eaſily it is loſt. They are fearful, which makes them provident. Commonly full of complaints from bodily infirmities, and a deficiency of ſpirits. Pleaſe themſelves rather with the memory of what is paſt, than any future proſpect, having ſo ſhort a view of life before them, in compariſon of what is already gone; for which reaſon alſo they love to talk of things paſt, and prefer them to what is preſent, of which they have but little reliſh, and know they muſt ſhortly leave them. They are ſoon angry, but not to exceſs. Laſtly, they are compaſſionate, from a ſenſe of their own infirmities, which makes them think themſelves of all perſons moſt expoſed. Perſons of a middle age, betwixt theſe two extremes, as they are freed from the raſhneſs and temerity of youth, ſo they have not yet ſuffered the decays of old age. Hence in every thing they generally obſerve a better conduct. They are neither ſo haſty in their aſſent as he one, nor ſo minutely ſcrupulous as the

2   other,

other, but weigh the reasons of things. They regard a decency in their actions, are careful and industrious; and as they undertake what appears just and laudable upon better and more deliberate consideration, than young persons; so they pursue them with more vigor and resolution, than those who are older.

As to the different *fortunes* of mankind, they may be considered as noble, rich, or powerful; and the contrary to these. Those of high birth, and noble extraction, are generally very tender of their honor, and ambitious to increase it; it being natural for all persons to desire an addition to those advantages, of which they find themselves already possessed. And they are apt to consider all others as much their inferiors, and therefore expect great regard and deference should be shewn them. Riches, when accompanied with a generous temper, command respect from the opportunities they give of being useful to others; but they usually elate the mind, and occasion pride. For as money is commonly said to command all things, those, who are possessed of a large share of it, expect others should be at their beck; since they injoy that, which all desire, and most persons

make

LECT.
X.
make the main purfuit of their lives to obtain. But nothing is more apt to fwell the
mind, than power. This is what all men
naturally covet, even when perhaps they
would not ufe it. But the views of fuch
perfons are generally more noble and generous, than of thofe, who only purfue riches,
and the heaping up of money. A ftate
contrary to thefe gives a contrary turn of
mind, and in lower life, perfons difpofitions
ufually differ according to their ftation and
circumftances. A citizen and a courtier, a
merchant and a foldier, a fcholar and a pea-
fant, as their purfuits are different, fo is generally their turn and difpofition of mind.

IT is the orator's bufinefs therefore to
confider thefe feveral characters, and circumftances of life, with the different bias
and way of thinking they give to the mind;
that he may fo conduct himfelf in his behaviour and manner of fpeaking, as will
render him moft acceptable, and gain him
the good efteem of thofe, to whom he addreffes.

LECTURE XI.

Of the Passions.

THE third and last part of rhetorical invention relates to the *Passions*, of which I am now to discourse. And as it is often highly necessary for the orator, so it requires his greatest skill, to ingage these in his interest. Quintilian calls this, *The soul and spirit of his art* [1]. And doubtless, nothing more discovers its empire over the minds of men, than this power to excite, appease, and sway their passions, agreably to the design of the speaker. Hence we meet with the characters of *admirable, divine,* and other splendid titles, ascribed to eloquence by antient writers. It has indeed been objected by some, that whatever high encomiums may be given of this art by the admirers of it; it is however disingenuous to deceive and impose upon mankind, as they seem to do, who, by ingaging their passions, give a bias to their minds, and take them off from the consideration of the truth; whereas every thing should be judged of from the reasons brought to support it, by the evidence of which

LECT. XI.

[1] *Inst. orat. Lib.* vi. *c.* 2.

LECT.
XI.
which it ought to ftand or fall. But in anfwer to this, it may be confidered, that all fallacy is not culpable. We often deceive children for their good, and phyficians fometimes impofe on their patients to come at a cure. And why therefore, when perfons will not be prevailed with by reafon and argument, may not an orator endeavour, by ingaging their paffions, to perfuade them to that, which is for their advantage? Befides, Quintilian makes it a neceffary qualification of an orator; that he be an honeft man, and one who will not abufe his art [1]. But fince thofe of a contrary character will leave no methods untried, in order to carry their point; it is requifite for thofe, who defign well, to be acquainted with all their arts, without which they will not be a match for them. As in military affairs, it is highly advantageous for the general of an army to get himfelf informed of all the defigns and ftratagems of the enemy, in order to counteract them. Indeed this part of oratory is not neceffary at all times, nor in all places. The better prepared perfons are to confider truth, and act upon the evidence of it, the lefs occafion there appears for it. But the greater part of mankind, either do not duly weigh the force

of

[1] *Inſt. orat.* *Lib.* xii. c. 1.

of arguments, or refuse to act agreably to
their evidence. And where this is the
case, that persons will neither be convinced
by reason, nor moved by the authority of
the speaker; the only way left to put
them upon action, is to ingage their paffions. For the paffions are to the mind,
what the wind is to a ship, they move,
and carry it forward; and he who is without them, is in a manner without action,
dull and lifelefs. There is nothing great
or noble to be performed in life, wherein
the paffions are not concerned. The ftoics
therefore, who were for eradicating the
paffions, both maintained a thing in itfelf
impoffible; and if it was poffible, would
be of the greateft prejudice to mankind.
For while they appeared fuch zealous af-
fertors of the government of reafon, they
fcarce left it any thing to govern; for the
authority of reafon is principally exercifed
in ruling and moderating the paffions, which,
when kept in a due regulation, are the
fprings and motives to virtue. Thus hope
produces patience, and fear induftry, and
the like might be shewn of the reft. The
paffions therefore are not to be extirpated,
as the ftoics afferted, but put under the
direction and conduct of reafon. Indeed
where

where they are ungovernable, and instead
of obeying command, they are, as some
have fitly called them, *diseases of the mind,*
and frequently hurry men into vice, and
the greatest misfortunes of life. Just as
the wind, when it blows moderately, carries on the ship; but if it be too boisterous
and violent, may overset her. The charge
therefore brought against this art, for giving rules to influence the passions, appears
groundless and unjust; since the proper use
of the passions is not to hinder the exercise
of reason, but to ingage men to act agreably to re son. And if an ill use be sometimes made of this, it is not the fault of
the art, but the artist. So moralists explain
the nature both of virtues and vices, that
men may know better how to practise one,
and avoid the other; but if their precepts
happen to have a different effect, they are
not answerable for that.

BUT that an orator may be enabled to
manage this part of his province to the
best advantage, it is necessary he should,
in some measure, be acquainted with the
nature, causes, and objects of the passions.
Now the passions, as defined by Aristotle,
are, *Commotions of the mind, under the influence of which men think differently con-*
cerning

cerning the same things [1]. Thus a thing appears good to him, who desires it; tho it may not appear so to another, or to the same person at a different time. Writers are not agreed as to the number of the passions. But I shall wave this dispute, as the more proper business of philosophy, and only consider them, as they come under the cognizance of the orator. And that I may procede in some order, I shall treat of them, as they may be separately refered, either to *demonstrative, deliberative,* or *judicial* discourses ; tho they are not wholly confined to any of them.

To the *demonstrative* kind, we may refer *Joy* and *Sorrow, Love* and *Hatred, Emulation* and *Contempt.*

JOY is an elation of the mind, arising from a sense of some present good. Such a reflection naturally creates a pleasant and agreable sensation, which ends in a delightful calm and serenity. This is hightened by a description of former evils, and a comparison between them and the present felicity. Thus Cicero endeavours to excite in the minds of his fellow citizens the highest sense of joy and delight at Catiline's departure from Rome, by representing to them the imminent danger,

which

LECT.
XI.

which threatened both them and the city, while he continued among them [1].

[1] *In Catil. Orat.* ii. *c.* 1.

SORROW, on the contrary, is an uneafinefs of mind, arifing from a fenfe of fome prefent evil. This paffion has generally a place in funeral difcourfes. And it may be hightened like the former by comparifon, when any paft happinefs is fet in oppofition to a prefent calamity. Hence Cicero aggravates the forrow at Rome, occafioned by the death of Metellus, from his character, and great fervices to the public while living [2].

[2] *Pro Coel. c.* 24.

LOVE excites us to efteem another for fome excellency, and to do him all the good in our power. It is diftinguifhed from *Freindfhip*, which is mutual; and therefore love may continue, where freindfhip is loft: that is, the affection may remain on one fide. And when we affift a perfon from no other motive, but to do him a kindnefs, Ariftotle calls this *good will* [3]. Love takes its rife from a variety of caufes. Generofity, benevolence, integrity, gratitude, courtefy, and other focial virtues, are great incitements to love any one indued with fuch qualities. And perfons generally love thofe, who are of a like difpofition with themfelves, and purfue the fame

[3] *De rhetor. Lib.*ii. *c.* 9.

fame views. It is therefore the cheif art of a flatterer to fuit himfelf in every thing to the inclination of the perfon, whofe good graces he courts. When the orator would excite this affection towards any perfon, it is proper to fhew, that he is poffeffed of fome at leaft, if not all thefe agreable qualities. When the confpirators with Catiline were to be brought to juftice, Cicero was very fenfible of the envy he fhould contract on that account, and how neceffary it was for him to fecure the love of the Roman fenate for his fupport and protection in that critical juncture. And this he endeavours to do in his fourth oration againft Catiline, by reprefenting to them, in the moft pathetic manner, that all the labors he underwent, the difficulties he conflicted with, and the dangers to which he was expofed, on that account, were not for his own fake, but for their fafety, quiet, and happinefs [1].

[1] *Cap.* 1.

HATRED is oppofed to love, and produced by the contrary difpofitions. And therefore perfons hate thofe, who never did them any injury, from the ill opinion they have of their bafe and vitious inclinations. So that the way to excite this paffion is, by fhewing that any one has

VOL. I. M com-

commited some heinous fact, with an ill intent. And the more nearly affected perſons are by ſuch actions, in what they account of the greateſt concern, the higher in proportion their hatred riſes. Since life therefore is eſteemed the moſt valuable good, Cicero endeavours to render Mark Antony odious to the citizens of Rome, by deſcribing his cruelty [1].

[1] *Philipp.* iv. c. 5.

EMULATION is a diſquiet, occaſioned by the felicity of another, not becauſe he enjoys it, but becauſe we deſire the like for ourſelves. So that this paſſion is in itſelf good and laudable, as it ingages men to purſue thoſe things, which are ſo. For the proper objects of emulation are any advantages of mind, body, or fortune, acquired by ſtudy or labor. And perſons are generally excited to an emulation of thoſe, with whom they converſe. So children are often ambitious of the like virtues or honors, which they ſee in their relations or freinds. And therefore it was a very proper queſtion of Andromache to Aeneas, concerning Aſcanius, which we have in Virgil:

> *What hopes are promis'd from his blooming*
> *years?*
> *How much of Hector's ſoul in him appears*[2]*?*

[2] *Aen.* Lib. iii. ℣. 342.

Emu-

Emulation therefore is excited by a lively representation of any defirable advantages, which appear to be attainable, from the examples of others, who are, or have been poffeffed of them. But where the felicity of another occafions an uneafinefs, not from the want of it, but becaufe he enjoys *it*; this paffion is called *Envy*, which the antients defcribe as an hideous monfter, feeding upon itfelf, and being its own tormentor [1]. Ariftotle obferves, that it moft ufually affects fuch perfons, who were once upon a level with thofe they envy [2]. For moft men naturally think fo well of themfelves, that they are uneafy to fee thofe, who were formerly their equals, advanced above them. But as this is a bafe and vitious paffion, the orator is not to be informed how to excite it, but how to leffen or remove it. And the method prefcribed by Cicero for this purpofe is, to fhew that the things, which occafioned it, have not happened to the envied perfon undefervedly; but are the juft reward of his induftry or virtue; that he does not fo much convert them to his own profit or pleafure, as to the benefit of others; and that the fame pains and difficulties are neceffary to preferve them, with which they were at firft acquired [3].

[1] *Ovid. Met. Lib.*i. *v.* 760.

[2] *Athenaeus, Lib.* i. *c.* 10.

[2] *De rhetor. Lib.*ii. *c.* 12.

[3] *De orat. Lib.* ii. *c.* 52.

M 2 CON-

L E C T.   CONTEMPT is oppofed to *Emulation,*
  XI.
⌣⌣⌣ and arifes from mifconduct in things, not
of themfelves vitious.   As where a perfon
either acts below his ftation and character;
or affects to do that, for which he is not
qualified.   Thus Cicero endeavours to expofe Caecilius, and bring him into contempt of the court, for pretending to rival
him in the accufation of Verres, for which
Cap. 12. he was altogether unfit [1].

To *deliberative* difcourfes may be refered
Fear, Hope, and *Shame.*

FEAR arifes from the apprehenfion of
fome great and impending evil.   For the
greateft evils, while they appear at a diftance, do not much affect us.   Such perfons occafion fear, who are poffeffed with
power, efpecially if they have been injured,
or apprehend fo.   Likewife thofe who are
addicted to do injuries, or who bear us an
ill will.   And the examples of others, who
have fuffered in a like cafe, or from the
fame perfons, help to excite fear.   From
the circumftances therefore either of the
thing, or perfon, it will not be difficult for
the orator to offer fuch arguments, as may
be proper to awaken this paffion.   So Demofthenes, when he would perfuade the
Athenians to put themfelves in a condition

of

of defence againſt king Philip, enumerates the ſeveral acts of hoſtility already com- mited by him, againſt the neighbouring ſtates [1]. And becauſe mens private con- cerns generally more affect them, than what relates to the public; it is proper ſometimes to ſhew the neceſſary connec- tion theſe have with each other, and how the ruin of one draws the other after it.

[1] *Philipp.* iii.

THE contrary paſſion to *Fear* is *Hope*, which ariſes, either from a proſpect of ſome future good, or the apprehenſion of ſafety from thoſe things, which occaſion our fear. Young perſons are eaſily induced to hope the beſt, from the vigor of their ſpirits. And thoſe, who have eſcaped former dan- gers, are encouraged to hope for the like happy ſucceſs for the future. The exam- ples of others alſo, eſpecially of wiſe and conſiderate men, have often the ſame good effect. To find them calm and ſedate, when expoſed to the like dangers, natu- rally creates confidence, and the hopes of ſafety. But nothing gives perſons that firmneſs and ſteadineſs of mind, under the apprehenſion of any difficulties, as a con- ſciouſneſs of their own integrity and in- nocence. Let dangers come from what quarter they will, they are beſt prepared

M 3   to

LECT. to receive them. They can calmly view
XI. an impending tempeft, obferve the way
of its approach, and prepare themfelves in
the beft manner to avoid it. In Cicero's
oration for the Manilian law, he encou-
rages the Roman citizens to hope for fuccefs againft Mithridates, if they chofe Pompey for their general, from the many inftances of his former fuccefſes, which he
there enumerates. We find in hiftory,
that artful men have frequently made ufe
of omens and prodigies with the populace,
either to awaken or expel their fears, and
that with the greateft fuccefs. But fuch
arguments are not much regarded by wife
and prudent men. In the time of the
civil wars between Caefar and Pompey,
when the affairs of Pompey's party were
very much broken and fhattered; one who
was in that intereft, endeavoured to animate the reft, and excite them to puſh on
the war with vigor, from a lucky omen
(as it was then thought) of feven eagles,
which were obferved to fettle in their camp.
But Cicero, who was then prefent, and
knew very well the vanity of fuch reafoning, immediately replied: *That fuch an hap-*
1 Plut. in *py incident might indeed prove of fervice to*
vit. Cicer. *them, if they were to fight with jackdaws* [1].

SHAME

SHAME arifes from the apprehenfion of thofe things, that hurt a perfon's character. *Modefty* has been wifely implanted in mankind by the great author of nature, as a guardian of virtue, which ought for this reafon to be cherifhed with the greateft care; becaufe, as Seneca has well obferved, *if it be once loft, it is fcarce ever to be recovered* [1]. Therefore the true caufe or foundation of fhame is any thing bafe or vitious; for this wounds the character, and will not bear reflection. And he muft arrive at no fmall degree of infenfibility, who can ftand againft fuch a charge, if he be confcious to himfelf that it is juft. Therefore to deter perfons from vitious actions, or to expofe them for the commiffion of them, the orator endeavours to fet them in fuch a light, as may moft awaken this paffion, and give them the greateft uneafinefs by the reflection. And becaufe the bare reprefentation of the thing itfelf is not always fufficient for this purpofe; he fometimes inforces it by inlarging the view, and introducing thofe perfons, as witneffes of the fact, for whom they are fuppofed to have the greateft regard. Thus when fome of the Athenians, in an arbitration about certain lands, which had

[1] *In Agamemn.*

M 4   been

been refered to them by the contending
parties, propofed it as the fhorteft way of
deciding the controverfy, to take the poffeffion of them into their own hands ;
Cydias, a member of the affembly, to diffuade them from fuch an unjuft action,
defired them to imagine themfelves at that
time in the general affembly of the ftates
of Greece (who would all hear of it
fhortly) and then confider how it was
proper to act [1]. But where perfons labour
under an excefs of modefty, which prevents
them from exerting themfelves in things
fit and laudable, it may fometimes be neceffary to fhew, that it is faulty and ill
grounded.   On the other hand, *immodefty*
or impudence, which confifts in a contempt
of fuch things, as affect the reputation, can
never be too much difcouraged and expofed.   And the way of doing this is, to
make ufe of fuch arguments, as are moft
proper to excite fhame.   We have a very
remarkable inftance of it in Cicero's fecond
Philippic, wherein he affixes this character
upon Mark Antony, thro every fcene of
his life.

    I COME now to thofe paffions, which
may be refered to *judicial* difcourfes.   And

[1] Arift.
De Rhet.
Lib. ii.
c. 8. §. 4.

thefe are *Anger* and *Lenity*, *Pity* and *In-*
dignation.

ANGER is a refentment, occafioned by fome affront, or injury, done without any juft reafon. Now men are more inclined to refent fuch a conduct, as they think they lefs deferve it. Therefore perfons of diftinction and figure, who expect a regard fhould be paid to their character, can the lefs bear any indications of contempt. And thofe who are eminent in any profeffion or faculty, are apt to be offended, if reflections are caft, either upon their reputation, or art. Magiftrates alfo, and perfons in public ftations, fometimes think it incumbent on them to refent indignities, for the fupport of their office. But nothing fooner inflames this paffion, than if good fervices are rewarded with flights and neglect. The inftance of Narfites, the Roman general, is remarkable in this kind; who, after he had been very fuccefsful in his wars with the Goths, falling under the difpleafure of the emperor Juftin, was removed from the government of Italy, and received by the emprefs with this taunt: *That he muft be fent to weave among the girls.* Which fo provoked him, that he faid, he would weave fuch a web, as they fhould

never

never be able to unravel. And accordingly he foon after brought down the Longo-
bards, a people of Germany, into Italy,
where they fettled themfelves in that part
of the country, which from them is now
called Lombardy [1]. The time and place,
in which an injury was done, and other
circumftances that attended it, may likewife contribute very much to highten the
fact. Hence Demofthenes, in his oration
againft Midias, endeavours to aggravate
the injury of being ftruck by him, both
as he was then a magiftrate, and becaufe
it was done at a public feftival. From
hence it appears, that the perfons, who
moft ufually occafion this paffion, are fuch,
who neglect the rules of decency, contemn
and infult others, or oppofe their inclinations; as likewife the ungrateful, and thofe
who violate the ties of freindfhip, or requite favors with injuries. But when the
orator endeavours to excite anger, he fhould
be careful not to excede due bounds in ag-
gravating the charge, left what he fais,
appear rather to procede from prejudice,
than a ftrict regard to the demerit of the
action.

LENITY is the remiffion of anger. The
defigns of mens actions are principally to

be

Paul.
Diacon.
De geft.
Long.
Lib. ii.
c. 5.

be regarded; and therefore what is done ignorantly, or thro inadvertency, is sooner forgiven. Also to acknowledge a fault, submit, and ask pardon, are the ready means to take off resentment. For a generous mind is soon cooled by submission. Besides he, who repents of his fault, does really give the injured party some satisfaction, by punishing himself; as all repentance is attended with greif, and uneasiness of mind: and this is apt very much to abate the desire of revenge. As, on the contrary, nothing is more provoking, than when the offender either audaciously justifies the fact, or confidently denies it. Men are likewise wont to lay aside their resentment, when their adversaries happen by some other means to suffer, what they think a sufficient satisfaction. Lastly, easy circumstances, a lucky incident, or any thing, which gives the mind a turn to mirth and pleasure, has a natural tendency to remove anger. For anger is accompanied with pain and uneasiness, which very ill suit joy and chearfulness. The orator therefore, in order to assuage and pacify the minds of his auditors, will endeavour to lessen their opinion of the fault, and by that means to take off the edge of their resentment. And

to

5

to this purpose, it will be proper either to represent, that the thing was not defigned; or that the party is forry for it; or to mention his former fervices; as alfo to fhew the credit and reputation, which will be gained by a generous forgivenefs. And this laft topic is very artfully wrought up by Cicero, in his addrefs to Caefar, in favor of Ligarius.

PITY arifes from the calamities of others, by reflecting that we ourfelves are liable to the like misfortunes. So that evils, confidered as the common lot of human nature, are principally the caufe of *pity*. And this makes the difference between *pity* and *goodwill*, which, as I have fhewn already, arifes merely from a regard to the circumftances of thofe, who want our affiftance. But confidering the uncertainty of every thing about us, he muft feem in a manner divefted of humanity, who has no compaffion for the calamities of others; fince there is no affliction, which happens to any man, but either that, or fome other as great, may fall upon himfelf. But thofe perfons are generally fooneft touched with this paffion, who have met with misfortunes themfelves. And by how much greater the diftrefs is, or the perfon appears lefs deferving it; the

higher

higher pity does it excite : for which reason persons are generally moft moved at the misfortunes of their relations and freinds, or thofe of the beft figure and character. The orator therefore, in order to excite the greater pity, will endeavour to highten the idea of the calamity, from the feveral circumftances, both of the thing itfelf, and the perfon who labours under it. A fine example of this may be feen in Cicero's defence of Muraena [1].

[1] *Cap.* 40. *&c.*

INDIGNATION, as oppofed to *pity*, is an uneafinefs at the felicity of another, who does not feem to deferve it. But this refpects only external advantages, fuch as riches, honors, and the like; for virtues cannot be the object of this paffion. Ariftotle therefore fais, *that pity and indignation are generally to be found in the fame perfons, and are both evidences of a good difpofition* [2]. Now the orator excites this paffion, by fhewing the perfon to be unworthy of that felicity which he enjoys. And as, in order to move compaffion, it is fometimes of ufe, to compare the former happy ftate of the perfon, with his prefent calamity; fo here, the greater indignation is raifed, by comparing his former mean circumftances with his prefent advancement:

[2] *De rhetor. Lib.* ii. *c.* 11.

LECT. vancement: as Cicero does in the cafe of
XI. Vatinius [1].

[1] *In Vatin. c. 5, &c.*

THESE are the paſſions, with which an orator is principally concerned. In addreſſing to which, not only the greateſt warmth and force of expreſſion is often neceſſary; but he muſt likewiſe firſt endeavour to impreſs his own mind with the ſame paſſion, he would excite in others, agreably to that of Horace:

> *My greif with others juſt proportion bears,*
> *To make me weep, you muſt be firſt in tears* [2].

[2] *Art. Poet. v. 102.*

I HAVE now finiſhed the firſt part of oratory, namely *Invention*; and ſhall procede to the ſecond, which is *Diſpoſition*, in my next diſcourſe.

LECTURE XII.

Of Difpofition in general, and particularly of the Introduction.

IN treating upon the *divifion* of oratory, I fhewed, that it confifts of four parts ; *Invention, Difpofition, Elocution,* and *Pronunciation.* And as I then propofed to confider each of thefe in their order, having explained the firft of them in feveral difcourfes, I fhall now procede to the fecond, which is *Difpofition.* For agreably to the fimilitude I formerly obferved between the arts of fpeaking and building, as *Invention* fupplies the orator with neceffary materials ; fo *Difpofition* directs him how to place them in the moft proper and fuitable order. And, as in both arts, the firft confideration of the artift is to collect and prepare his materials, fo the next is to put them together [1]. *Difpofition* therefore, confidered as a part of oratory, naturally follows *Invention.* And what is here cheifly intended by it is, the placing the feveral parts of a difcourfe in a juft method, and dependance upon each other. Tho indeed the feveral things contained under each

[1] See Lect. III.

part,

part, require likewife a fuitable order and
difpofition, as will be fhewn in their proper
place. Order and regularity is always pleafant and agreable ; we admire it in nature,
and it is no lefs beautiful in art, and particularly in difcourfe. For, as that judicious
writer Quintilian has well obferved : *A
difcourfe that wants difpofition, muft neceffarily be confufed, and without connection,
liable to frequent tautologies, and omiffions,
and, like one wandering in the dark, be con-*
ducted by chance, rather than defign [1]. And
want of order is certainly a very great
prejudice to a difcourfe in other refpects.
For what is methodically delivered, is heard
with more attention, better underftood, and
longer retained. But as *Invention* requires
thought, and a lively imagination, fo judgement and prudence are neceffary in *Difpofition.*

WRITERS are not all agreed in deter-
mining the parts of an oration ; tho the
difference is rather in the manner of confidering them, than in the things themfelves. Ariftotle mentions four ; *Introduction, Propofition, Proof,* and *Conclufion* [2].
Two of thefe, that is, *Propofition* and *Proof,*
are always neceffary. For in every difcourfe
there ought to be fome fubject propofed,
which

[1] *Inft. orat.
Lib.* vii.
prooem.

[2] *De rhe-
tor. Lib.* iii.
c. 13.

which muſt afterwards be proved or illuſtrated. The other two ſeem to have
been introduced, not ſo much from neceſſity, as from other conſiderations. For
as the tempers of mankind are exceding
various, it is often neceſſary to prepare the
way for a candid reception of a diſcourſe,
by firſt gaining their benevolence, and attention ; and after the matter has been
fully repreſented, and ſupported by proper
arguments, it is further requiſite to engage
their paſſions in the purſuit of what has
been offered. For theſe reaſons therefore,
the uſe of the *Introduction* is to make way
for a kind and attentive hearing, and the
deſign of the *Concluſion* is to gain that by
an addreſs to the paſſions, which perhaps
could not be done by cool reaſoning. Quintilian makes five parts, *Introduction, Narration, Confirmation, Refutation,* and *Concluſion* [1]. But Cicero enlarges them to ſix;
namely, *Introduction, Narration, Propoſition, Confirmation, Confutation,* and *Concluſion* [2]. Tho Ariſtotle may be ſuppoſed
to include *Narration* under *Propoſition,* and
both *Confirmation* and *Confutation* under
Proof; as, on the contrary, Quintilian ſeems
to have included *Propoſition* under *Narration.* However, I ſhall chooſe to follow

[1] *Inſt. orat. Lib.* iii. *c.* 9.

[2] *De Invent. Lib.* i. *c.* 14.

Cicero's divifion, as moft full and explicit;
and treat upon each part in the order now
mentioned. Not but that this order is
fometimes changed by the beft orators,
and for good reafons, as will be fhewn
hereafter.

THE firft part of a difcourfe is the *In-troduction*, the defign of which is to prepare the minds of the hearers for a fuitable
reception of the remaining parts, that are
to follow. And for this end, three things
are requifite; that the orator gain the *good
opinion* of his hearers, that he fecure their
attention, and give them fome *general no-tion* of his fubject. I fhall fpeak to each
of thefe heads feparately, begining with
Benevolence.

Now the topics made ufe of for gaining
the efteem and *good opinion* of the hearers,
are *Perfons*, or *Things*.

THE *Perfons* are cheifly the fpeaker himfelf, or thofe to whom he addreffes. When
the orator introduces his difcourfe with his
own perfon, he will be careful to do it
with modefty, and feem rather to extenuate
his virtues and abilities, than to magnify
them. And where the nature of the fubject may feem to require it, he will endeavour to fhew, that fome juft and good
reafon

reason induced him to ingage in it. We have a very fine example of this, in Cicero's *oration* for the poet Aulus Licinius Archias, which begins thus : *If I have any natural genius, which I am sensible how small it is ; or any ability in speaking, wherein I own I have been very conversant ; or any skill acquired from the study and precepts of the best arts, to which my whole life has been devoted : this Aulus Licinius has, in a particular manner, a right to demand of me the fruit of all these things. For as far back as I can remember, and call to mind what passed in my youth, to the present time, he has been my cheif adviser and encourager, both to undertake and pursue this course of studies.* When the orator sets out with the persons of those, to whom the discourse is made, it is not unusual to commend them for their virtues, and those especially, which have a more immediate relation to the present subject. Thus Cicero begins his oration of thanks for the pardon of Marcellus, with an encomium upon the mildness, clemency, and wisdom of Caesar, to whom it was addressed. But sometimes he expresses his gratitude for past favors ; as Cicero has done in his orations, both to the people and senate of

N 2 Rome,

Rome, after his return from banishment.
And at other times he declares his concern
for them and their interest; in which manner Cicero begins his fourth oration against
Catiline, which was made in the senate.
I perceive, sais he, *that all your countenances
and eyes are turned on me; I perceive that
you are solicitous, not only for your own danger, and that of the state, but for mine likewise, if that should be removed. Your affection for me is pleasant in misfortunes, and
grateful in sorrow; but I adjure you to lay
it aside, and forgeting my safety, consider
yourselves and your children.* But in *judicial*
cases, both the character of the person,
whose cause he espouses, and that of the
adverse party, likewise furnishes the orator
with arguments for *Benevolence.* The former, by commemorating his virtues, dignity, or merits; and sometimes his misfortunes, and calamities. So Cicero in his
defence of Flaccus, begins his oration in
commending him on the account of his
services done to the public, the dignity of
his family, and his love to his country.
And Demosthenes, in his oration against
Midias, sets out with a recital of his vices,
in order to recommend his own cause to
the favorable opinion of the court. And
Cicero,

Cicero, in his defence of Quintius, with the fame view, joins his antagonift Hortenfius with Nevius the plaintif : *Both thofe things,* fais he, *at prefent make againft us, which bear the cheif fway in this city, the greateft intereft, and the greateft eloquence. As I am concerned at the one, fo I fear the other.   For as I am fomewhat apprehenfive, left the eloquence of Hortenfius fhould prejudice what I fay ; fo I very much dread, left the intereft of Nevius fhould prove hurtful to Quintius* [1].   [1] *Cap.* 1.

THE other topic above mentioned, for gaining *Benevolence,* was *Things.*   And thefe are principally taken from the fubject ; as its *Juftice, Importance, Advantage,* or *Pleafure.*   Thus Cicero recommends the caufe of Rabirius, whom he defended, from the juftice of it, when he fais : *No crime, envy, vice, or inveterate, reafonable, and heavy refentments of his fellow citizens, have brought Caius Rabirius in danger of his life; but a defign to take away that power and authority, which has been delivered to us from our anceftors, that neither the authority of the fenate, the commands of the conful, nor the confent of good men, fhould be able to withftand thofe, who aim at the ruin and deftruction of the ftate* [2].   Again, in his [2] *Cap.* 1.

N 3   oration

oration for the recovery of his house, made
to the preifts, to whom that caufe was
committed, he reprefents the importance of
it, with the fame defign : *If a weighty
caufe has at any time come under the cognizance and decifion of the preifts of the Roman people ; this truly is fo great, that the
dignity of the whole ftate, the fafety of all
the citizens, their lives, liberty, religious
rights, both public and private, goods, fortunes, and habitations, feem all to be committed and intrufted to your wifdom, integrity,*
[1] Cap. 1. *and power* [1]. And at the entrance of his
charge againft Verres before the fenate,
he endeavours to recommend it to their
good opinion, from the advantage it might
bring to themfelves. *I have, fais he, undertaken this caufe with the greateft approbation and expectation of the Roman people,
not to increafe the envy of your order, but to
remove the common infamy, under which it
lies.* But in his oration for the Manilian
law, he propofes the fame thing, from the
pleafure of the fubject. *It affords me, fais
he, a particular delight and fatisfaction, that
in fpeaking from this place, to which I have
not been accuftomed, I am furnifhed with
fuch a fubject, in which no one can want
matter of difcourfe. For I am to fpeak of*
the

the singular and excellent virtues of Cneius
Pompey; in treating upon which, it is more
difficult to know how to end, than where to
begin [1].　But tho I have reprefented thefe [1] *Cap.* 1.
feveral ways of gaining *Benevolence* feparately, that they might appear in a clearer
light; yet feveral of them are frequently
made ufe of by orators in the fame introduction.

THE fecond thing propofed in the introduction, is, to gain the *Attention* of the
hearers.　And in fpeaking of this head,
Cicero fais: *We fhall be heard attentively*
by one of thefe three things; if we propofe
what is great, neceffary, or for the intereft
of thofe, to whom the difcourfe is addreffed [2].　[2] *Orat*
So that according to him, the topics of *Partit.*
c. 8.
Attention are much the fame, with thofe
of *Benevolence*, when taken from the fubject.　And indeed, people are naturally led
to attend either to thofe things or perfons,
of which they have entertained a favorable opinion.　But in order to gain this
point, the orator fometimes thinks it proper
to requeft the attention of his audience.
Thus Cicero, in his defence of Cluentius,
after having fhewn the heinoufnefs of the
charge againft him, concludes his introduction in the following manner, fpeaking

　　　　to

to the judges: *Wherefore I intreat, that while I breifly and clearly reply to a charge of many years standing, you will, according to your usual custom, give me a kind and attentive hearing* [1]. And again, in his second Philippic, addressing himself to the senate: *But as I must say something for myself, and many things against Mark Antony; one of these I beg of you, that you will hear me kindly, while I speak for myself; and the other I will undertake for, that when I speak against him, you shall hear me with attention* [2]. But tho the introduction be the most usual and proper place for gaining attention; yet the orator finds it convenient sometimes to quicken and excite his hearers in other parts of his discourse, when he observes they flag, or has something of moment to offer.

[1] *Cap.* 3.

[2] *Cap.* 5.

THE third thing required in an introduction, is, some *general account* of the subject of the discourse. This is always necessary, which the two others are not. And therefore it must be left to the prudence of the orator, when to use or omit them, as he shall judge proper, from the nature of his discourse, the circumstances of his hearers, and how he stands with them. But some account of the subject is what

I   cannot

cannot be neglected. For every one ex-
pects to be soon informed of the design of
the speaker, and what he proposes to treat
of. Nor when they are all made use of,
is it necessary they should always stand in
the order I have here placed them. Cicero
sometimes enters immediately upon his
subject, and introduces the other heads
afterwards. As in his third oration against
Catiline, made to the body of the Roman
people, which begins thus : *You see that*
the state, all your lives, estates, fortunes,
wives and children, and this seat of the
greatest empire, the most flourishing and beau-
tiful city, having by the favor of heaven
towards you, and my labors, counsels, and
dangers, been this day rescued from fire and
sword, and the very jaws of destruction, are
preserved and restored to you. And then
he procedes to recommend himself to their
esteem and benevolence, from the consideration of these benefits.

THESE are the heads, which commonly
furnish matter for this part of a discourse.
But orators often take occasion from the
time [1], place [2], largeness of the assembly [3],
or some other proper circumstance [4], to
compliment their hearers, recommend
themselves, or introduce the subject, upon
which

[1] Cic. *Pro Cat-lio, & Phi-lipp.* v.
[2] *Pro Leg. Man. & Pro reg. Dejotaro.*
[3] *Philipp.* iv.
[4] *Pro Mi-lon.*

which they are about to treat. Inſtances of each of theſe may be met with in ſeveral of Cicero's orations. And ſometimes they ſet out with ſome remarkable cuſtom, compariſon, ſimilitude, or other ornament, which they accommodate to the occaſion of their diſcourſe. So Pliny begins his panegyric upon the emperor Trajan with an antient cuſtom. *Our anceſtors, ſais he, have very well and prudently appointed, that both our actions and ſpeeches ſhould begin with prayers; ſince men can enter upon nothing in a proper and becoming manner, without the aſſiſtance, direction, and favor of the deities. And by whom ought that cuſtom to be more regarded and practiſed, than by the conful? or on what occaſion, than when by order of the ſenate, and authority of the ſtate, we are ingaged to return thanks to the beſt of princes?* And Iſocrates enters upon his celebrated panegyric in praiſe of his countrymen, the Athenians, with the following compariſon: *I have often wondered, what could be their deſign, who brought together theſe aſſemblies, and inſtituted the gymnical ſports, to propoſe ſo great rewards for bodily ſtrength; and to vouchſafe no honor to thoſe, who applied their private labors to ſerve the public, and*

ſo

fo cultivated their minds as to be ferviceable L E C T.
to others, to whom they ought to have fhewn XII.
greater regard. For altho the ftrength of
a champion was doubled, no benefit would
from thence accrue to others; but all enjoy
the prudence of one man, who will hearken
to his advice. But when the fubject will
admit of it, the orator will fometimes introduce his difcourfe in a merry and face-
tious manner. As Cicero has done in his
defence of Ligarius, which begins thus:
My kinfman Quintus Tubero has brought a
new crime before you, Caius Caefar, and to
this day unheard of, that Quintus Ligarius
was in Africa. But fuch freedoms are
fcarce to be ventured upon, unlefs by fpeakers of an eftablifhed reputation and authority; which was the cafe of Cicero at
that time. Moreover, in fome cafes, orators have recourfe to a more covert and
artful way of opening their fubject, endeavour to remove jealoufies, apologize for
what they are about to fay, and feem to
refer it to the candor of the hearers to
judge of it as they pleafe. Cicero appears to have been a perfect mafter of this
art, and ufed it with great fuccefs. I fhall
recite one example of it, from his feventh
Philippic, where he feems to exprefs the

greateft

LECT.
XII.

greateſt concern, leſt what he was about to ſay, ſhould give any offence to the ſenate, to whom he was ſpeaking: *I*, ſais he, *who always declared for peace, and to whom peace among ourſelves, as it is wiſhed for by all good men, was in a particular manner deſirable; who have employed all my induſtry in the forum, in the ſenate, and in the defence of my freinds, whence I have arrived to the higheſt honors, a moderate fortune, and what reputation I enjoy; I therefore, who owe what I am to peace, and without it could not have been the perſon I am, be that what it will, for I would arrogate nothing to myſelf; I ſpeak with concern and fear, how you will receive what I am going to ſay; but I beg and intreat you from the great regard I have always expreſſed for the ſupport and advancement of your honor, that if any thing ſaid by me ſhould at firſt appear harſh or unfit to be received, you will notwithſtanding pleaſe to hear it without offence, and not reject it, till I have explained myſelf: I then, for I muſt repeat it again, who have always approved of peace, and promoted it,* [1] *am againſt a peace with Mark Antony* [1]. This is called *Inſinuation*, and may be neceſſary, where a cauſe is in itſelf doubtful, or may be thought ſo from the received notions

[1] *Cap. 3.*

notions of the hearers, or the impreſſions
already made upon them by the contrary
ſide. An honeſt man would not knowingly
ingage in a bad cauſe; and yet thro prevailing prejudice that may be ſo eſteemed,
which is not ſo in itſelf. In theſe caſes
therefore great caution and prudence are
neceſſary to give ſuch a turn to things, and
place them in that view, as may be leaſt
liable to offence. And becauſe it ſometimes happens, that the hearers are not ſo
much diſpleaſed at the ſubject, as the perſon, Quintilian's rule ſeems very proper,
when he ſais : *If the ſubject diſpleaſes, the
character of the perſon ſhould ſupport it;
and when the perſon gives offence, he ſhould
be helped by the cauſe* [1].

[1] *Inſt. orat.
Lib.* iv.
c. 1.

I HAVE done with the ſeveral things
requiſite to form an introduction ; but before I conclude, it may not be amiſs to add
a few remarks proper to be obſerved in its
compoſition. And firſt, it ought to appear
eaſy and natural, and ſo connected with the
reſt of the diſcourſe, as the head to the
body. Again, it ſhould be ſuited to the
length of the diſcourſe ; leſt otherwiſe, as
we ſay, the porch ſhould not appear pro-
portioned to the building. The language
of it ſhould alſo be juſt, eaſy, and pleaſant.

For

L E C T. For the orator has not yet fecured his hea-
XII.
rers, and a little matter may give them a
diftafte. Whereas afterwards, when their
minds are warmed and ingaged in his favor, a fmall flip will be fooner overlooked,
or more eafily forgiven. And therefore
Quintilian facetioufly compares a faulty introduction to a fcarred face; which is prefently difcerned, and very difagreable. But
further, it ought neither to be wholly without paffions, nor too violent and impetuous.
Soft and fmooth language, with an eafy
and modeft addrefs, infenfibly win upon
the hearers; when a more vehement and
boifterous attack upon them at firft may
poffibly alarm them, excite their fufpicion,
and preclude all accefs to their minds.
Laftly, it ought not to be too general, or
fo formed, as may equally ferve both parties, or be turned by the contrary party to
his advantage.

But altho the introduction be the firft
part of a difcourfe, yet it is not what the
orator fhould firft think of, and form in
his mind; but when he has laid the whole
fcheme of what he defigns to fay in his
thoughts, then is the proper time to confider in what manner to introduce it. And
thofe, who take the contrary method, feem

3   liable

liable to this inconvenience among others, that instead of suiting the introduction to the body of their discourse, they are many times obliged to accommodate their discourse to the introduction; and in order to prevent being inconsistent with themselves, are forced to say, not what they would, but what will best agree with those things they had said before.

I SHALL only add, that as the introduction is not an essential part of a discourse, so it is sometimes omited by the best orators. We find instances of it in Cicero, as in his first invective against Catiline, and that against Piso, where he begins immediately with his subject, without any previous address to his audience. Nay, sometimes this is not only unnecessary, but would be very improper; as where the hearers are already apprised of the subject, and expect brevity; or in cases that require dispatch. Such are many of the speeches we meet with in Livy, and other historians, made by generals to their armies, and upon other emergent occasions.

LECTURE XIII.
Of Narration.

THE orator having prepared his hearers to receive his difcourfe with candor and attention, and acquainted them with his general defign in the *Introduction,* before he procedes directly to his fubject, often finds it neceffary to give fome account of what preceded, accompanied, or followed upon it. And this he does in order to enlarge the view of the particular point in difpute, and place it in a clearer light. This is called *Narration,* the nature and properties of which I now propofe to explain.

NARRATION then is a recital of fomething done, in the order and manner in which it was done. Hence it is eafy to perceive, what thofe things are, which properly enter into a narration. And fuch are the caufe, manner, time, place, and confequences of an action; with the temper, fortune, views, ability, affociates, and other circumftances of thofe concerned in it. Not that each of thefe particulars is neceffary in every narration; but fo many

of

LECT.
XIII.

of them at least, as are requisite to set the matter in a just light, and make it appear credible. Besides, in relating a fact, the orator does not content himself with such an account of it, as is barely sufficient to render what he sais intelligible to his hearers; but describes it in so strong and lively a manner, as may give the greatest evidence to his relation, and make the deepest impression upon their minds. And if any part of it appears at present less probable, he promises to clear up and remove any remaining doubts in the progress of his discourse. For the foundation of his reasoning afterwards is laid in the narration, from whence he takes his arguments for the confirmation. And therefore it is a matter of no small importance, that this part be well managed; since the success of the whole discourse so much depends upon it.

THERE are four properties required in a good narration; that it be *short*, *clear*, *probable*, and *pleasant* [1]. I shall speak to each of these in their order.

AND first, the *brevity* of a narration is not to be judged of barely from its length: for that may be too long, which contains but a little; and that too short, which

[1] Cic. *Orat. Part.* c. 9.

comprehends a great deal. Wherefore this depends upon the nature of the subject, since some things require more words to give a just representation of them, and others fewer. That may properly therefore be called a short narration, which contains nothing, that could well have been omited; nor omits any thing, which was necessary to be said. Now in order to avoid both these extremes, care should be taken not to go further back in the account of things, nor to trace them down lower, than the subject requires; to say that only in the general, which does not need a more particular explication; not to assign the causes of things, when it is enough to shew they were done; and to omit such things which are sufficiently understood, from what either preceded, or was consequent upon them. So historians frequently satisfy themselves with relating how things were ordered to be done, and leave their readers to conclude, they were accordingly executed, or had answerable events. But the orator should be careful, lest while he endeavours to avoid prolixity, he run into obscurity. Horace was very sensible of this danger, when he said:

[1]*Art. Poet.*
v. 25.   *By striving to be short, I grow obscure* [1].

THE

THE second property of a narration therefore is *perspicuity*, which may justly be esteemed the cheif excellency of language. For as the design of speech is to communicate our thoughts to others, that must be its greatest excellence, which contributes most to this end, and that doubtless is perspicuity [1]. As perspicuity therefore is requisite in all discourse, so it is particularly serviceable in a narration, which contains the substance of all that is to be said afterwards. Wherefore if this be not sufficiently understood, much less can those things, which receive their light from it. Now the following things render a narration clear and plain : proper and significant words, whose meaning is well known and determined; short sentences, tho full and explicit, whose parts are not perplexed, but placed in their just order ; proper particles to join the sentences, and shew their connexion, and dependance on each other; a due regard to the order of time, and other circumstances necessary to be expressed; and lastly, suitable transitions.

THE third property of a narration is *probability*. And things appear probable, when the causes assigned for them appear natural; the manner, in which they are de-

[1] See *Lect.* XXII.

described, is eafy to be conceived; the consequences are such, as might be expected;
the characters of the persons are justly represented; and the whole account is well
attested, confistent with itself, and agreable
to the general opinion. Simplicity likewife in the manner of relating a fact, as
well as in the stile, without any referve or
appearance of art, contributes very much
to its credibility. For truth loves to appear naked and open, stript of all coloring
or difguife. The confpiracy of Catiline
was so daring and extravagant, that no one,
but fuch a defperado, could ever have undertaken it with any hopes of fuccefs.
However Cicero's account of it to the fenate was so full and exact, and so well
fuited to the character of the person, that

[1] *In Catil.*
c. 1.
it presently gained credit [1]. And therefore, when upon the conclusion of Cicero's
speech, Catiline, who was present, immediately stood up, and defired they would
not entertain fuch hard thoughts of him,
but confider how much his family had always been attached to the public interest,
and the great services they had done the
ftate; their refentments rofe so high, that
he could not be heard; upon which he
im-

immediately left the city, and went to his affociates [1].

[1] See Flor. *Lib.* iv. *c.* 1. *& ibi* Camert.

THE laft thing required in a narration is, that it be *pleafant* and entertaining. And this is more difficult, becaufe it does not admit of that accurate compofition, and pompous drefs, which delight the ear, and recommend fome other parts of a dif-courfe. For it certainly requires no fmall fkill in the fpeaker, while he endeavours to exprefs every thing in the moft natural, plain, and eafy manner, not to grow flat, and tirefome. For Quintilian's remark is very juft, that, *the moft experienced orators find nothing in eloquence more difficult, than what all, who hear it, fanfy they could have faid themfelves* [2]. And the reafon of this

[2] *Inft. orat. Lib.* iv. *c.* 2.

feems very obvious. For as all art is an imitation of nature, the nearer it refembles that, the more perfect it is in its kind. Hence unexperienced perfons often ima-gine that to be eafieft, which fuits beft with thofe natural ideas, to which they have been accuftomed; till, upon trial, they are convinced of their miftake. Wherefore to render this part of a difcourfe pleafant and agreable, recourfe muft be had to va-riety, both in the choice of words, and turns of the expreffion. And therefore

O 3 que-

queſtions, admirations, interlocutions, ima-
gery, and other familiar figures, help very
much to diverſify and inliven a narration,
and prevent it from becoming dull and tedious, eſpecially when it is carried on to
any conſiderable length.

HAVING given a breif account of the
nature and properties of a narration, I
ſhall now procede to conſider the uſes
of it.

LAUDATORY orations are uſually as it
were a ſort of continued narration, ſet off
and adorned with florid language and fine
images, proper to grace the ſubject, which
is naturally ſo well fited to afford pleaſure
and entertainment. Wherefore a ſeparate
narration is more ſuited to *deliberative* and
judicial diſcourſes. In Cicero's oration for
the Manilian law (which is of the former
kind) the deſign of the narration is to
ſhew the Roman people the neceſſity of
giving Pompey the command of the army
againſt king Mithridates, by repreſenting
the nature of that war, which is done in
the following manner. *A great and dangerous war*, ſais he, *threatens your revenues
and allies from two very powerful kings,
Mithridates and Tigranes; one of whom not
being purſued after his defeat, and the other*

pro-

provoked, think they have an opportunity to
seize Asia. Letters are daily brought from
those parts to worthy gentlemen of the eque-
strian order, who have large concerns there
in farming your revenues; they acquaint me,
as freinds, with the state of the public af-
fairs, and danger of their own; that many
villages in Bithynia, which is now your pro-
vince, are burnt down; that the kingdom
of Ariobarzanes, which borders upon your
revenues, is intirely in the enemies power;
that Lucullus, after several great victories,
is withdrawn from the war: that he who
succedes him, is not able to manage it; that
all the allies and Roman citizens wish and
desire the command of that war may be
given to one particular person; and that he
alone, and no other, is dreaded by the ene-
mies. You see the state of the case, now
consider what ought to be done [1]. Here is [1] *Cap.* 2.
an unhappy scene of affairs, which seemed
to call for immediate redress. The causes
and reasons of it are assigned, in a very
probable manner, and the account well
attested by persons of character and figure.
And what the consequences would be, if
not timely prevented, no one could well
be ignorant. The only probable remedy
suggested in general is, the commiting that

affair

affair to one certain perſon, which he afterwards ſhews at large could be no other than Pompey. But in Cicero's defence of Milo (which is of the *judicial* kind) the deſign of the narration, which is greatly commended by Quintilian, is to prove, that in the combat between Clodius and Milo, the former was the aggreſſor. And in order to make this appear, he gives a ſummary account of the conduct of Clodius the preceding year, and from the courſe of his actions and behaviour ſhews the inveterate hatred he bore to Milo, who obſtructed him in his wicked deſigns. For which cauſe he had often threatened to kill him, and given out, that he ſhould not live beyond ſuch a time. And accordingly he went from Rome without any other apparent reaſon, but that he might have an opportunity to attack him in a convenient place near his own houſe, by which he knew Milo was then obliged to paſs. Milo was in the ſenate that day, where he ſtaid till they broke up, then went home, and afterwards ſet forward on his journey. When he came to the place, in which he was to be aſſaulted, Clodius appeared every way prepared for ſuch a deſign, being on horſeback, and attended

with

with a company of desperate ruffians, ready to execute his commands. Whereas Milo was with his wife in a chariot, wraped up in his cloak, and attended with servants of both sexes. These were all circumstances, which preceded the fact. And as to the action itself, with the event of it, the attack, as Cicero sais, was begun by the attendants of Clodius, from an higher ground, who killed Milo's coachman. Upon which, Milo throwing off his cloak, leaped out, and made a brave defence, against Clodius's men, who were got about the chariot. But Clodius in the heat of the skirmish, giving out that Milo was killed, was himself slain by the servants of Milo, to avenge, as they thought, the death of their master. Here seems to be all the requisites proper to make this account credible. Clodius's open and avowed hatred of Milo, which proceded so far as to threaten his life, the time of his leaving Rome, the convenience of the place, his habit and company so different from those of Milo, joined with his known character of a most profligate and audacious wretch, could not but render it very probable, that he had formed that design to kill Milo. And which of them began the
attack,

attack, might very reasonably be credited from the advanced ground, on which Clodius and his men were placed; the death of Milo's coachman at the begining of the combat; the skirmish afterwards at the chariot; and the reason of Clodius's own death at laft, which does not appear to have been intended, till he had given out that Milo was killed. It would be eafy to shew, that all the other properties of a fine narration are likewife to be found in this. But that could not be done without tranfcribing the whole; which would be too long to recite here, and therefore I can only refer to it as fuch, upon the authority of Quintilian.

But a diftinct and feparate narration is not always neceffary in any kind of difcourfe. For if the matter was well known before, a fet and formal narrative will be tedious to the hearers. Or if one party has done it already, it is needlefs for the other to repeat it. But there are three occafions efpecially, in which it may feem very requifite; when it will bring light to the fubject, when different accounts have already been given out concerning it, or when it has been mifreprefented by the adverfe party. If the point in controverfy
be

be of a dubious nature, or not sufficiently known to the hearers, a distinct account of the matter, with the particular circumstances attending it, must be very serviceable, in order to let them into a true state of the case, and inable them to judge of it with greater certainty. At the time of the Mithridatic war, Pompey had so large a share in the administration of affairs, and his power was so great, that some good freinds to the constitution began to grow uneasy at it. And therefore had not Cicero first represented the greatness and danger of that war, and the necessity of commiting it to Pompey, as the only general then equal to so important a trust; it would have been very difficult for him to prevail with the Roman people to make choice of him. And in the case of Milo so many stories had been raised, and such different relations industriously divulged by the freinds of Clodius concerning that action; that Cicero could not but think it necessary to obviate them, by so large and particular a narrative of the fact. Moreover, where the opposite party has set the matter in a false light by some artful and invidious turn, or loaded it with any odious circumstances, it seems no less necessary

that

2

LECT. XIII. that endeavours fhould be ufed to remove any ill impreſſions, which otherwife might remain upon the minds of the hearers, by a different and more favorable reprefentation. And if any thing can be fixed upon to make the contrary account appear abfurd or incredible, it ought particularly to be remarked. Thus Cicero in his defence of Sextus Rofcius, fhews that he was many miles diftant from Rome, at the time he was charged to have killed his father there. *Now, fais he, while Sextus Rofcius was at America, and this Titus Rofcius* [his accufer] *at Rome, Sextus Rofcius* [the father] *was killed at the baths on mount Palatine, returning from fupper. From whence I hope there can be no doubt, who ought to be fufpected of the murder. And was not the thing plain of itfelf, there is this further fufpicion to fix it upon the profecutor, that after the fact was committed, one Manlius Glaucia, an obfcure fellow, the freedman, client, and familiar of this Titus Rofcius, firft carried the account of it to America, not to the fon of the deceafed, but to the houfe of Titus Capito his enemy. And the fact being done in the evening, this meſſenger arrived at America by break of day, having rode fifty fix miles in a chaife in ten hours*

hours by night, to carry this acceptable news [1].
With more to the fame purpofe. But
what I bring it for is to fhew the ufe,
which Cicero makes of this narration, for
retorting the crime upon the profecutors.

BUT the orator fhould be very careful
in conducting this part, to avoid every
thing which may prejudice the caufe he
efpoufes. Falfehood and a mifreprefenta-
tion of facts are not to be juftified; but no
one is obliged to fay thofe things, which
may hurt himfelf. I fhall juft mention
one inftance of this from Cicero, where
he has fhewn great fkill in this refpect, in
pleading before Caefar, for the pardon of
Ligarius, who had joined with Pompey in
the civil war. For Ligarius having been
reprefented by the adverfe party as an enemy to Caefar, and fo efteemed by Caefar
himfelf; Cicero very artfully endeavours
in his narration to take off the force of
this charge, by fhewing, that when the
war firft broke out, he refufed to ingage in
it, which he would not have done, had he
borne any perfonal hatred to Caefar. *Quintus Ligarius,* fais he, *before there was any
fufpicion of a war, went into Africa as a
legate to the proconful Caius Confidius, in
which office he fo approved himfelf, both to*

I   *the*

the Roman citizens and allies, that when Confidius left the province, the inhabitants would not be satisfied he should leave the government in the hands of any other person. Therefore Quintus Ligarius having excused himself in vain for some time, accepted of the government against his will, which he so managed during the peace, that both the citizens and allies were greatly pleased with his integrity and justice. The war broke out on a sudden, which those in Africa did not hear of, till it was begun; but upon the news of it, partly thro inconsiderate haste, and partly from blind fear, they looked out for a leader, first for their own safety, and then as they were affected; when Ligarius thinking of home, and desirous to return to his freinds, would not be prevailed on to ingage in any affairs. In the mean time, Publius Accius Varus, the pretor, who was formerly governor of Africa, coming to Utica, recourse was immediately had to him, who very eagerly took upon himself the government. If that can be called a government, which was confered on a private man, by the clamor of the ignorant multitude, without any public authority. Ligarius therefore, who endeavoured to avoid every thing of that kind, ceased to [1] *act soon after the arrival of Varus* [1]. Here
Cicero

[1] *Cap.* 1.

Cicero ends his narrative. For tho Ligarius afterwards joined with Pompey's party, yet to have mentioned that, which was nothing more than what many others had done, whom Caesar had already pardoned, could have served only to increase his displeasure against him. And therefore he doubtless shewed great skill in so managing his account, as to take off the main force of the accusation, and by that means make way for his pardon, which he accordingly obtained.

L E C-

L E C T U R E XIV.

Of the Propofition.

IN every juft and regular difcourfe, the
fpeaker's intention is to prove or illuftrate fomething. And when he lais down
the fubject, upon which he defigns to treat,
in a diftinct and exprefs manner, this is
called the *Propofition*. But as I fhewed
before concerning the *Introduction*, that it
is the laft thing, which comes under the
confideration of the orator, tho it be firft
pronounced [1]; fo the propofition is what
firft imploys his thoughts, altho it ufually
follows both the introduction and narration
in the order of the difcourfe. For this is
the bafis and foundation of his whole defign, and his main view is to fupport and
maintain it thro his whole oration. It is
therefore neceffary, in the firft place, that
this be duly weighed, and reprefented to
his mind in all the different views, in which
he can place it ; that he well confider the
nature of it, the feveral parts of which it
confifts, and the particular force of each
part. By this means he will be the better
inabled to offer fuch arguments, as may be

[1] See *Lect*. XII.

proper in its defence; and to refute any objections, which may be brought against it. For, as it sometimes happens, that persons, by wanting a command of language, are at a loss to convey their thoughts to others, even of such things, whereof they themselves have very right sentiments; so it must be much more difficult for any one to demonstrate that clearly to another, of which he has only a confused and imperfect notion himself. And therefore Isocrates sais: *I have been used to tell my hearers, that they ought first to consider, how the subject and each part of it is to be treated; and when that has been duly weighed and examined, then to think of arguments, and a proper dress to support and recommend it, that it may answer the end we propose by it* [1]. This was certainly very good advice, for unless the speaker be master of his subject, and every branch of it, the most he can hope to do, is to entertain his hearers with fine language, and a florid harangue, not much to the purpose.

ORATORS use several ways in laying down the subject of their discourses. Sometimes they do it in one general proposition. We have an instance of this in Cicero's *speech to the senate*, the day after

[1] *Epist.* 6. *ad Jasonis liberos.*

[*Lib:* xliv.
p. 250
ed. Leun-
clav.
See alfo
Fabric.
Bibl. Lat.
Tom. i.
p. 148.
ed. 4to.]

Caefar was killed (as it is given us by Dion Caffius [1]) in which his defign was to perfuade them to peace and unanimity. *This,* fais he, *being the ftate of our affairs, I think it neceffary that we lay afide all the difcord and enmity, which have been among us, and return again to our former peace and agreement.* And then he procedes to offer his reafons for this advice.

AT other times, to give a clearer and more diftinct view of their difcourfe, they fubjoin to the propofition the general heads of argument, by which they endeavour to fupport it. This method Cicero ufes in his *feventh Philippic,* where he fais : *I who have always commended and advifed to peace, am againft a peace with Mark Antony. But why am I averfe to peace? Becaufe it is bafe, becaufe it is dangerous, and becaufe it is impracticable. And I befeech you to hear me with your ufual candor, while I make out thefe three things* [2].

[*Cap.* 3.]

BUT when the fubject relates to feveral different things, which require each of them to be feparately laid down in diftinct propofitions, it is called a *Partition.* Tho fome have made two kinds of *Partition* ; one of which they call *Separation,* and the other *Enumeration.* By the former of thefe, the

the orator shews in what he agrees with LECT.
his adversary, and wherein he differs from XIV
him. So in the case I formerly mentioned,
of a person accused of sacrilege for stealing
private money out of a temple, he who
pleads for the defendant sais: *He owns the
fact; but it being private money, the point
in question is, whether this be sacrilege* [1]. [1] See
And in the *cause of* Milo, Cicero speaking *Lect.* IX.
of Clodius sais: *The point which now comes
before the court, is not, whether he was
killed, or not, that we confess; but whether
justly or unjustly* [2]. Now in reality here is [2] *Cap.* 11.
no partition, since the former branch of
the proposition is what is agreed upon,
and given up; and consequently it is only
the latter, that remains to be disputed.
It is called *Enumeration*, when the orator
acquaints his hearers with the several parts
of his discourse, upon which he designs to
treat. And this alone properly speaking
is a *Partition*. Thus Cicero states his plea
in his *defence of* Muraena: *I perceive the
accusation consists of three parts: the first
respects the conduct of his life; the second
his dignity; and the third contains a charge
of bribery* [3]. But as it is frequent with [3] *Cap.* 5.
him in every part of his discourse, not
barely to inform his hearers, but likewise

P 2

to

to endeavour fo to influence their minds, as may beft anfwer his defign ; fometimes he difcovers a peculiar air of modefty in dividing and laying down the feveral branches of his fubject. For by this means, while he feems as it were diftruftful of himfelf, and to appeal to them for the equity of his procedings ; he artfully removes all fufpicion of defign to fupprefs any thing, which might make againft himfelf ; or to advance what was improper. In his *defence of* Sextus Rofcius, he thus befpeaks the judges : *As far as I am able to perceive, there are three things, which make againft Rofcius ; the crime he is charged with, the boldnefs, and the power of his adverfaries. And of each of thefe I think it will be proper for me to fpeak, tho not in the fame manner : for the firft belongs to my province, the other two the Roman people have injoined upon you : I muft clear him of the crime ; and it will depend on you to check the infolence, and break the pernicious and infufferable power* ¹ *Cap.* 13. *of thofe men, as foon as poffible* ¹. But elfewhere, when he thinks it for his purpofe, he takes the contrary method, and addrefles either his adverfary, the judges, or the whole audience with that franknefs, as if he was already affured of his caufe.

We

We have a remarkable instance of this in his *defence of* Quintius, where he sais : *I will do what I have always observed you to do, Hortensius, I will divide my whole cause into certain parts. You always do this, because you always can do it ; I shall do it in this case, because I think I can. What nature inables you to do at all times, that my cause inables me to do at present. I shall prescribe to myself certain bounds and limits, which I cannot excede, if I would : that I myself may be at a certainty what to speak to ; and you, what to answer ; and you likewise, Caius Aquilius, may be apprised before hand, what you are to hear. We deny, Sextus Nevius, that you was admitted to the possession of the estate of Publius Quintius by the pretor's edict. This is what we have ingaged to contest with you. And first, I shall shew, that you had no just cause to desire the pretor would admit you to the possession of the estate of Publius Quintius ; then, that you could not possess it by the edict ; and lastly, that you did not so possess it. And I beseech you, Caius Aquilius, and the rest of the judges, that you would be careful to remember what I have promised ; for by this means you will better understand what I say, and more easily prevent me from exceding*

P 3 *those*

LECT.
XIV.
*those bounds I have marked out for myself.
I deny that he had any foundation to solicit
for possession: I deny that he could have possession by the edict: and I deny that he had
possession by it. And when I have proved*
^¹*Cap.* 10. *these three things, I shall conclude* ¹. That
air of assurance, which Cicero here difco-
vers in stating the cafes, and his addressing
in so frank a manner, both to his antago-
nist, and the judges, was doubtless designed
to intimidate the one, and induce the other
to a favorable opinion of what he proposed
to say.

THERE are three things requisite in a
good *Partition*; that it be *short*, *complete*,
and consist but of a *few members*.

A PARTITION is said to be *short*, when
each proposition contains in it nothing
more, than what is necessary. So that the
brevity here required is different from that
of a narration; for that confifts cheifly in
things, this in words. And, as Quintilian
justly obferves, brevity feems very proper
here, where the orator does not fhew what
he is then speaking of, but what he defigns
^²*Inst. orat.* to discourse upon ¹.
Lib. iv.
c. 5.　　AGAIN, it ought to be *complete* and
perfect. And for this end, care must be
taken to omit no necessary part in the enumeration　　　　　　　　　BUT

BUT however there should be as few heads, as is consistent with the nature of the subject. The antient rhetoricians prescribe three or four at the most. And I do not remember that Cicero ever excedes that number. But it is certain, the fewer they are, the better, provided nothing necessary be omitted. For as it is the design of the partition to give the hearers a summary view of the several things, on which the orator proposes to treat, which they may carry in their minds thro the whole discourse; the fewer they are, the better they will be able to retain them, and too large a number is apt to introduce that confusion, which partition is designed to prevent.

I HAVE been hitherto speaking only of those heads, into which the subject, or general argument of the discourse, is at first divided. For it is sometimes convenient to divide these again, or at least some of them, into several parts or members. And when this happens, it is best done, as the speaker comes to each of them, in the order at first laid down; by which means the memory of the hearers will be less burdened, than by a multitude of particulars at one and the same

time

LECT.
XIV.

time. Thus Cicero in his *oration for the Manilian law*, comprifes what he defigns to fay, under three general heads. *Firft*, fais he, *I fhall fpeak of the nature of the war, then of its greatnefs, and laftly, about the choice of a general.* And when he comes to the firft of thefe, he divides it again into four branches, and fhews, *how much the glory of the Romans, the fafety of their allies, their greateft revenues, and the fortunes of many of their citizens, were all concerned in that war* [1]. The fecond head, in which he confiders the greatnefs of the war, has no divifion. But when he comes to the third head, concerning the choice of a general, he divides that likewife into four parts, and fhews, that fo many virtues are neceffary in a confummate general, fuch an one as was proper to have the management of that war, namely: *fkill in military affairs, courage, authority, and fuccefs* [2], all which he attributes to Pompey. And this is the fcheme of that celebrated oration. But in making the partition, it is of great fervice fo to difpofe the feveral parts, that they may appear to have a natural dependance upon each other. For, as by this means, what goes before will give light to that which follows ; fo, on the other hand,

[1] *Cap.* 2.

[2] *Cap.* 11.

it

it will receive ftrength and fupport from it. And the feveral heads ought to be treated on in the fame order, wherein they were at firft laid down, from which the hearers form to themfelves a fcheme of the difcourfe.

As the properties above mentioned are neceffary to a good partition, fo whatever is contrary to them, muft be a fault. But there are likewife fome other miftakes incident to a partition, which ought to be avoided. And firft, care fhould be taken not to infert any thing fuperfluous. And therefore, as Quintilian informs us, fome have blamed Cicero's partition in his *defence of* Cluentius on this account. Cluentius had formerly profecuted his father in law for a defign to poifon him, and got him convicted. But afterwards lay under the reproach of having bribed fome of the judges in that profecution. And being now himfelf profecuted upon a like charge of poifon, Cicero thought it requifite to clear him of the former fcandal. And this he propofes to do under three heads, by fhewing, *that no one was ever profecuted upon better evidence than his father in law; that fome of his accomplices had been convicted before him; and that he had bribed*

3 *the*

the judges, and not Cluentius [1]. Now if this laſt head could be proved, the two former were thought by ſome to be ſuperfluous. But Cicero had doubtleſs his reaſons to inſiſt on them at that time, tho they might not be ſo obvious afterwards. Again, it is wrong to mix things of a different order. As if a perſon ſhould ſay: *My deſign is to treat of virtue, juſtice, and temperance.* For juſtice and temperance are two particular virtues, and therefore ought not to be placed in the ſame order with virtue in general. But further, ſome divide their ſubject into two parts; and propoſe to treat upon it *negatively* and *poſitively*; by ſhewing firſt what it is not, and then what it is. But while they are imployed to prove what it is not, they are not properly treating upon that, but ſomething elſe; which ſeems as irregular, as it is unneceſſary. For he who proves what a thing is, does at the ſame time ſhew what it is not. However in facts there is a ſort of diviſion by affirmation and negation, which may ſometimes be conveniently uſed. As if a perſon, charged with killing another, ſhould thus ſtate his defence: *I had done right if I had killed him, but I did not kill him.* Here indeed, if the latter

can

can be plainly made to appear, it may
feem needlefs to infift upon the former.
But if that cannot be fo fully proved, but
there may be room left for fufpicion, it
may be proper to make ufe of both : for
all perfons do not fee things in the fame
light, and he who beleives the fact, may
likewife think it juft ; while he who
thinks it unjuft, may not beleive it, but
rather fuppofe, had it really been committed by the party, he would not have
denied it, fince he looked upon it as de-
fenfible. And this method of proceding
Quintilian compares to a cuftom often
ufed in traffic, when perfons make a large
demand at firft, in order to gain a reafonable price [1]. Cicero ufes this way of
reafoning, in his *defence of* Milo, but in the
contrary order, that is, he firft anfwers the
charge, and then juftifies the fact, upon
the fuppofition that the charge was true.
For he proves firft, that Clodius was the
aggreffor, and not Milo, as the contrary
party had afferted [2] ; and then to give the
greater advantage to his caufe, he procedes
to fhew, that if Milo had been the aggreffor, it would however have been a glo-
rious action to take off fuch an abandoned
wretch, who was not only a common enemy

[1] *Inft. orat. Lib.* iv. *c.* 5.

[2] *Cap.* 12.

my to mankind, but had likewife often threatned his life.

A GOOD and juft partition is attended with confiderable advantages. For it gives both light and ornament to a difcourfe. And it is alfo a great releif to the hearers, who, by means of thefe ftops and refts, as I may call them, are much better inabled to keep pace with the fpeaker without confufion, and by cafting their thoughts either way, from what has been faid, both know, and are prepared for what is to follow. And as perfons in travelling a road, with which they are acquainted, go on with greater pleafure and lefs fatigue, becaufe they know how far it is to their journey's end; fo to be apprifed of the fpeaker's defign, and the feveral parts of his difcourfe, which he propofes to treat on, contributes very much to releive the hearer, and keep up his attention. This muft appear very evident to all, who confider how difficult it is to attend long and clofely to one thing, efpecially when we do not know how long it may be, before we are like to be releafed. Whereas, when we are before hand acquainted with the fcheme, and the fpeaker procedes regularly from one thing to another, opportunity

nity is given to eafe the mind, by relaxing
the attention, and recalling it again when
neceffary.

BUT fome orations, efpecially of the *demonftrative* kind, do not require any particular propofition, being, as I obferved in my laft difcourfe, little more than a continued narrative or illuftration of the fubject. Of this fort is that of Cicero, in which he *returns thanks to* Caefar, in the name of the fenate, *for pardoning* Marcellus ; and his *invective againft* Pifo ; as likewife Pliny's *panegyric in praife of the emperor* Trajan. Not but that fuch difcourfes are difpofed in a regular order, and under proper heads, tho they are not laid down at firft in diftinct propofitions. Thus Cicero, in his *oration* for Marcellus, firft commends the clemency of Caefar, and then removes his fufpicions of any defigns formed againft him. And the *invective* againft Pifo likewife contains two parts, his public and private views ; as Pliny's panegyric does the public and private virtues of Trajan, which he there highly extols. Befides, as Quintilian obferves [1], orators fometimes avoid laying down any direct propofition, when the cheif thing they have in view, may be difagreable to thofe,

Inft. orat.
Lib. iv.
c. 5.

to

to whom they addrefs; for which reafon they take them off from attending to it, till they have firft prepared them for it, by offering fomething elfe, which, when proved, the other may with lefs difficulty be admited. Cicero makes ufe of this art in his *defence* of Ligarius, where his cheif defign was to perfuade Caefar, that Ligarius had not acted againft him in the late war from any perfonal enmity. However he does not directly undertake the proof of this, which he was fenfible, would have been an ungrateful fubject; but endeavours to convince him of it as a neceffary confequence of his conduct at that time, as was fhewn more at large in my laft difcourfe. Again, at other times orators omit fomething in their partition, which they defign in a particular manner to imprefs upon their hearers, and afterwards introduce it, by faying: *But I muft not omit, or I muft by no means forget:* or fome fuch expreffion, that may excite their regard and clofer attention to it; which will be the more eafily gained, by the fudden and unexpected manner of propofing it. But as this does not often happen, it muft be left to the prudence of the fpeaker, when it may be proper to make ufe of it.

L E C-

LECTURE XV.

Of Confirmation by Syllogism and En-thymem.

THE orator having acquainted his hearers in the *Proposition* with the subject, on which he designs to discourse, usually procedes either to prove or illustrate, what he has there laid down. For some discourses require nothing more than an inlargement or illustration, to set them in a proper light, and recommend them to the hearers. For which reason likewise they have often no distinct proposition, as was observed in my last lecture. But where arguments are brought in defence of the subject, this is properly *Confirmation*. For, as Cicero defines it, *Confirmation is that, which gives proof, authority and support to a cause by reasoning* [1]. And for this end, if any thing in the proposition seems obscure, or liable to be misunderstood, the orator first takes care to explain it, and then goes on to offer such arguments for the proof of it, and represent them in such a light, as may be most proper to gain the assent of his hearers. But we must di-

[1] *De Invent. Lib.* i. *c.* 24.

2   stinguish

LECT.
XV.
stinguish here between the *Arguments* themselves, and *Argumentation*, or the various ways of reasoning from them. Tho in common speech, the word *Argument* is often used for both. But *Arguments*, in the strict sense of the word, are the medium, by which other things are proved, and belong to *Invention*, which as I have formerly shewn, directs to the several topics or heads, from whence they may be taken [1].

[1] See
Lect. V.

My present business therefore is to treat of *Argumentation*, or the several forms and methods of reasoning made use of by orators. For there are different ways of reasoning suited to different arts. The mathematician treats his subject after another manner than the logician, and the orator in a method different from them both. Now as to these forms of reasoning used by orators, the Greek writers make them four; *Syllogism*, *Enthymem*, *Induction*, and *Example*. But Cicero reduces them to two, which he calls *Ratiocination* and *Induction*; comprizing both *Syllogism* and *Enthymem* under *Ratiocination*, and *Example* under *Induction:* so that the difference lies cheifly in their manner of dividing them. I shall follow the division of the Greeks, as more plain and distinct.

A

A SYLLOGISM then (for I shall begin with that) is a form of reasoning, which consists of three propositions, the last of which is deduced from the two former. The first of these is called the *major Proposition*, or, for brevity, the *Major :* the second, the *minor Proposition*, or *Minor :* and the third, the *Conclusion*. But as the last is opposed to the other two jointly, they are called the *Premises*, and this the *Conclusion*. So we may reduce Cicero's argument, by which he endeavours to prove, that Clodius assaulted Milo, and not Milo Clodius, to a syllogism in this manner :

> *He was the aggressor, whose advantage it was to kill the other.*
> *But it was the advantage of Clodius to kill Milo, and not Milo's to kill him.*
> *Therefore Clodius was the aggressor, or he assaulted Milo.*

The thing to be proved was, that Clodius assaulted Milo, which therefore comes in the conclusion: and the argument, by which it is proved, is taken from the head of profit or advantage. Thus the logician would treat this argument, and if either of the premises was questioned, he would support it with another syllogism. But this short and dry way of reasoning does not at all suit the orator, who, not only for variety changes the order of the parts, begining sometimes with the minor, and at other times with the conclusion, and ending with the major; but likewise cloaths each part with such ornaments of expression, as are proper to inliven the subject, and render it more agreable and entertaining. And he frequently subjoins, either to the major proposition, or minor, and sometimes to both, one or more arguments to support them; and perhaps others to confirm or illustrate them, as he thinks it requisite. Therefore as a logical syllogism consists of three parts or propositions, a rhetorical syllogism frequently contains four, and many times five parts. And Cicero reckons this last the most complete [1].

[1] *De invent. Lib. i. c. 37.*

But all that is said in confirmation of either of the premises, is accounted but as one part. This will appear more evident by examples: and therefore I shall endeavour to explain it by an instance or two from Cicero. By a short syllogism then he thus proves, that the Carthaginians were not to be trusted: *Those who have often deceived us, by violating their engagements, ought not to be trusted. For if we receive any damage*

by

*by their treachery, we can blame no body
but ourfelves.* But the Carthaginians have
often *fo deceived us. Therefore it is madnefs to truft them* [1]. Here the major propofition is fupported by a reafon. The
minor needed none; becaufe the treachery
of the Carthaginians was well known. So
that this fyllogifm confifts of four parts.
But by a fyllogifm of five parts he proves
fomewhat more largely and elegantly, that
the world is under the direction of a wife
governor. The major is this: *Thofe things
are better governed, which are under the
direction of wifdom, than thofe which are
not.* This he proves by feveral inftances:
*A houfe managed with prudence has every
thing in better order, and more convenient,
than that which is under no regulation. An
army commanded by a wife and fkilful general, is in all refpects better governed, than
one which has a fool or a madman at the
head of it. And the like is to be faid of a
fhip, which performs her courfe beft under
the direction of a fkilful pilot.* Then he
procedes to the minor thus: *But nothing
is better governed than the univerfe.* Which
he proves in this manner: *The rifing and
feting of the heavenly bodies keep a certain*

[1] *De in-
vent. Lib.i.
c. 93.*

Q 2   de-

LECT. *determined order ; and the several seasons of*
XV. *the year do not only necessarily return in the same manner, but are suited to the advantage of the whole ; nor did the vicissitudes of night and day ever yet become prejudicial, by altering their course.* From all which he concludes, *That the world must be under the direction of a wife governor* [1]. In both these examples, the regular order of the parts is observed. I shall therefore produce another, in which the order is directly con‑trary ; for begining with the conclusion, he procedes next to the minor proposition, and so ends with the major. This method is not uncommon with Cicero, but the example I shall fix on, is in his *defence of* Coelius. His design is to prove that Coelius had not led a loose and vicious life, with which his enemies had charged him. And this he does, by shewing he had closely followed his studies, and was a good ora‑tor. This may probably at first sight ap‑peal but a weak argument ; tho to him who considers, what Cicero every where declares necessary to gain that character, it may perhaps be thought otherwise. The sense of what he sais here may be reduced to this syllogism.

[1] *De In-vent. Lib.i. c.* 34.

Those

Those who have pursued the study of ora-
tory, so as to excel in it, cannot have
led a loose and vicious life.

But Coelius has done this.

Therefore his enemies charge him wrong-
fully.

But let us hear Cicero himself. He begins, as I said, with the conclusion, thus:
Coelius is not chargeable with profuseness,
extravagancy, contracting of debts, or in-
temperance, a vice which age is so far from
abating, that it rather increases it. Nay,
he never ingaged in amours, and those plea-
sures of youth, as they are called, which are
soon thrown off, as reason prevails. Then
he procedes to the minor, and shews from
the effects, that Coelius had closely applied himself to the best arts, by which he
means those necessary for an orator: *You*
have now heard him make his own defence,
and you formerly heard him ingaged in a
prosecution (I speak this to vindicate, not to
applaud him) you could not but perceive his
manner of speaking, his ability, his good sense,
and command of language.   Nor did he only
discover a good genius, which will oftentimes
do much of itself, when it is not improved by
industry; but what he said (if my affection
for him did not bias my judgement) appeared

Q 3   *to*

LECT.
XV.
to be the effect of learning, application, and study. And then he comes to the major: *But be assured, that those vices charged upon Coelius, and the studies upon which I am now discoursing, cannot meet in the same person. For it is not possible that a mind disturbed by such irregular passions, should be able to go thro what we orators do, I do not mean only in speaking, but even in thinking.* And this he proves by an argument taken from the scarcity of good orators. *Can any other reason be imagined, why so few, both now, and at all times, have ingaged in this province, when the rewards of eloquence are so magnificent, and it is attended with so great delight, applause, glory, and honor? All pleasures must be neglected; diversions, recreations, and entertainments omitted; and even the conversation of all our freinds must in a manner be laid aside. This it is which deters persons from the labor and study of oratory;* [1] *not their want of genius, or education* [1].

³ Cap. 19.

But sometimes, as I hinted above, several arguments, and those of a different kind, are brought to support each proposition, which draw out the syllogism to a great length. Nay sometimes a whole discourse shall be formed upon one principal syllogism. It is necessary therefore to observe, what

what the orator cheifly defigns to prove;
and for what end every particular argument is offered; and whether it be immediately connected with either of the
propofitions, or with fomething brought
to fupport them: for the propofitions may
both be true, and the conclufion fairly
deduced from them; tho fome of the reafons brought to fupport them, confidered
feparately, appear weak and inconclufive.
For in popular difcourfes, orators often
interfperfe fome things in the courfe of
their reafoning, which they know to be
agreable to the fentiments of their hearers, tho in themfelves of lefs weight, and
which they would not offer upon other
occafions.

BUT orators do not often ufe complete
fyllogifms, but moft commonly *Enthymems,*
which make the fecond kind of reafoning,
I propofed to explain. Now an *Enthymem*
is an imperfect fyllogifm, confifting of two
parts; the *Conclufion,* and one of the *Premifes.* And in this kind of fyllogifm, that
propofition is omitted, whether it be the
major or minor, which is fufficiently ma-
nifeft of itfelf, and may eafily be fupplied
by the hearers. But the propofition that
is expreffed, is ufually called the *Antecedent,*

Q 4   and

LECT.
XV.
and the conclusion the *Consequent*. So if
the major of that syllogism be omitted, by
which Cicero endeavours to prove, that
Clodius assaulted Milo, it will make this
Enthymem :

> The death of Milo would have been an
> advantage to Clodius,

> Therefore Clodius was the aggressor ;

> or, therefore he assaulted Milo [1].

¹ *Pro Mi-*
lon. c. 12.

In like manner that other syllogism above
mentioned, by which he shews that the
Carthaginians ought not to be trusted, by
omitting the minor, may be reduced to the
following *Enthymem* :

> Those who have often broke their faith,
>   ought not to be trusted.

> For which reason the Carthaginians
>   ought not to be trusted.

Every one would readily supply the minor,
since the perfidiousness of the Carthaginians was known to a proverb. But it is
reckoned a beauty in *Enthymems*, when
they consist of contrary parts : because the
turn of them is most acute and pungent.
Such is that of Micipsa in Sallust : *What*
stranger will be faithful to you, who are an
enemy to your freinds [2]? And so likewise
that of Cicero for Milo, speaking of Clodius : *You sit as avengers of his death* ;
                                        whose

² *Bell Jug.*
c. 10.

*whose life you would not restore, did you
think it in your power* [1]. Orators manage
Enthymems in the same manner they do
syllogisms, that is, they invert the order
of the parts, and confirm the proposition
by one or more reasons : and therefore
a rhetorical *Enthymem* frequently consists
of three parts, as a syllogism does of five.
Tho strictly speaking, a syllogism can consist of no more than three parts, and an
Enthymem but of two ; and the arguments
brought to support either of the propositions constitute so many new *Enthymems,*
of which the part they are designed to
prove is the conclusion. I will endeavour
to illustrate this by the following example :

> *An honest man thinks himself under the
>   highest obligations to his country.
> Therefore he should shun no danger
>   to serve it.*

In this *Enthymem* the major is wanting,
which would run thus : *He who is under
the highest obligations to another, should shun
no danger in order to serve him.* This last
proposition is founded upon the common
principle of gratitude, which requires, that
to the utmost of our power, a return should
be made in proportion to the kindness re-

[1] *Cap.* 29.

I   ceived.

ceived. And this being a maxim generally allowed, it is omitted by the orator. But now this *Enthymem*, confifting of the minor and conclufion, might be managed in fome fuch manner as this, begining with the conclufion : *An honeft man ought to fhun no danger, but readily expofe his life for the fafety and prefervation of his country.* Then the reafon for this conduct might be added, which is the antecedent of the *Enthymem*, or minor of the fyllogifm : *For he is fenfible, that his obligations to his country are fo many, and fo great, that he can never fully requite them.* And this again might be confirmed by an enumeration of particulars : *He looks upon himfelf indebted to his country for every thing he enjoys, for his freinds, relations, all the pleafures of life, and even for life itfelf.* Now the orator, as I have faid, calls this one *Enthymem*, tho in reality there are two. For the fecond reafon or argument added to the firft becomes the antecedent of a new *Enthymem*, of which the firft reafon is the confequent. And if thefe two *Enthymems* were expreffed feparately in the natural order of the parts, the former would ftand thus : *An honeft man thinks himfelf under the higheft obligations to his country. Therefore he ought to fhun no danger*

ger for its preservation. The latter thus :
*An honest man esteems himself indebted to his
country for every thing he injoys. Therefore
he thinks he is under the highest obligations
to it.* The same thing might be proved in
the like way of reasoning, by arguments of
a different kind. From comparison thus :
*As it would be thought base and ungrateful
in a son not to hazard himself for the preservation of his father ; an honest man must
certainly esteem it so, when his country is in
danger.* Or from an example in this manner : *An honest man in like circumstances
would propose to himself the example of De-
cius, who freely gave up his life for the service of his country.* He gave up his life indeed, but did not lose it ; for he cannot be
said to have lost his life, who lives in immortal honor.* And orators frequently intermix
such arguments to adorn and illustrate their
subject, with others taken from the nature
and circumstances of things. And now, if
we consider a little this method of reasoning, we shall find it the most plain and
easy imaginable. For when any proposition
is laid down, and one or more reasons sub-
joined to prove it, each reason joined with
the proposition makes a distinct *Enthymem,*
of which the proposition is the conclusion.

Thus

LECT.
XV.
Thus Cicero in his seventh Philippic, lais down this as the foundation of his discourse. *That he is against a peace with Mark Antony.* For which he gives three reasons: *Because it is base, because it is dangerous, and because* [1] *it is impracticable* [1]. These severally joined with the proposition form three *Enthymems*, and upon each of these he discourses separately, which make up that oration. And this method is what persons for the most part naturally fall into, who know nothing of the terms *Syllogism* or *Enthymem*. They advance something, and think of a reason to prove it, and another perhaps to support that, and so far as their invention will assist them, or they are masters of language, they endeavour to set what they say in the plainest light, give it the best dress, embellish it with proper figures, and different turns of expression, and, as they think convenient, illustrate it with similitudes, comparisons, and the like ornaments, to render it most agreable, till they think what they have advanced sufficiently proved. As this method of arguing therefore is the most plain, easy and natural; so it is what is most commonly used in oratory. Whereas a strict syllogistical way of discoursing is dry and jejune, cramps the mind, and does not admit

[1] *Cap.* 3.

admit of thofe embellifhments of language, L E C T.
XV.
which are a great advantage to the orator :
for which reafon he feldom ufes complete
fyllogifms, and when he does, it is with
great latitude.   However fyllogiftical reafoning is very ufeful, tho not in popular
difcourfes : for every argument may be reduced to a fyllogifm, and if it will not
hold in that form, there is certainly fome
flaw in it, which by that means will moft
eafily be difcovered.

I HAVE now gone thro the two firft
ways of reafoning made ufe of by orators ;
there are two others yet remaining, but
thefe I muft defer to my next difcourfe.

L E C-

LECTURE XVI.

Of Confirmation by Induction and Example.

THAT there are different ways of reasoning, suited to different arts, was shewn in my last discourse. The forms made use of by orators are four; *Syllogism, Enthymem, Induction,* and *Example*: the two first of which I then explained, and shall now procede to confider the other two, begining with *Induction.*

Now it is called *Induction,* when one thing is infered from several others, by reason of the similitude between them. And this way of reasoning is often very useful in popular difcourses. For many persons are sooner moved by examples, and similitudes, than by arguments taken from the nature of things. Every one either endeavours to think right, or at least would be esteemed so to do. But it is often no easy matter to take in the force of an argument, especially for those, who have not been accustomed to examine things closely, and weigh them duly in their minds. And therefore when this cannot be done without some pain and uneafinefs to the mind,

till

till it become habitual by practice; it is
not to be wondred at, if such persons are
beft pleafed with that way of reafoning,
by which they imagine they can form a
judgement of things with the greateft eafe
and facility. But tho inductions are made
from all kinds of fimilitudes; yet thofe
ufually carry the greateft force with them,
which are drawn from like facts. Such is
that of Cicero in his *oration for the Manilian law.* For when fome perfons objected
to Pompey's being intrufted with the Mithridatic war, as a thing not cuftomary to
put fuch an acceffion of power into the
hands of one man: Cicero removes that
objection, by producing feveral inftances
of the like nature, and particularly fhews,
that more new honors had already been
confered on Pompey, than upon any other
Roman citizen before him, which had all
been employed to the advantage of the
ftate. *I will not,* fais he, *take notice that
two very great wars, the Punic and Carthaginian, were both managed by one general; and two very powerful cities, which
threatned this empire moft, Carthage and
Numantia, both deftroyed by the fame Scipio.
I will not obferve, that both you and your
fathers thought fit to place the fafety of*

I   *the*

*the government alone in Caius Marius, and
that the same person should carry on the war
with Jugurtha, with the Cimbrians, and the
Teutons. You remember how many new
powers have already been confered on Pompey ;*
which he then procedes to enumerate, and
from thence infers, that the objection of novelty was no juft reafon againſt his being in-
truſted with the conduct of that important
war [1]. And as to other fimilitudes, it may
thus be fhewn by *Induction*, that virtuous
habits are gained and improved by practice : Bodily ſtrength is increaſed and confirmed by daily exerciſe. All manual arts
are acquired by repeated trials and experi-
ments. The liberal ſciences are alſo attained by conſtant ſtudy and application.
And in like manner the mind is formed to
virtue, and improved in it, by the continued practice of right actions.

BUT there is one particular form of *Induction*, called *Socratic* ; becauſe Socrates
very frequently uſed that way of reaſoning. It procedes by ſeveral queſtions,
which being ſeparately granted, the thing
defigned to be infered is afterwards put,
which, by reaſon of its fimilitude with the
ſeveral caſes allowed before, cannot be denied. But this is a captious way of reaſoning,

[1] *Pro Leg. Man. c. 20.*

ning, for while the respondent is not aware
of what is designed to be infered, he is easily induced to make those concessions, which otherwise he would not. Besides, it is not so well suited to continued discourses, as to those which are interlocutory; and therefore we meet with it oftenest in the *Socratic dialogues* both of Plato and Xenophon. However it may be made use of in oratory by a figure called *Subjection* [1], when the same person first puts the question, and then makes the answer. So in the famous *cause of* Epaminondas, general of the Thebans, who was accused for refusing to surrender his command to his successor, appointed by the state, till after he had engaged the enemy, and given them a total defeat. Cicero thus represents his accuser pleading for the words of the law against Epaminondas, who alleged the intention of it in his defence: *Should Epaminondas add that exception to the law, which, he fais, was the intention of the writer, namely:* Except any one refuse to give up his command, when it is for the interest of the public he should not, *Would you admit of it? I beleive not Should you yourselves, which is a thing most remote from your justice and wisdom, to skreen*

[1] See *Lect.* XXXII. *in Hypobole.*

LECT.	*him, order this exception to be added to the*
XVI.	*law, without the command of the people,*
Would the Thebans suffer it to be done? No
certainly. Can it be right then to come into
that, as if it was writen, which it would be
a crime to write? I know it cannot be agre-
[1] De In-	*able to your wisdom to think so* [1].
vent Lib.i.
c. 33.	I COME now to the fourth and last man-
ner of reasoning above mentioned, and that
is *Example.* But rhetoricians use this word
in a different sense from the common acceptation. For that is usually called an
example, which is brought either to prove
or illustrate some general assertion. As if
any one should say, that *human bodies may
be brought to sustain the greatest labors by
use and exercise* ; and in order to prove
this should relate, what is said of Milo of
Croton, that *by the constant practice of
carrying a calf several furlongs every day,
he could carry it as far after it was grown*
[2] Erasm.	*to its full size* [2]. But in oratory the word
Chil.
p. 193.	*Example* is used for any kind of similitude :
or, as Vossius defines it, *When one thing is
infered from another, by reason of the like-*
[3] Orat.	*ness which appears between them* [3]. Hence
Partit.
Lib. iii.	it is called an *imperfect Induction*, which
c. 7. §. 16.	infers something from several others of a
like nature. But, as was observed before,
in

in fpeaking of induction, fo likewife in examples, thofe have the greateft force in reafoning, which are taken from facts. Now facts may be compared with refpect to fome agreement or fimilitude between them, which in themfelves are either equal or unequal. Of the former kind this is an inftance: *Cato acted as became a patriot, and a lover of his country's liberty, in oppofing the arms of Caefar; and therefore fo did Cicero.* The reafon of the inference is founded in the parity of the cafe, which equally concerned all good fubjects of the Roman government at that time. For all were alike obliged to oppofe a common enemy, who endeavoured to fubvert the conftitution, and fubject them to his own arbitrary power. But tho an example confifts in the comparifon of two fingle facts, yet feveral perfons may be concerned in each fact. Of this kind is that which follows: *As Pompey, Caefar, and Craffus, acted illegally in the firft triumvirate, by ingroffing the fole power into their own hands, and by that means violating the public liberty; fo likewife did Auguftus, Mark Antony, and Lepidus, in the fecond triumvirate, by purfuing the fame meafures.* But when Cicero defends Milo

R 2 for

for killing Clodius, from the like instances of Ahala Servilius, Scipio Nasica,
Lucius Opimius, and others, that is not
an example, but an induction; because one
thing is there infered from its similitude
to several others. But when a comparison
is made between two facts that are unequal, the inference may be either from
the greater to the less, or from the less to
the greater. From the greater to the less
in this manner: *Caesar had no just pre-
tensions to the Roman government, and therefore much less had Antony.* The reason lies in the difference between the two
persons. Caesar had very much enlarged
the bounds of the Roman empire by his
conquests, and greatly obliged the populace
by his generosity; but as he had always
acted by an authority from the senate and
people of Rome, these things gave him no
claim to a power over them. Much less
then had Antony any such pretence, who
always acted under Caesar, and had never
performed any signal services himself. Cicero has described the difference between
them in a very beautiful manner in his
second Philippic, thus speaking to Antony:
*Are you in any thing to be compared to him?
He had a genius, sagacity, memory, learning,*

care,

care, thought, diligence; he had performed
great things in war, tho detrimental to the
state; he had for many years designed to get
the government into his hands, and obtained
his end by much labor and many dangers;
he gained over the ignorant multitude by
public shows, buildings, congiaries, and feasts;
obliged his freinds by rewards, and his ene-
mies by a shew of clemency. In a word, he
subjected a free state to slavery, partly thro
fear, and partly compliance. I can liken you
to him for ambition of power, but in other
things you are in no respect to be compared
with him [1]. By a comparison from the [1] *Cap.* 45.
less to the greater, Cicero thus argues
against Catiline : *Did the brave Scipio,*
when a private man, kill Tiberius Gracchus,
for attempting to weaken the state; and shall
we consuls bear with Catiline endeavouring
to destroy the world by fire and sword [2] ? [2] *In Catil.*
i. *c.* 1.
The circumstances of these two cases were
very different; and the comparison runs
between a private man, and a consul intrusted with the highest authority; between a design only to raise a tumult, and
a plot to destroy the government : whence
the orator justly infers, that what was
esteemed lawful in one case, was much
more so in the other. The like way of

LECT
XVI.

reasoning is sometimes used from other similitudes, which may be taken from things of all kinds, whether animate or inanimate. Of the former sort is that of Cicero speaking of Muraena, when candidate for the consulship, after he had himself gone thro that office : *If it is usual,* sais he, *for such persons, who are safely arrived in port, to give those, who are going out, the best account they can, with relation to the weather, pirates, and coasts ; because thus nature directs us to assist those, who are entering upon the same dangers, which we ourselves have escaped : how ought I, who now after a great storm am brought within a near prospect of land, to be affected towards him, who, I perceive, must be exposed to the greatest tempests of the state* [1]*?* He alludes to the late disturbances and tumults occasioned by the conspiracy of Catiline, which had been so happily suppressed by him in the time of his consulate. Of the latter kind is that of Quintilian : *As the ground is made better and more fruitful by culture, so is the mind by instruction* [2]. There is both a beauty and justness in this simile.

[1] *Pro Muraen. c. 2.*

[2] *Inst. orat. Lib. viii. c. 3.*

BUT comparisons are sometimes made between facts and other things, in order

to

to infer fome difference or oppofition between them. In comparing two facts,
on the account of fome difagreement and
unlikenefs, the inference is made from the
difference between one and the other in
that particular refpect only. As thus :
Tho it was not efteemed cruelty in Brutus
to put his two fons to death, for endea-
vouring to betray their country ; it might
be fo in Manlius, who put his fon to
death, only for ingaging the enemy with-
out orders, tho he gained the victory. The
difference between the two facts, lies in
the different nature of the crime. The
fons of Brutus entered into a confpiracy to
betray their country, and tho they mif-
carried in it, yet the intention and endeavours they ufed to accomplifh it were criminal in the higheft degree. But young
Manlius could only be charged with rafh-
nefs. His defign was honorable, and intended for the intereft of his country ;
only it was irregular, and might have
proved of ill confequence to military dif-
cipline. Now in all fuch cafes, the force
of the argument is the ftronger, the greater the difference appears. But the fame
facts, which differ in one refpect, may
agree in many others. As in the example

R 4   here

here mentioned, Brutus and Manlius were both magistrates as well as fathers; they both killed their sons, and that for a capital crime by the Roman law: in any of which respects they may be compared in a way of similitude. As, *If Brutus might lawfully put his son to death for a capital crime; so might Manlius.* But now contrary facts do not only differ in some certain respect, but are wholly opposite to each other; so that what is affirmed of the one, must be denied of the other; and if one be a virtue, the other is a vice. Thus Cicero compares the conduct of Marcellus and Verres in a way of opposition. *Marcellus,* fais he, *who had engaged, if he took Syracuse, to erect two temples at Rome, would not beautify them with the spoils he had taken: Verres, who had made no vows to honor and virtue, but to Venus and Cupid, endeavoured to plunder the temple of Minerva. The former would not adorn the gods with the spoils of other deities: the latter carried the ornaments of Minerva, a virgin, into the house of a strumpet* [1]. If therefore the conduct of Marcellus was laudable and virtuous, that of Verres must bear the contrary character. But this way of reasoning has likewise place in other re-

[1] *In Verr.* iv. c. 55.

respects. Thus Cicero in the quarrel between Caesar and Pompey, advised to peace
from the difference between a foreign and
domestic war: That the former might
prove beneficial to the state; but in the
latter, which ever side conquered, the
public must suffer. And thus the ill effects of intemperance may be shewn in a
way of opposition. That as temperance
preserves the health of the body, keeps
up the vigor of the mind, and prolongs
life; so excess must necessarily have the
contrary effects.

FROM what has been said upon these
heads of *Induction* and *Example*, they appear to consist of three parts; the thing
designed to be proved, that which is
brought to prove it, and the similitude or
dissimilitude between them according to
the nature of the inference. And great
care must be taken, that what is introduced, on the account of which it is expected some other thing should be granted,
be itself very plain and evident. The similitude likewise or dissimilitude between
that, and the thing it is brought to prove,
ought to be no less obvious. For in every
induction and example, the thing or things,
from a comparison with which we infer

3   our

LECT. our conclusion, carries in it the force of a
XVI. medium or argument, and the whole induction or example has the nature of an
Enthymem or imperfect syllogism. However rhetoricians have thought fit to sepa-
rate these from other *Enthymems*, because
they seemed to require a distinct and particular explication.

THUS I have given a breif account of
the principal ways of reasoning commonly
made use of by orators. And it is very
proper to vary them in a discourse, and not
keep too close to the same form; for a
want of variety in this, as well as in other
cases, will soon create a disrelish. As to
the disposition of arguments, or the order
of placing them, some advise to put the
weaker, which cannot wholly be omitted,
in the middle; and such as are stronger,
partly in the begining, to gain the esteem
of the hearers, and render them more attentive; and partly at the end, because
what is last heard, is likely to be retained
longest: but if there are but two arguments, to place the stronger first, and then
the weaker; and after that to return again
to the former, and insist principally upon
that. But this must be left to the prudence
of the speaker, and the nature of the subject.

LECT.
XVI.

ject. Tho to begin with the ftrongeft, and fo gradually defcend to the weakeft, can never be proper, for the reafon laft mentioned. Nor ought arguments to be crouded too clofe upon one another; for that takes off from their force, as it breaks in upon the attention of the hearers, and does not leave them fufficient time duly to confider them. Nor indeed fhould more be ufed than are neceffary, becaufe the fewer they are, the more eafily they are remembered. And the obfervation of a great mafter of eloquence upon this fubject is certainly very juft, that, *Arguments ought rather to be weighed, than numbered* [1].

[1] Cic. *De orat. Lib.* ii. *c.* 76.

L E C-

LECTURE XVII.
Of Confutation.

CONFIRMATION, of which I laſt diſcourſed, is often attended with a *Confutation* of what either has been, or may be advanced to the contrary. And in treating of *Diſpoſition*, rhetoricians generally place this after *Confirmation*, which ſeems agreable to the natural method of thinking upon any ſubject. For perſons firſt endeavour to find out ſuch arguments, as are proper to maintain that ſide of a queſtion, which they eſpouſe, before they conſider, what objections may be offered againſt it. Tho in ſpeaking it may be requiſite to vary the order, according to the nature of the diſcourſe. And the method preſcribed by Quintilian is this, that, *If we bring a charge, we ſhould firſt prove it, and then anſwer objections; but if we ſtand upon the defence, we ought to begin with* confutation [1]. And there ſeems to be good reaſon for this different procedure. For he who either ſpeaks alone, or firſt, endeavours to ſupport what he ſais with reaſon and arguments; and till that be done,

[1] *Inſt orat.*
Lib. v.
c. 13.

done, there is no room to move objections. But, on the contrary, to confute what another has before offered, is sometimes sufficient to carry a cause. And when it is otherwise, it is however frequently necessary to take off the force of what has been advanced, in order to make way for a candid reception of the opposite opinion. Wherefore, unless there be some particular reason to the contrary, it seems generally most commodious to follow this method, which from several orations of Cicero appears to have been his usual custom.

THE forms of reasoning are the same here, as have been already explained under *Confirmation*. And therefore what I propose at present, is only to give a brief account of the different ways of *Confutation* made use of by orators, which is often the more difficult task ; because he, who is to prove a thing, comes usually prepared ; but he, who is to confute it, is frequently left to a sudden answer. For which reason in *judicial* cases Quintilian sais : *It is as much easier to accuse, than to defend; as it is to make a wound, than to heal it* [1]. There-fore not only a good judgement, but a readiness of thought also, seems necessary for this province. But in all disputes it

[1] *Ubi supra.*

is

is of the greateſt conſequence to obſerve, where the ſtreſs of the controverſy lies. For without attending to this, perſons may cavil about different matters without underſtanding each other, or deciding any thing. And in confutation, what the adverſary has advanced ought carefully to be conſidered, and in what manner he has expreſſed himſelf. As to the things themſelves ; whether they immediately relate to the matter in diſpute, or are foreign to it. Thoſe things that are foreign to the ſubject, may either be paſt over in ſilence, or in a very few words ſhewn to be inſignificant. And there ought likewiſe to be a diſtinction made between ſuch things as relate to the ſubject, according to their importance. Thoſe that appear to have no great weight, ſhould be ſlightly remarked. For to inſiſt largely upon ſuch matters is both tireſome to the hearers, and apt to bring the judgement of the ſpeaker into queſtion. And therefore things of that nature are generally better turned off with an air of neglect, a pungent queſtion, or an agreable jeſt ; than confuted by a ſerious and laboured anſwer. But thoſe things, which relate to the merits of the cauſe, may be confuted either by *contradicting*

tradicting them, or by shewing some *mi-stake* in the reasoning, or their *invalidity* when granted.

THINGS may be *contradicted* several ways. What is apparently false, may be expresly *denied*. Thus Cicero in his *defence of* Cluentius : *When the accuser had said, that the man fell down dead, after he had drunk off his cup ; denies, that he died that day* [1]. And things which the adver- [1] *Cap.* 60. sary cannot prove, may likewise be denied. Of which we have also an instance in Cicero, who first upbraids Mark Antony as guilty of a breach not only of good breeding, but likewise of freindship, for reading publicly a private letter he had sent him. And then adds : *But what will you say now, if I should deny that ever I sent you that letter ? How will you prove it ? By the hand writing ? In which I confess you have a peculiar skill, and have found the benefit of it. But how can you make it out ? For it is in my secretary's hand. I cannot but envy your master, who had so great a reward for teaching you to understand just nothing. For what can be more unbecoming not only an orator, but even a man, than for any one to offer such things, which if the adversary denies, he has nothing more*

to

to *fay* [1]? It is an handſome way of contradicting a thing, by ſhewing, that the
adverſary himſelf maintained the contrary.
So when Oppius was charged with de-
frauding the ſoldiers of their proviſions,
Cicero refutes it, by proving, that the ſame
perſons charged Oppius with a deſign to
corrupt the army by his liberality [2].   An
adverſary is never more effectually ſilenced,
than when you can faſten contradictions
upon him; for this is ſtabing him with
his own weapon.   Sometimes a thing is
not in expreſs terms denied, but repreſented to be utterly incredible.   And this
method expoſes the adverſary more than
a bare denial.   So when ſome perſons re-
proached Cicero with cowardice, and a
ſhameful fear of death; he recites their
reaſons in ſuch a manner, that any one
would be inclined to think the charge entirely falſe.   *Was it becoming me,* ſais he,
*to expect death, with that compoſedneſs of
mind, as ſome have imagined? Well, and did
I then avoid it? Nay, was there any thing
in the world that I could apprehend more
deſirable? Or when I had done the greateſt
things in ſuch a crowd of ill minded perſons
about me, do you think baniſhment, and death,
were not always in my view? and conti-
nually*

*nually founding in my ears, as my certain
fate, while I was so employed? Was life de-
sirable, when all my freinds were in such
sorrow, and myself in so great distress, deprived of all the gifts both of nature and
fortune? Was I so unexperienced, so ignorant, so void of reason and prudence? Had
I never seen, nor heard any thing in my
whole life? Did all I had read, and studied
avail nothing? What? did not I know that
life is short, but the glory of generous actions
permanent? When death is appointed for all,
does it not seem eligible, that life, which
must be wrested from us, should rather be
freely devoted to the service of our country,
than reserved to be worn out by the decays
of nature. Was not I sensible, there has
been this controversy among the wisest men,
that some say, the minds of men and their
consciousness utterly perish at death; and
others, that the minds of wise and brave
men are then in their greatest strength and
vigor, when they are set free from the body?
The first state is not greatly to be dreaded,
to be void of sense; but the other, of in-
joying larger capacities, is greatly to be de-
sired. Therefore since I always aimed at
dignity, and thought nothing was worth living for without it; how should I, who am*

paft the confulfhip, and did fo great things in it, be afraid to die [1] *?* Thus far Cicero.

[1] *Pro Sext. c. 21.*

There is likewife an ironical way of contradicting a thing, by retorting that and other things of the like nature upon the adverfe party. Thus Cicero in his *oration againft* Vatinius fais: *You have objected to me, that I defended Cornelius, my old freind, and your acquaintance. But pray why fhould I not have defended him? Has Cornelius carried any law contrary to the omens? Has he violated any law? Has he affaulted the conful? Did he take poffeffion of a temple by force of arms? Did he drive away the tribune, who oppofed the paffing a law? Has he thrown contempt upon religion? Has he plundered the treafury? Has he pillaged the ftate?*

[2] *Cap. 2.*

No, thefe, all thefe, are your doings [2] *?* Such an unexpected return is fometimes of great fervice to abate the confidence of an adverfary.

A second way of *Confutation* is, by obferving fome *flaw* in the reafoning of the adverfe party. I fhall endeavour to illuftrate this from the feveral kinds of reafoning, treated of before under *Confirmation*. And firft as to *Syllogifms,* they may be refuted either by fhewing fome miftake in the premifes, or that the conclufion

clusion is not justly deduced from them.
So when the Clodian party contended, that
Milo ought to suffer death for this reason,
because he had confessed that he had killed
Clodius, that argument reduced to a syllo-
gism, would stand thus :

> *He who confesses he has killed another,*
> *ought not to be allowed to see the light.*
> *But Milo confesses this.*
> *Therefore he ought not to live.*

Now the force of this argument lies in
the major or first proposition, which Cicero
refutes by proving, that the Roman people
had already determined contrary to what
is there asserted : *In what city*, sais he, *do*
these men dispute after this weak manner?
In that wherein the first capital trial was
in the case of the brave Horatius, who, be-
fore the city enjoyed perfect freedom, was
saved by the suffrages of the Roman people,
tho he confessed, that he killed his sister with
his own hand [1]. But when Cicero accused
Verres for male administration in his government of Sicily, Hortensius, who defended him, being sensible the allegations
brought against him could not be denied,
had no other way left to bring him off,
but by pleading his military virtues in a-
batement, which at that time were much

[1] *Pro Mi-*
lon. c. 3.

wanted,

wanted, and very ferviceable to the ftate.
The form of the argument was this :

> *That the Romans then wanted good*
> *generals.*
>
> *That Verres was fuch.*
>
> *And confequently, that it was for the in-*
> *tereft of the public he fhould not be*
> *condemned.*

But Cicero, who knew his defign, ftates
the argument for him in his charge, and
then anfwers it by denying the confequence, fince the crimes of Verres were
of fo heinous a nature, that he ought by
no means to be pardoned, on the account
of any other qualifications. Tho indeed
he afterwards refutes the minor or fecond
propofition, and fhews that he had not
merited the character of a good general [1].
Enthymems may be refuted, either by fhewing that the antecedent is falfe, or the confequent not juftly infered from it. As thus,
with refpect to the former cafe :

> *A ftrict adherence to virtue has often*
> *proved detrimental.*
>
> *Therefore virtue ought not conftantly to*
> *be embraced.*

Here the antecedent may be denied. For
virtue is always beneficial to thofe, who
fteadily adhere to it, both in the prefent

[1] *Lib.* 5. *in Verr.* *c.* 1.

fa-

satisfaction it affords them, and the future
rewards they may certainly expect from
it. And as to the latter case in this
manner:

> *She is a mother*.
> *Therefore she loves her children*.

Now as the certainty of that inference depends upon this general assertion, That all mothers love their children, which is not true, the mistake of the reasoning may be shewn from the instance of Medea and others, who destroyed their own children. As to *Induction* and *Example*, by which the truth or equity of a thing is proved from its likeness to one· or more other things, the reasoning in either is invalid, if the things so compared can be shewn not to have that similitude or agreement, on which the inference is founded. One instance therefore may serve for both. As when Cicero, after the death of Caesar, pleaded for the continuance of his laws, but not of those, which were made afterwards by Mark Antony. Because tho both were in themselves invalid, and impositions upon the public liberty; yet some of Caesar's were useful, and others could not be set aside without disturbance to the state, and injuring particular persons; but

those

those of Antony were all detrimental to the public [1].

THE laſt method of *Confutation* before mentioned was, when the orator does in ſome ſenſe *grant* the adverſary his argument, and at the ſame time ſhews its *invalidity*. And this is done by a variety of ways, according to the different nature of the ſubject. Sometimes he allows what was ſaid may be true, but pleads, that what he contends for is neceſſary. This was the method, by which Hortenſius propoſed to bring off Verres, as I have already ſhewn from Cicero, whoſe words are theſe, addreſſing himſelf to the judges : *What ſhall I do? which way ſhall I bring in my accuſation? where ſhall I turn myſelf? for the character of a brave general is placed like a wall againſt all the attacks I can make. I know the place, I perceive where Hortenſius intends to diſplay himſelf. He will recount the hazards of war, the neceſſities of the ſtate, the ſcarcity of commanders ; and then he will intreat you, and do his utmoſt to perſuade you, not to ſuffer the Roman people to be deprived of ſuch a commander, upon the teſtimony of the Sicilians ; nor the glory of his arms to be ſullied by a charge of avarice* [2]. At other times the orator pleads, that

that altho the contrary opinion may seem to be attended with advantage, yet that his own is more juſt or honorable. Such was the caſe of Regulus, when his freinds endeavoured to prevail with him to continue at Rome, and not return to Carthage, where he knew he muſt undergo a cruel death. But as this could not be done without violating his oath, he refuſed to hearken to their perſuaſions [1]. Another way of *Confutation* is, by retorting upon the adverſary his own argument. Thus Cicero in his *defence of* Ligarius ſais: *You have, Tubero, that which is moſt deſirable to an accuſer, the confeſſion of the accuſed party; but yet ſuch a confeſſion, that he was on the ſame ſide that you, Tubero, choſe yourſelf, and your father too, a man worthy the higheſt praiſe. Wherefore, if there was any crime in this, you ought firſt to confeſs your own, before you attempt to faſten any upon Ligarius* [2]. The orator takes this advantage, where an argument proves too much, that is, more than the perſon deſigned it for, who made uſe of it. Not much unlike this is, what they call *Inverſion*, by which the orator ſhews, that the reaſons offered by the oppoſite party make for him. So when Caecilius urged,

[1] See *Lect.* VIII.

[2] *Cap*

S 4

urged, that the province of accusing Verres ought to be granted to him, and not to Cicero, becaufe he had been his treafurer in Sicily, at the time thofe crimes were committed, with which he was charged, and confequently knew moft of that affair: Cicero turns the argument upon him, and fhews, for that very reafon he was the moft unfit of any man to be intrufted with his profecution; fince having been concerned with him in his crimes, he would certainly do all in his power to conceal, or

¹ *In Caecil.*
c. 18.

leffen them ¹. Again, fometimes the charge is acknowledged, but the crime fhifted off to another. Thus when Sextius was accufed of fedition, becaufe he had got together a body of gladiators, and brought them into the forum, where a warm engagement happened between them and Clodius's faction; Cicero owns the fact, but charges the crime of fedition upon

² *Pro Sext.*
c. 36.

Clodius's party in being the aggreffors ². Another method made ufe of for the fame purpofe is, to alleviate the charge, and take off the force of it, by fhewing, that the thing was not done with that intention, which the adverfary infinuates. Thus Cicero in his *defence of king* Dejotarus,

owns

owns he had raifed fome forces, tho not to invade the Roman territories, as had been alleged, but only to defend his own borders, and fend aid to the Roman ge- nerals [1]. Some other ways might be men- tioned, efpecially in *judicial* cafes; but I have formerly treated fo largely upon them in their proper place, that I need not here repeat them.

[1] *Cap.* 8.

I HAVE hitherto been fpeaking of the methods of *Confutation* ufed by orators, in anfwering thofe arguments, which are brought by the contrary party. But fome- times they raife fuch objections them- felves, to what they have faid, as they imagine may be made by others; which they afterwards anfwer, the better to in- duce their hearers to think, that nothing confiderable can be offered againft what they have advanced, but what will ad- mit of an eafy reply. I fhall endeavour to illuftrate this by one inftance. When Cicero, at the requeft of the Sicilians, had undertaken the accufation of Verres, it came under debate, whether he, or Cae- cilius, who had been Verres's quæftor in Sicily, fhould be admitted to that pro- vince. Cicero therefore in order to fet
him

him afide, among other arguments, fhews
his incapacity for fuch an undertaking,
and for that end recounts at large the qualifications neceffary for an orator. Which
he reprefents to be fo many and great,
that he thought it neceffary to ftart the
following objection, to what he had himfelf faid upon that fubject. *But you will
fay perhaps: Have you all thefe qualifications?* To which he thus replies: *I wifh
I had; but it has been my conftant ftudy
from my youth to gain them. And if from
their greatnefs and difficulty I have not
been able to attain them, who have done
nothing elfe thro my whole life; how far
do you imagine, you muft be from it, who
never thought of them before; and even
now, when you are entering upon them,
have no apprehenfion, what, and how great
they are* [1]*?* This is an effectual way of
defeating an adverfary, when the objection is well founded, and clearly anfwered.
But I fhall have occafion to confider this
matter more largely hereafter, under the
figure *Prolepfis,* to which it properly relates.

As to the order and difpofition of the
arguments, proper to be ufed in confutation :

[1] *In Caecil.
c.* 12.

tion: whether to follow the adverfe party, or alter his method, and range them in a different manner, as likewife whether to attack the weakeft, or ftrongeft arguments firft; thefe things muft be left to the difcretion of the fpeaker.

LEC-

LECTURE XVIII.

Of the Conclusion.

*I*N *speaking*, fais Cicero, *nature itself pre-scribes this method, to say something before we come to our subject, then to propose the subject, after that to support it by our own arguments, and refute those brought against it, and so to conclude* [1]. And in this order I proposed to treat of the several parts, which conftitute a complete and regular difcourfe; and have accordingly gone thro each of them, except the laft, namely, the *Conclufion*, which at prefent remains to be confidered. Now as the defign of the *Introduction* is to prepare the hearers for a favorable regard and attention, to what the fpeaker propofes to fay; fo in the *Conclufion* his view is to prevail with them, to fall in with what he has faid. And agreably to the methods proper for this purpofe, rhetoricians make the *Conclufion* of a difcourfe to confift of two parts: *Recapitulation*, and *an addrefs to the Paffions*.

RECAPITULATION is a fummary account of what the fpeaker has before offered in maintenance of his fubject; and

[1] *De orat. Lib.* ii. *c.* 76.

is

is defigned both to refrefh the memory of
the hearers, and to bring the principal arguments together into a narrow compafs,
that they may appear in a ftronger light.
Now there are feveral things neceffary to
a good repetition.

AND firft, it muft be fhort and concife,
fince it is defigned to refrefh the memory,
and not to burden it. For this end therefore the cheif things only are to be touched
upon; thofe on which the caufe principally depends, and which the orator is
moft defirous fhould be regarded by his
hearers. Now thefe are the general heads
of the difcourfe, with the main arguments
brought to fupport them. But either to
infift particularly upon every minute circumftance, or to inlarge upon thofe heads,
which may be thought proper to mention,
carries in it not fo much the appearance
of a repetition, as of a new difcourfe.

AGAIN, it is convenient in a repetition
to recite things in the fame order, in which
they were at firft laid down. By this
means the hearers will be enabled much
better to keep pace with the fpeaker, as
he goes along; and if they happen to have
forgot any thing, they will the more readily recall it. And befides, this method

appears

LECT.
XVIII.

appears moſt ſimple and open, when the ſpeaker reviews what he has ſaid in the ſame manner it was before delivered, and ſets it in the cleareſt light, for others to judge of it. And hence he ſometimes uſes ſuch expreſſions as theſe: *This I have ſhewn:* and, *This I hope, has been made very evident* [1]. And, at other times, as it were appealing to his hearers, he inquires: *Whether any thing has been omitted:* or, *If he has not fully made out his point.* But tho a repetition contains only the ſame things, which had been more largely treated of before; yet it is not neceſſary they ſhould be expreſſed in the ſame words. Nay this would many times be tireſome, and unpleaſant to the hearers; whereas a variety of expreſſion is grateful, provided the ſenſe be the ſame. Beſides every thing ought now to be repreſented in the ſtrongeſt terms, and in ſo lively a manner, as may at the ſame time both entertain the audience, and make the deepeſt impreſſion upon their minds. We have a very exact and accurate example of repetition in Cicero's oration for Quintius. Cicero was then a young man, and ſeems to have kept more cloſely to the rules of art, than afterwards, when by uſe and practice he had gained

[1] Cic.
De Invent.
Lib. i.
c. 52.

gained a greater freedom of speaking. I
formerly cited the partition of this speech
upon another occasion [1], which runs thus : 1 See
Lect.XIV.
p. 213.
*We deny, Sextus Nevius, that you was put
into the possession of the estate of P.
Quintius, by the pretor's edict. This is the
dispute between us. I will therefore show
first, that you had no just cause to apply to
the pretor for possession of the estate of P.
Quintius : Then, that you could not possess it by the edict : And lastly, that you did
not possess it. When I have proved these
three things I will conclude.* Now Cicero
begins his conclusion with a repetition of
those three heads, and a summary account
of the several arguments he made use of
under each of them [2]. But I am obliged 2 Cap. 28.
here to refer to the original, and must forbear to give a translation of it, by reason
of its length. In his *oration for the Manilian law*, his repetition is very short. He
proposed in the partition to speak to three
things : *The nature of the war against king
Mithridates, the greatness of it, and what
sort of general was proper to be intrusted
with it* [3]. And when he has gone thro 3 See
Lect.XIV.
each of these heads, and treated upon
them very largely, he reduces the substance
of what he had said to this general and
short

LECT. XVIII. fhort account: *Since therefore the war is fo neceffary, that it cannot be neglected; and fo great, that it requires a very careful management; and you can intruft it with a general of admirable fkill in military affairs, of fingular courage, the greateft authority, and eminent fuccefs: do you doubt to make ufe of this fo great bleffing, confered and beftowed upon you by heaven, for the prefer-*

[1] *Cap.* 16. *vation and inlargement of the Roman ftate* [1]?

Indeed this repetition is made by Cicero, before he procedes to the confutation, and not at the end of his difcourfe, where it is ufually longer, and more particular; however this may ferve to fhew the nature of fuch a recital.

But fometimes a repetition is made, by runing a comparifon between the fpeaker's own arguments, and thofe of the adverfe party; and placing them in oppofition to each other. And this method Cicero takes in the conclufion of his *third*

[2] *Cap.* 4. *oration upon the Agrarian law* [2]. And here fometimes the orator takes occafion to find fault with his adverfary's management, in thefe and fuch like expreffions: *This part he has entirely dropt. To that he has given an invidious turn, or a falfe coloring. He leaves arguments, and flies to intreaties; and*

not

not without good reason, if we consider the weakness of his cause [1].

BUT when the difcourfe is very long, and the arguments infifted on have been many, to prevent the hearers growing out of patience by a more particular recital, the orator fometimes only juft mentions fuch things, which he thinks of leaft confequence, by faying that, he *omits* or *paffes over them,* till he comes to what is of greater moment, which he reprefents more fully. This method Cicero has taken in his *defence of* Cluentius; where, having run over feveral leffer heads in the manner now defcribed, he then alters his expreffion, and introduces what was of more importance, by faying: *What I firft complain of, is that wickednefs, which is now difcovered.* And fo he procedes more particularly to recite thofe things, which immediately related to Cluentius [2]. And this is what the writers upon this art call *Preterition.* But thus much may ferve for repetition or *Recapitulation.*

I NOW procede to the other part of the conclufion, which confifts in *an addrefs to the Paffions.* Indeed the orator fometimes endeavours occafionally to work upon the paffions of his hearers in other parts of

[1] Quint. *Inft. orat.* *Lib.* vi. *c.* 1.

[2] *Cap.* 65.

T　his

LECT.
XVIII.

his difcourfe, but more efpecially in the conclufion, where he is warmeft himfelf, and labours to make them fo. For the main defign of the *Introduction* is to conciliate the hearers, and gain their attention; of the *Narration*, *Propofition*, and *Confirmation* to inform them; and of the *Conclufion* to move them. And therefore, to ufe Quintilian's words: *Here all the fprings of eloquence are to be opened. It is here we fecure the minds of the hearers, if what went before was well managed. Now we are paft the rocks and fhallows, all the fails may be hoifted. And as the greateft part of the conclufion confifts in illuftration, the moft pompous language, and ftrongeft figures have place here* [1]. Now the paffions,

[1] *Inft. orat. Lib. vi. c. 1.*

to which the orator more particularly addreffes, differ according to the nature of the difcourfe. In *demonftrative* orations, when laudatory, love, admiration, and emulation are ufually excited; but in invectives hatred, envy, and contempt. In *deliberative* fubjects, either the hope of gratifying fome defire is fet in view; or the fear of fome impending evil. And in *judicial* difcourfes, almoft all the paffions have place, but more efpecially refentment and pity; infomuch that moft of the antient

rhe-

rhetoricians mention only thefe two. But
I have treated upon the nature of the paffions, and the methods fuited both to excite and allay them, in a former difcourfe [1];
and therefore at prefent I fhall only add
a few general obfervations, which may not
be improper in this place, where the fkill
of the orator in addreffing to them is more
efpecially required.

Now the objects of the *Paffions* are either *Things* or *Perfons*, and orators make
ufe of both, for puting in motion thefe
fprings of the human mind. With regard to *Things*, the nature and circumftances of them are to be confidered; and
different paffions applied to, in order to
induce people either to purfue or avoid
them. *Perfons* may be confidered either
as agents or patients. In the former fenfe,
different regards are due to them, according to the different qualities, with which
they are poffeffed, and a fuitable courfe of
actions. So becaufe virtue excites efteem,
and vice hatred; anfwerable regards are
paid to virtuous, or vicious men. But in
confidering them as patients, whatever be-
fals them according to their demerits, be
the thing good or ill, others are generally
pleafed; and if the contrary happens, it

gives

LECT.
XVIII.
gives them an uneafinefs. So that if fome
good thing accrues to one, who does not
deferve it, it caufes indignation ; and where
a misfortune happens to a good man, it
occafions pity. And thus perfons are apt
to be affected with refpect to the circumftances of others. But every one is naturally inclined to think well of himfelf, that
every profperous occurrence is but anfwerable to his merit, and that every misfortune comes undefervedly. And fometimes
there is joined with the occurrence the confideration of the agent, or perfon, who occafioned it ; and the defign in doing it is
often more regarded, than the thing itfelf.
The orator therefore will obferve what circumftances either of things, or perfons, or
both, will furnifh him with motives, proper
to apply to thofe paffions, he defires to excite in the minds of his hearers. Thus
Cicero in his *orations for* Plancus and Sylla,
moves his hearers from the circumftances
of the men ; but in his *accufation of* Verres
very frequently from the barbarity and
horrid nature of his crimes ; and from both
in his *defence of* Quintius.

But the fame paffion may be excited
by very different methods. This is plain
from the writings of thofe Roman fatyrifts,

which

which are yet extant; for they have all the same design, and that is to ingage men to a love of virtue, and hatred of vice; but their manner is very different, suited to the genius of each writer. Horace endeavours to recommend virtue, by laughing vice out of countenance. Persius moves us to an abhorrence and detestation of vice, with the gravity and severity of a philosopher. And Juvenal by open and vehement invectives. So orators make use of all these methods in exciting the passions, as may be seen by their discourses, and particularly those of Cicero. But it is not convenient to dwell long upon the same passion. For the image thus wrought up in the minds of the hearers, does not last a great while, but they soon return to reflection. When the emotion therefore is once carried as high as it well can be, they should be left under its influence, and the speaker procede to some new matter, before it declines again [1]. Moreover, orators sometimes endeavour to raise contrary passions to each other, as they are concerned for opposite parties. So the accuser excites anger and resentment, but the defendant pity and compassion. At other times, one thinks it sufficient to allay and

[1] See Quint. *Inst. orat.* *Lib.* vi. *c.* 1.

T 3   take

take off that paſſion, which the other has raiſed, and bring the hearers to a calm and ſedate conſideration of the matter before them.

But this eſpecially is to be regarded, that the orator expreſs the ſame paſſion himſelf, with which he endeavours to affect others, and that not only in his action, and voice, but likewiſe in his language; and therefore his words, and manner of expreſſion, ſhould be ſuited to that perturbation and diſorder of mind, which he deſigns to repreſent. However a decency and propriety of character is always carefully to be obſerved. For as Cicero very well remarks: *A neglect of this is not only very culpable in life, but likewiſe in diſcourſe. Nor do the ſame things equally become every ſpeaker, or every audience; nor every time, and every place* [1]. And therefore he greatly commends that painter, who deſigning to repreſent in a picture the ſacrifice of Iphigenia, Agamemnon's daughter, drew Calchas the preiſt with a ſad countenance; Ulyſſes, her father's great freind, more dejected; and her uncle Menelaus, moſt diſconſolate; but threw a veil over the face of Agamemnon himſelf, as being unable to expreſs that exceſs of ſorrow, which he thought

[1] *Orat. Cap.* 21.

thought was proper to appear in his countenance [1]. And this juftnefs of character
is admirably well obferved by Cicero himfelf, in his *defence of* Milo. For as Milo
was always known to be a man of the
greateft refolution, and moft undaunted
courage, it was very improper to introduce
him, as the ufual method then was in capital cafes, moving pity, and beging for
mercy. Cicero therefore takes this part
upon himfelf, and what he could not do
with any propriety in the perfon of Milo,
he performs in his own, and thus addreffes
the judges: *What remains, but that I intreat and befeech you, that you would fhew
that compaffion to this brave man, for which
he himfelf does not folicit, but I, againft his
inclination, earneftly implore and requeft. Do
not be lefs inclined to acquit him, if in this
our common forrow, you fee no tear fall from
Milo's eyes; but perceive in him the fame
countenance, voice, and language, as at other
times, fteady and unmoved. Nay I know not
whether for this reafon you ought not much
fooner to favour him. For if in the contefts
of gladiators, perfons of the loweft condition
and fortune in life, we are wont to be difpleafed with the timorous, and fuppliant, and
thofe who beg for their life; but interpofe*

in

[1] *Ibid.*
c. 22.

in favor of the brave, and courageous, and such who expose themselves to death ; and we shew more compassion to those, who do not sue for it, than to such who do : with how much greater reason ought we to act in the same manner towards the bravest of our fellow citizens? And as these words were agreable to his own character, while soliciting in behalf of another; so immediately after he introduces Milo speaking like himself, with a generous and undaunted air : *These words of Milo,* fais he, *quite sink and dispirit me, which I daily hear from him. Farewell, farewell, my fellow citizens farewell; may you be happy, flourish, and prosper; may this renowned city be preserved, my most dear country, however it has treated me ; may it continue in peace, tho I cannot continue in it, to whom it ows its peace. I will retire, I will be gone* [1].

¹ Cap. 34.

B U T as persons are commonly more affected with what they see, than what they hear, orators sometimes call in the assistance of that sense in moving the passions. For this reason it was usual among the Romans in *judicial* cases, for accused persons to appear with a dejected air, and a sordid garb, attended by their parents, children, or other relations and freinds, with the like dress and

and afpect; as likewife to fhew their fcars, wounds, bloody garments, and other things of the like nature, in open court. So when upon the death of Caefar Mark Antony harangued the populace, he at the fame time expofed to their view the garment, in which he was ftabed, fixed upon a pole; at which fight they were fo inraged, that immediately they ran with lighted torches to fet fire to the houfes of the confpirators [1]. But this cuftom at laft became fo common, and was fometimes fo ill conducted, that the force of it was greatly abated, as we learn from Quintilian [2]. However, if the Romans proceded to an excefs on the one hand; the ftrictnefs of the Areopagites at Athens may perhaps be thought too rigid on the other. For in that court, if the orator began to fay any thing, which was moving, an officer immediately ftood up, and bad him be filent [3]. There is certainly a medium between thefe two extremes, which is fometimes not only ufeful, but even neceffary. For, as Quintilian very juftly fays: *It it neceffary to apply to the paffions, when thofe things which are true, juft, and of common benefit, cannot be come at any other way* [4].

[1] Suet. *in Vit. c.* 84.

[2] *Inft. orat. Lib.* vi. *c.* 1.

[3] *Ibid.*

[4] *Ibid.*

To

To conclude in an handſom and decent manner, is doubtleſs of great conſequence to an orator; ſince, as we ſay: *It is the end, which crowns the work.* And it can neither be for the advantage of his cauſe, nor his own character, to be cold and life-leſs, where the greateſt warmth and ſpirit is neceſſary. But a ſet and diſtinct concluſion is not always requiſite. For to what end ſhould he make a recital, where his diſcourſe is but ſhort, or conſiſts but of a few particulars? Nor is it at all proper to inflame the paſſions on light ſubjects, or where the hearers are already ingaged in his favor. And beſides to overact a thing is often of ill conſequence, and apt to raiſe a jealouſy of ſome wrong deſign. Wherefore in this, and all other caſes, the rules of art muſt ſubmit to the conduct of reaſon and prudence; leſt by being miſapplied, they both fail in their intention, and loſe their eſteem.

LECTURE XIX.

Of Digreſſion, Tranſition, and Amplification.

THE number, order, and nature of the parts, which conſtitute a complete and regular oration, I have endeavoured to explain in ſeveral preceding lectures. But there are two or three things yet remaining, very neceſſary to be known by an orator, which ſeem moſt properly to come under the ſecond branch of his art. And theſe are *Digreſſion, Tranſition,* and *Amplification,* upon each of which I ſhall now treat; not that they are connected with each other, but becauſe I think all, that is requiſite to be ſaid concerning them, may be compriſed in one diſcourſe.

DIGRESSION then, as defined by Quintilian, is, *A going off from the ſubject we are upon to ſome different thing, which may however be of ſervice to it* [1]. We have a very beautiful inſtance of this in Cicero's *defence of* Coelius, who was accuſed of having firſt borrowed money of Clodia, and then ingaging her ſervants to poiſon her. Now as the proof of the fact depended upon ſeveral circumſtances, the orator examines

[1] *Inſt. orat. Lib.* iv. *c.* 3.

amines them feparately; and fhews them
to be all highly improbable. *How, fais
he, was the defign of this poifon laid? Whence
came it? how did they get it? by whofe affiftance, to whom, or where was it delivered?*
Now to the firft of thefe queries he makes
the accufer give this anfwer : *They fay
Coelius had it at home, and tried the force
of it upon a flave provided on purpofe, whofe
fudden death proved the ftrength of the poifon.*
Now, as Cicero reprefents the whole charge
againft Coelius as a fiction of Clodia, invented out of revenge for fome flights he
had put upon her; to make this the more
probable he infinuates, that fhe had poi-
foned her hufband, and takes this opportunity to hint it, that he might fhew how
eafy it was for her to charge another with
poifoning a fervant, who had done the
fame to her own hufband. But not con-
tented with this, he fteps out of his way,
and introduces fome of the laft words of
her hufband Metellus, to render the fact
more barbarous and fhocking, from the
admirable character of the man. This digreffion is brought in immediately upon
the words I laft read from Cicero, in the
following manner: *O immortal gods, why
do you fometimes wink at the greateft crimes*

of

*of mankind, or delay the punishment of them
to futurity! For I saw, I myself saw (and
it was the dolefulest scene of my whole life)
when Q. Metellus was taken from the bosom
of his country ; and when he, who thought
himself born to be serviceable to this state,
within three days after he had appeared with
such advantage in the senate, in the forum,
and every where in public, was snatched from
us in the flower of his age, and prime of his
strength and vigor. At which time, when
he was about to expire, and his mind had
lost the sense of other things, still retaining
a concern for the public, he looked upon me,
as I was all in tears, and intimated in broken
and dying words, how great a storm hung
over the city, and threatened the whole state,
often striking the wall, which separated his
house from that of Quintus Catulus, and
frequently calling both upon him and me, and
seeming to greive not so much at the approach of his own death, as that both his
country and I should be deprived of his assistance. Had he not been wickedly taken off
on a sudden, how would he after his consulship have withstood the fury of his kinsman,
Publius Clodius, who, while in that office,
threatened, in the hearing of the senate, to
kill him with his own hand, when he first*
began

*began to break out.   And will this woman
dare to come out of those doors, and talk of
the force of poison? will not she fear, left the
house itself should speak the villainy? will
not she dread the conscious walls, nor that
sad and mournful night? But I return to*
[1] *Cap.* 24. *the accusation* [1].   And then he procedes to
confider, and refute the feveral circum-
ftances of the accufation.   What I have
therefore cited here, was no part of his argument; but having mentioned the charge
of poifon, he immediately takes occafion
to introduce it, in order to excite the indignation of the hearers againft Clodia,
and invalidate the profecution, as coming
from a perfon of her character.   *Digreffion*
cannot properly be faid to be a neceffary
part of a difcourfe, but it may fometimes
be very convenient, and that upon feveral
accounts.

As firft, where a fubject is of itfelf flat
and dry, or requires clofe attention, it is of
ufe to releive and unbend the mind by
fomething agreable and entertaining.   For
which reafon Quintilian obferves, that the
orators of his time generally made an ex-
curfion in their harangues upon fome pleafing topic, between the narration and the
proof.   But he condemns the practice, as
too

too general; for while they seemed to
think it neceſſary, it obliged them ſometimes to bring in things trifling and fo-
reign to the purpoſe [1].   Beſides, a *Digreſ-* [1] *Inſt. orat.*
ſion is confined to no one part of a diſ- *Lib.* iv.
courſe, but may come in any where, as *c.* 3.
occaſion offers; provided it fall in naturally with the ſubject, and be made ſome
way ſubſervient to it.   We never meet
with it in Cicero, without ſome evident
and good reaſon.   I have already ſhewn
the uſe he makes of it, in the example
above mentioned.   So in his *proſecution of*
Verres, for his barbarous and inhuman
outrages againſt the Sicilians, he takes an
occaſion to launch out into a beautiful de-
ſcription of the iſland, and to recount the
advantages, which accrued from it to the
Romans.   His ſubject did not neceſſarily
lead him to this, but his view in it was
to highten and aggravate the charge againſt
Verres [2].   [2] *Lib.* ii.
                                           init.
AGAIN, as a *Digreſſion* ought not to be
made without ſufficient reaſon, ſo neither
ſhould it be too frequent.   And he who
never does it, but where it is proper and
uſeful, will not often ſee occaſion for it.
Frequently to leave the ſubject, and go off
to other things, breaks the thread of the
                                        diſ-

difcourfe, and is apt to introduce confufion. Indeed fome kinds of writing admit
of a more frequent ufe of digreffions than
others. In hiftory they are often very ferviceable. For as that confifts of a feries
of facts, and a long continued narrative
without variety is apt to grow dull and
tedious; it is neceffary at proper diftances
to throw in fomething entertaining, in order to inliven it, and keep up the attention. And accordingly we find the beft
hiftorians often imbellifh their writings
with defcriptions of cities, rivers, and countries, as likewife with the fpeeches of eminent perfons upon important occafions, and
other ornaments, to render them the more
pleafing and delightful. Poets ftill take a
greater liberty in this refpect; for as their
principal view is moft commonly to pleafe,
they do not attend fo clofely to connection;
but as an image offers itfelf, which may
be agreably wrought up, they bring it in,
and go off more frequently to different
things, than other writers.

ANOTHER property of a *Digreffion* is,
that it ought not to be too long, left the
hearers forget what preceded, before the
fpeaker returns again to his fubject. For
a digreffion being no principal part of a
dif-

difcourfe, nor of any further ufe, than as
it ferves fome way or other to inforce, or
illuftrate the main fubject; it cannot anfwer this end, if it be carried to fuch a
length, as to caufe that either to be forgot, or neglected. And every one's memory will not ferve him to connect together two parts of a difcourfe, which lie at
a wide diftance from each other. The
better therefore to guard againft this, it is
not unufual with orators, before they enter
upon a digreffion of any confiderable length,
to prepare their hearers, by giving them
notice of it, and fometimes defiring leave
to divert a little from the fubject. And
fo likewife at the conclufion they introduce the fubject again by a fhort tranfition. Thus Cicero in the example cited
above, when he has finifhed his digreffion
concerning the death of Metellus, procedes to his fubject again with thefe words:
But I return to the accufation.

INDEED we find orators fometimes, when
fore preffed, and the caufe will not bear a
clofe fcrutiny, artfully run into digreffions
with a defign to divert the attention of the
hearers from the fubject, and turn them
to a different view. And in fuch cafes,
as they endeavour to be unobferved, fo

VOL. I.   U   they

they do it tacitly without any tranſition, or intimation of their deſign ; their buſineſs being only to get clear of a difficulty, till they have an opportunity of entering upon ſome freſh topic. I do not mention this as a conduct proper for imitation, tho it is fit to be remarked, in order to guard againſt it.

But as *Tranſitions* are often uſed not only after a *Digreſſion,* but likewiſe upon other occaſions, I ſhall explain the nature of them a little more particularly. A *Tranſition* therefore is, *A form of ſpeech, by which the ſpeaker in a few words tells his hearers both what he has ſaid already, and what he next deſigns to ſay* [1]. Where a diſcourſe conſiſts of ſeveral parts, this is often very proper in paſſing from one to another, eſpecially when the parts are of a conſiderable length; for it aſſiſts the hearers to carry on the ſeries of the diſcourſe in their mind, which is a great advantage to the memory. It is likewiſe a great releif to the attention, to be told when an argument is finiſhed, and what is to be expected next. And therefore we meet with it very frequently in hiſtory. But I conſider it at preſent only as made uſe of by orators. Cicero, as I have had occaſion

[1] Voſſ.
Inſt. orat.
Lib. v.
c. 6. §. 3.

to

to obferve formerly, divides his *oration for* LECT.
the Manilian law into three parts, and pro- XIX.
pofes to fpeak, *firft of the nature of the*
war againft king Mithridates, then of its
greatnefs, and laftly of the choice of a ge-
neral [1]. And when he has gone thro the ¹ *Cap.* 2.
firft head, which is pretty long, he connects it with the fecond, by this fhort
tranfition : *Having fhewn the nature of the*
war, I fhall now fpeak a few things of its
greatnefs [2]. And again, at the conclufion ² *Cap.* 8.
of his fecond head, he reminds his hearers
of his method in the following manner : *I*
think I have fufficiently fhewn the neceffity
of this war from the nature of it, and the
danger of it from its greatnefs. What re-
mains is to fpeak concerning the choice of a
general, proper to be intrufted with it [3]. ³ *Cap.* 10.
And in his *fecond oration againft* Catiline,
who had then left Rome, having at large
defcribed his conduct and defigns, he adds :
But why do I talk fo long concerning one
enemy, and fuch an one ; who owns himfelf
an enemy, and whom I do not fear, fince,
what I always defired, there is now a wall
between us ; and fay nothing of thofe, who
conceal themfelves, who remain at Rome, and
are among us [4]. And then he procedes to ⁴ *Cap.* 8.
give an account of the other confpirators.

LECT.
XIX.

BUT fometimes in paffing from one thing to another, a general hint of it is thought fufficient to prepare the hearers, without particularly fpecifying what has been faid, or is next to follow. Thus Cicero in his *fecond Philippic* fais : *But thofe things are old, this is yet frefh* [1]. And again : *But I have infifted too long upon trifles, let us come to things of greater moment* [2]. And at other times, for greater brevity, the tranfition is imperfect, and mention made only of the following head, without any intimation of what has been faid already. As in Cicero's *defence of* Muraena, where he fais : *I muft now procede to the third part of my oration concerning the charge of bribery* [3]. And foon after : *I come now to Cato, who is the fupport and ftrength of this charge* [4].

[1] *Cap.* 11.
[2] *Cap.* 32.
[3] *Cap.* 26.
[4] *Cap.* 28.

THE third and laft head, to which I propofed to fpeak, is *Amplification*. Now by *Amplification* is meant not barely a method of inlarging upon a thing ; but fo to reprefent it in the fulleft and moft comprehenfive view, as that it may in the livelieft manner ftrike the mind, and influence the paffions. Cicero fpeaking of this, calls it, *The greateft commendation of eloquence* ; and obferves, *that it confifts not only in magnifying*

fying and hightening a thing, but likewise
in extenuating and leſſening it [1].   But tho

it conſiſts of theſe two parts, and may be
applied either way, yet to amplify is not
to ſet things in a falſe light; but to paint
them in their juſt proportion and proper
colors, ſuitable to their nature, and qualities.   Rhetoricians have obſerved ſeveral
ways of doing this, the cheif of which I
ſhall here mention.

ONE is to aſcend from a particular thing
to a general.   Thus Cicero in his *defence
of* Archias, having commended him as an
excellent poet, and likewiſe obſerved, that
all the liberal arts have a connection with
each other, and a mutual relation between
them, in order to raiſe a juſt eſteem of
him in the minds of his hearers, takes occaſion to ſay many things in praiſe of polite literature in general, and the great
advantages, that may be received from it.
You will aſk me, ſais he, *why we are ſo de-
lighted with this man? Becauſe he ſupplies
us with thoſe things, which both refreſh our
minds after the noiſe of the forum, and delight our ears, when wearied with contention.
Do you think we could either be furniſhed
with matter for ſuch a variety of ſubjects,
if we did not cultivate our minds with lear-*

U 3   *ning;*

LECT.
XIX.

ning; or bear such a constant fatigue, without affording them that refreshment. I own I have always pursued these studies; let those be ashamed, who have so given up themselves to learning, as neither to be able to convert it to any common benefit, nor discover it in public. But why should it shame me, who have so lived for many years, that no advantage or ease has ever diverted me, no pleasure allured me, nor sleep retarded me from this pursuit. Who then can blame me, or who can justly be displeased with me, if I have imployed that time in reviewing these studies, which has been spent by others in managing their affairs, in the celebration of festivals, or other diversions, in refreshments of mind and body, in unseasonable banquets, in dice, or tennis? And this ought the rather to be allowed me, because my ability as an orator has been improved by these pursuits, which, such as it is, was never wanting to assist my freinds. And if it be esteemed but small, yet I am sensible from what spring I must draw those things, which are of the

[1] Cap. 6.   *greatest importance* [1]. With more to the same purpose, from which he draws this inference: *shall I not therefore love this man? shall I not admire him? shall I not by all*

[2] Cap. 8.   *means defend him* [2]?

A

A CONTRARY method to the former is
to defcend from a general to a particular.
As if any one, while fpeaking in commendation of eloquence, fhould illuftrate
what he fais from the example of Cicero,
and fhew the great fervices he did his
country, and the honors he gained to himfelf by his admirable fkill in oratory. Our
common way of judging of the nature and
importance of things is from what we
obferve in particular inftances, by which
we form general notions concerning them.
When therefore we confider the character
of Cicero, and the figure he made in the
world, it leads us to conclude, there muft
be fomething very admirable in that art,
by which he became fo celebrated. And
this method he has taken himfelf in his
oration for the Manilian law, where having
firft intimated the fcarcity of good generals
at that time among the Romans, he then
defcribes the virtues of a complete commander as a proof of it, and fhews how
many and great qualifications are neceffary
to form fuch a character, as courage, prudence, experience, and fuccefs ; all which
he afterwards applies to Pompey [1].   [1] *Cap.* 10.

A THIRD method is by an enumeration
of parts. So when Cicero upon the defeat

U 4   of

of Mark Antony before Mutina, propofed
that a funeral monument fhould be erected
in honor of the foldiers, who were killed
in that battle, as a comfort to their fur-
viving relations, he does it in this way, to
give it the greater weight. *Since, fais he,
the tribute of glory is paid to the beft and
moft valiant citizens by the honor of a monument, let us thus comfort their relations,
who will receive the greateft confolation in
this manner ; their parents, who produced
fuch brave defenders of the ftate ; their children, who will enjoy thefe domeftic examples
of fortitude; their wives, for the lofs of fuch
hufbands, whom it will be more fiting to extol
than lament ; their brethren, who will hope
to refemble them no lefs in their virtues, than
their afpect. And I wifh we may be able to
remove the greif of all thefe by our refolu-
tions* [1]. Such reprefentations greatly inlarge the image of a thing, and afford the
mind a much clearer view of it, than
if it were contracted into one fingle propofition.

[1] *Philipp.
xiv. c.* 13

AGAIN, another method not much unlike the former is, when any thing is illuftrated from a variety of caufes. Thus
Cicero juftifies his behaviour in retiring,
and not oppofing his enemies, when they
fpirited

spirited up the mob in order to banish
him, from the following reasons, which
at that time determined him to such a
conduct. *When, sais he, unless I was given
up, so many armed fleets seemed ready to
attack this single ship of the state, tossed with
the tempests of seditions and discords, and the
senate was now removed from the helm ;
when banishment, murder, and outrage were
threatened ; when some from an apprehension
of their own danger would not defend me,
others were incited by an inveterate hatred
to all good men, others thought I stood in
their way, others took this opportunity to
express their resentment, others envied the
peace and tranquillity of the state, and upon
all these accounts I was particularly struck
at : should I have chosen rather to oppose
them (I will not say to my own certain destruction, but to the greatest danger both of
you and your children) than alone to submit
to, and undergo what threatened us all in
common* [1]?* Such a number of reasons brought [1] *Pro Sext.*
together must set a thing in a very strong *c. 20.*
and clear light.

THE like may be said of a number and
variety of effects. Thus Cicero describes
the force and excellence of oratory from
its great and surprizing effects, when he sais:

Nothing

*Nothing seems to me more excellent than by
discourse to draw the attention of an whole
assembly, delight them, and sway their inclinations different ways at pleasure. This in
every free state, and especially in times of peace,
and tranquillity, has been always in the highest
esteem and reputation. For what is either so
admirable, as for one only, or a very few, out
of a vast multitude to be able to do that,
which all have a natural power of doing?
or so delightful to hear, as a judicious and
solid discourse in florid and polite language?
or so powerful and grand, as to influence the
populace, the judges, the senate, by the charms
of eloquence? Nay, what is so noble, so generous, so munificent, as to afford aid to suppli-
cants, to support the afflicted, give safety, deliver from dangers, and preserve from exile?
Or what is so necessary, as to be always furnished with arms to guard yourself, assert your
right, or repel injuries? and not to confine
our thoughts wholly to the courts of justice,
or the senate; what is there in the arts of
peace more agreable and entertaining, than
good language, and a fine way of speaking?
For it is this especially, wherein we excel other
animals, that we can discourse together, and
convey our thoughts to each other by words.
Who therefore would not esteem, and in a particular*

*ticular manner endeavour to surpass others
in that, wherein mankind principally excels
brute beasts? But to procede to its cheif advantages: what else would have drawn men
into societies; or taken them off from a wild
and savage life, and softened them into a polite and civilized behaviour; or when settled
in communities have restrained them by laws* [1]? ¹ *De Orat.*
Who but after such a description must con- *Lib.* i.
ceive the strongest passion for an art, at- *c.* 8.
tended with so many great and good effects?

A THING may likewise be illustrated by
its opposite. So the blessings and advantages of peace may be recommended from
the miseries and calamities of war. And
thus Cicero endeavours to throw contempt
upon Catiline and his party, by comparing
them with the contrary side: *But if omitting all these things, with which we abound,
and they want, the senate, the knights, the
populace, the city, treasury, revenues, all
Italy, the provinces, and foreign nations, if,
I say, omitting these things, we compare the
causes themselves, in which each side is ingaged, we may learn from thence how de-
spicable they are. For on this side modesty
is ingaged, on that impudence; on this chastity, on that lewdness; on this integrity, on
that fraud; on this piety, on that profaneness;*

ness; on this constancy, on that fury; on this honor, on that baseness; on this moderation, on that unbridled passion; in a word equity, temperance, fortitude, prudence, and all virtues contend with injustice, luxury, cowardise, rashness, and all vices; plenty with want, reason with folly, sobriety with madness, and lastly good hope with despair. In such a contest did men desert us, would not heaven ordain, that so many, and so great vices should be defeated by these most excellent virtues [1].*

[1] *In Catil.*
ii. *c.* 11.

GRADATION is another beautiful way of doing this. So when Cicero would aggravate the cruelty and barbarity of Verres, for crucifying a Roman citizen; which was a sort of punishment only inflicted upon slaves; he chooses this way of doing it. *It is a crime,* sais he, *to bind a Roman citizen, wickedness to whip him, and a sort of parricide to kill him; what then must I call it to crucify him? No name can sufficiently express such a villany* [2]. And the images of things may thus be hightened, either by ascending, as in this instance, or descending, as in that which follows, relating to the same action of Verres: *Was I not to complain of, or bewail these things to Roman citizens, nor the freinds of our state,*

[2] *Lib.* v.
c. 66.

nor

nor thofe who had heard of the Roman name,
nay if not to men but beafts; or to go yet
further, if in the moft defert wilderneſs to
ſtones and rocks; even all mute and inani-
mate creatures would be moved by ſo great
and heinous cruelty [1].

[1] *Cap.* 67.

AND to name no more, facts may be
amplified from their circumſtances, as time,
place, manner, event, and the like. But
inſtances of this would carry me too far,
and therefore I ſhall only add, that as the
defign of *amplification* is not barely to prove
or evince the truth of things, but alſo to
adorn and illuſtrate them, it requires a
florid and beautiful ſtile, confiſting of ſtrong
and emphatical words, flowing periods,
harmonious numbers, lively tropes, and
bright figures. But the confideration of
theſe things will come under the third part
of oratory, namely *Elocution,* upon which
I ſhall enter in my next difcourfe.

L E C-

LECTURE XX.

Of Elocution in general, and particularly of Elegance, and Purity.

CICERO tells us, *An orator ought to confider three things, what to fpeak, in what order, and in what manner* ¹. As it is therefore the defign of the art of rhetoric to prepare and form the orator, it ought to treat of each of thefe. On which account I have formerly had occafion more than once to obferve its fimilitude with the art of building; in which the workman firft collects his materials, then puts them together in their proper order, and laftly gives them fuch ornaments, as are fuited to the nature of the ftructure. But fince the manner of fpeaking refpects both the *Language* and *Pronunciation,* this art is ufually divided into four parts : *Invention,* which teaches what to fpeak; *Difpofition,* which refpects the order; *Elocution,* which regards the propriety and ornaments of language ; and *Pronunciation,* which gives rules for a graceful delivery. I have hitherto, in the courfe of thefe lectures, treated upon the two firft of thefe, and

fhall

fhall now procede to the third, which is
Elocution.

Now *Elocution* directs us to fuit both
the words and expreffions of a difcourfe
to the nature of the fubject, or to fpeak
with propriety and decency. This faculty
is in one word called *Eloquence*, and thofe
perfons, who are poffeffed of it, are therefore ftiled *eloquent*. This has always been
efteemed fo neceffary and effential to an
orator, that fome have placed the whole
art of oratory only in *Elocution*. That it
is the moft difficult part is very certain,
and fo peculiar to it, that the rules for it
are given no where elfe; but it is evident
from what I have formerly faid both upon
Invention and *Difpofition*, that this art contains many other things, befides what particularly relates to *Elocution*. And therefore when Cicero, in his *Book of a perfect
orator*, tells us, that *to invent what things
are proper to fay, and to difpofe them in a
juft order, are indeed great matters, and like
the foul in the body; but yet more proper
to prudence, than eloquence*; he immediately
adds: *But what caufe can be fupported
without prudence? Let the orator therefore,
who would excel, be acquainted with the
heads of invention* [1]. From whence it is
plain,

[1] *Cap.* 14.

plain, that Cicero did not think the whole
art of an orator to confift in *Eloquence* or
Elocution. But Quintilian has expreffed
himfelf more fully upon this head. I fhall
recite the paffage, by which you will perceive his judgement concerning it. *Without elocution,* fais he, *invention and difpofition are ufelefs, and like a fword in the fcab-
bard. This is therefore what is principally
taught; this no one can arrive at, but by
the help of art; this requires ftudy, practice,
and obfervation; this is the exercife of our
whole life; by this one orator excels another;
this gives one kind of eloquence the preference
to another; what is either commendable, or
culpable in oratory, is found here.* But he
adds: *However the whole care is not to be
employed about words. For I muft declare
againft thofe, who neglect all concern about
things, which are the nerves of a caufe; and
fpend their whole age in a vain attendance
to words. And this they do for the fake of
being exact, which in my opinion is very or-
namental in fpeaking; but when it appears*
Inft. orat. *natural, and without affectation* [1]. Thus
Lib. viii.
prooem. far Quintilian. It appears therefore from
the authority of thefe great mafters of oratory, that perfons may run into an extreme
either way. And a little obfervation will
con-

convince us, that thofe orators, who attend only to the matter of their difcourfe, and the truth of their reafoning, and neglect all beauty and decency of expreffion; tho they inform their hearers, yet it is in fuch a way, as neither to delight, nor move them. And accordingly, as what is faid gives them lefs entertainment, their attention muft neceffarily flag; by which means the main end defigned is in proportion fruftrated, which was *Perfuafion*. And we often find that a fpeech fet off with good language, and agreable turns of expreffion, tho perhaps but weak arguments, ingages the minds of the hearers, and is received with applaufe; while more juft and clofe reafoning, but expreffed in a coarfe and unpolite manner, is lefs attended to, and difregarded. For many perfons are of that make, that you muft pleafe their ears in order to imprefs their minds; and truth muft be fet off in a very agreable drefs, before it will be received by them. So that a due attention to words, and this part of oratory, feems neceffary for all thofe, who would render what they fay acceptable to others. But, on the other hand, to regard founds only, and the flowers of language; and to be more foli-

X   citous

citous about the turn of a period, than the sense of it; is a sign of a weak mind, and trifling genius. And besides, an anxious concern about words cools the imagination, and checks the mind in its pursuits of things; and by that means commonly produces either a stiffness, or levity of expression. A medium therefore in this case is undoubtedly the best. And what Quintilian advises here is worth remarking. *Be as careful, sais he, as you please about your language, only remember, that nothing is to be done merely for the sake of words; since words were first invented for the sake of things. And they seem to be most preferable, which best express our ideas, and most affect the minds of the hearers* [1]. This part of oratory was much more cultivated by the antients, than it has been of late ages; and by none more than Cicero, who is generally largest upon it in his treatises upon this art. And in all his writings he appears to have been very exact and careful of his language; but always shews an equal regard to good sense, and solid reasoning. And therefore he tells us, that, *wisdom is the foundation of eloquence* [2]. And in another place, that, *eloquence is nothing else, but copious and florid wisdom* [3]. And indeed
where

Ubi supra

[2] *Orat. c.* 21.
[3] *Orat. Partit. c.* 23.

where these two do not meet, the one wants a necessary ornament to recommend it; and the other is of little value with wise men, tho it has often a considerable influence in popular harangues. But where they are united, they make one of the highest accomplishments of human nature.

ELOCUTION is twofold, *general* and *particular*. The former treats of the several properties and ornaments of language in common; the latter considers them, as they are made use of to form different sorts of stile. I shall begin with general elocution, which rhetoricians make to consist of three parts: *Elegance, Composition,* and *Dignity*. *Elegance* respects the purity, and clearness of the language. *Composition* regards the turn and harmony of the periods. And *Dignity* explains the nature and various kinds of tropes and figures. A discourse, which has all these properties suitably adjusted, must, with respect to the language, be perfect in its kind, and delightful to the hearers.

ELEGANCE, which makes the first part of *Elocution*, consists, as we have seen, in two things; *Purity,* and *Perspicuity:* and both these, as well with respect to single

X 2

words,

LECT.
XXᛜ

words, as their conſtruction in ſentences.
Theſe properties in language give it the
name of *elegant*; for a like reaſon that we
call other things ſo, which are clean and
neat in their kind. But in the common
uſe of our tongue, we are apt to confound
elegance with eloquence, and ſay, *a diſcourſe is elegant*; when we mean by the
expreſſion, that it has all the properties of
fine language.

Now by *purity* (upon which I propoſe
to treat at preſent) we are to underſtand
the choice of ſuch words and phraſes, as
are ſuited and agreable to the uſe of the
language, in which we ſpeak. And ſo
grammarians reduce the faults, they op-
poſe to it, to two ſorts, which they call
barbariſm and *ſoleciſm*; the former of which
reſpects ſingle words, and the latter their
conſtruction. But I ſhall conſider them
jointly, and in a manner different from
grammarians. For with them all words
are eſteemed pure, which are once adopted
into a language, and authoriſed by uſe.
And as to phraſes, or forms of expreſſion,
they allow them all the ſame claim, which
are agreable to the analogy of the tongue.
But in oratory neither all words, nor all
expreſſions are ſo called, which occur in
any

any language; but fuch only, as come
recommended by the authority of thofe,
who fpeak or write with accuracy and po-
litenefs. Indeed it is a common faying,
*that we fhould think with the learned, and
fpeak with the vulgar.* But the meaning
of that expreffion is no more, than that
we fhould fpeak agreably to the common
ufage of the tongue, that every one may
underftand us; and not choofe fuch words
or expreffions, as are either difficult to be
underftood, or may carry in them an appearance of affectation and fingularity.
But in order to fet this matter in a clearer
light, I fhall here recount the principal
things, which vitiate the purity of language.

AND firft, it often happens, that fuch
words and forms of fpeaking, as were introduced by the learned, are afterwards
dropt by them, as mean and fordid, from
a feeming bafenefs contracted by vulgar
ufe. For polite and elegant fpeakers diftinguifh themfelves by their difcourfe, as
perfons of figure do by their garb; one
being the drefs of the mind, as the other
is of the body. And hence it comes to
pafs, that both have their different fafhions,
which are often changed; and as the vul-

X 3   gar

gar affect to imitate those above them in
both, this frequently occasions an alteration, when either becomes too trite and
common. But besides these sordid words
and expressions, which are rendered so by
the use of the vulgar; there is another
sort first introduced by them, which is carefully to be avoided by all those, who are
desirous to speak well. For the vulgar
have their peculiar words and phrases,
suited to their circumstances, and taken
from such things, as usually occur in their
way of life. Thus in the old comedians,
many things are spoken by servants, agreable to their character, which would be
very unbecoming from the mouth of a
gentleman. And we cannot but daily observe the like instances among ourselves.

AGAIN, this is common to language
with all other human productions, that it
is in its own nature liable to a constant
change and alteration. For as Horace has
justly observed :

All human works shall waste :
Then how can feeble words pretend to
last [1] *?*

[1] *Art Poet.*
v. 68.

Nothing could ever please all persons, or
at least for any length of time. And there
is nothing, from which this can less be

ex-

expected, than language. For as the thoughts of men are exceding various, and words are the figns of their thoughts; they will be conftantly inventing new figns to exprefs them by, in order to convey their ideas with more clearnefs, or greater beauty. If we look into the different ages of the Latin writers, what great alterations and changes do we find in their language? How few now underftand the remaining fragments of the *twelve tables?* Nay how many words do we meet with even in Plautus, the meaning of which has not yet been fixed with certainty by the fkill of the beft critics? And if we confider our own language, it will appear to have been in a manner intirely changed, from what it was a few ages fince. To mention no others, our celebrated Chaucer is to moft perfons now almoft unintelligible, and wants an expofitor. And even fince our own memory, we cannot but have obferved, that many words and expreffions, which a few years ago were in common ufe, are now in a manner laid afide and antiquated; and that others have conftantly, and daily do fuccede in their room. So true is that obfervation of the fame poet:

Some

*Some words that have, or else will feel
    decay,*

Shall be restor'd, and come again in play;

*And words now fam'd, shall not be fancied
    long,*

*They shall not please the ear, nor move
    the tongue;*

*As use shall these approve, and those con-
    demn,*

*Use the sole rule of speech, and judge su-
    preme* [1].

[1] *Ibid.*
v. 70.

We muſt therefore no leſs abſtain from
antiquated, or obſolete words and phraſes,
than from ſordid ones. Tho all old words
are not to be thought antiquated. By the
former I mean ſuch, which tho of an antient ſtanding, are not yet entirely diſuſed,
nor their ſignification loſt. It is the opinion of Quintilian, that theſe may ſometimes be admitted, tho ſparingly. *Not
only the beſt judges,* ſais he, *allow the uſe of
old words; but they give both a majeſty, and
an agreable pleaſure to a diſcourſe. For they
have the authority of antiquity, and a kind
of novelty from their diſuſe. But they ought
neither to be frequent, nor glaring; becauſe
nothing is more diſtaſteful than affectation:
nor muſt they be ſuch, as are entirely antiquated, and thro length of time wholly for-
                                                        got.*

got [1]. We are not therefore in the opinion
of this judicious writer, to be wholly de-
bared from the use of old words, especially [1] *Inst. orat.*
Lib. i.
when they appear more significant, than *c.* 6.
any others we can fix upon. But as to
phrases or expressions, greater caution seems
still necessary, and such as are old, should
doubtless, if at all, be used more sparingly.
The Latin tongue was brought to its greatest perfection in the reign of Augustus,
or somewhat sooner ; and he himself studied it very carefully. For, as Suetonius
tells us : *He applied himself to eloquence, and
the study of the liberal arts, from his child-
hood, with great diligence and labor. He
chose a manner of speaking, which was smooth
and elegant; and avoided the ill favour, as
he used to call it, of antiquated words. And
he was wont to blame Tiberius for his affectation of them* [2]. In our own language, [2] *Suet. in*
such words are to be esteemed antiquated, *Vit.* 84.
&c.
which the most polite persons have droped,
both in their discourse, and writings; whose
example we should follow, unless we would
be thought to converse rather with the
dead, than the living.

But further, as on the one hand we
must avoid obsolete words and phrases ; so
on the other, we should refrain from new
ones ;

LECT.
XX.
ones; or such, whose use has not been yet
sufficiently established, at least among those
of the best taste. Custom rules here, but,
as we have observed before, every custom
is not to be followed: a distinction must
be made between the use of the vulgar,
and that of the learned. Quintilian has
very well determined this matter, when
he sais: *We must settle first, what that is,*
which we call custom. Which, if it take
its name from that, which most persons prac-
tise, it will be an ill guide, not only in lan-
guage; but what is of greater consequence,
in life. For when has the world been so
happy, that what is right, has pleased the
majority? Therefore that is not to be taken
for a rule in language, which many have
corruptly fallen into. But I shall call the
consent of the learned the custom of language,
as the consent of the good the custom of
living [1]. A language is not the progeny
of one age. It requires a much longer
series of time to complete it, and bring it
to perfection. And besides, there is a certain agrement and harmony both in the
words, and modes of expression, proper to
every language, by which it is distinguished
from others. Therefore when any thing
new is introduced, it often seems harsh at
first,

[1] *Inst. orat.*
Lib. i.
c. 6.

firſt, and diſpleaſing to the ear; till time
has ſoftened it, and the uſe of the learned,
as it were, wrought it into the language.
The antient Romans, while their language
continued in its purity, were very ſcrupulous of admitting any thing new into
it, by which it might be vitiated. Nor
would they preſently ſubmit to the greateſt authority in this caſe. *So when Pom-*
ponius, who (as Suetonius informs us) *was*
a moſt zealous defender of the purity of the
Latin tongue, once excepted to an expreſſion,
which was uſed by the emperor Tiberius;
and Atteius Capito attempted to defend it,
by ſaying that it was Latin, or at leaſt would
then be ſo, ſince the emperor had uſed it:
Capito is miſtaken, replied Pomponius; for
tho you, Caeſar, can make men free, you
cannot make words free [1]. Now words may
be conſidered as new in two reſpects; either when they are firſt brought into a language, or when they are uſed in a new
ſenſe. As the former of theſe may ſometimes leave us in the dark, by not being
underſtood; ſo the latter are moſt apt to
miſlead us: for when we hear a word,
that has been familiar to us, we are preſently led to fix that idea to it, with which

it

[1] *De illuſtr. gram.* 22.

LECT.
XX.

it has ufually been attended. And therefore in both cafes, fome previous intimation may be neceffary. Cicero, who perhaps inlarged the furniture of the Roman tongue more than any one perfon befides, appears always very cautious, how he introduces any thing new, and generally gives notice of it, when he attempts it; as appears in many inftances fcattered thro his works. What bounds we are now to fix to the purity of the Latin tongue, in the ufe of it, the learned are not well agreed. It is certain our furniture is much lefs, than when it was a living language, and therefore the greater liberty muft of neceffity be fometimes taken. So that their opinion feems not unadvifable, who direct us to make choice principally of what we are furnifhed with from the writers of the Auguftan age, and where we cannot be fupplied from them, to make ufe of fuch authors as lived neareft to them, either before, or fince. And as to our own tongue, it is certainly prudent to be as careful, how we admit any thing into it, that is uncouth, or difagreable to its genius; as the antient Romans were into theirs: for the perfection of a lan-

guage

guage does in a great meafure confift
in a certain analogy, and harmony runing
thro the whole, by which it may be capable of being brought to a ftandard.

BUT befides thofe things already mentioned, any miftake in the fenfe of words,
or their conftruction, is oppofed to purity. For to fpeak purely, is to fpeak
correctly. And fuch is the nature of thefe
faults in elocution, that they are often
not fo eafy to be obferved by hearing,
as by reading. Whence it is, that many
perfons are thought to fpeak better, than
they write; for while they are fpeaking,
many flips and inaccuracies efcape difregarded, which in reading would prefently appear. And this is more efpecially
the cafe of perfons unacquainted with arts
and literature; who, by the affiftance of
a lively fancy, and flow of words, often
fpeak with great eafe and freedom, and
by that means pleafe the ear; when, at
the fame time, what they fay, would not
fo well bear reading.

I SHALL only add, that a diftinction
ought likewife to be made between a
poetic diction, and that of profe writers.
For poets in all languages have a fort

of

LECT.
XX.
of peculiar dialect, and take greater liberties, not only in their figures, but alfo
in their choice and difpofition of words;
fo that what is a beauty in them, would
often appear unnatural and affected in
profe.

L E C-

LECTURE XXI.

Of Perspicuity.

ELEGANCE, as I have already observed, confifts of two parts, *Purity*
and *Perspicuity*: the former of which renders a difcourfe correct, and the latter
makes it intelligible. As the one therefore is agreable and pleafant, the other is
neceffary, and for that reafon principally
to be regarded. For the moft accurate
and exact language is of little ufe, if it be
not fufficiently clear; fince it is much the
fame thing not to fpeak at all, and not to
be underftood, when we do fpeak. And
therefore Quintilian feems very juftly to
place the cheif excellency of fpeech in
perfpicuity [1]. Tho to render a difcourfe [1] *Inft. orat.*
entertaining, as well as clear, efpecially to *Lib.* viii,
perfons of a good tafte, both thefe pro- *c.* 2.
perties muft be joined. They expect to
be pleafed, at the fame time they are informed; and think, that the beft fenfe
always deferves the beft language: but
ftill the cheif regard is to be had to perfpicuity.

I

LECT.   I TREATED of *Purity* in my laſt diſ-
XXI.
‿‿‿   courſe, and ſhall therefore now procede to
ſpeak of *Perſpicuity.* And this, as well as
the former, conſiſts partly in *ſingle words,*
and partly in their *conſtruction.*

As to *ſingle words,* thoſe are generally
cleareſt and beſt underſtood, which are
uſed in their proper ſenſe. But it requires
no ſmall attention and ſkill to be well
acquainted with the force and propriety
of words; which ought to be duly regarded, ſince the perſpicuity of a diſcourſe
depends ſo much upon it. Caeſar ſeems
plainly to have been of this mind, when
he tells us, *The foundation of eloquence con-*
[1]Ap. Cic. *ſiſts in the choice of words* [1]. It may not
De clar.
orat. c. 72. be amiſs therefore to lay down ſome few
obſervations, by which the diſtinct notions
of words, and their peculiar force may
more eaſily be perceived. Indeed it is the
buſineſs of a grammarian to give us all the
different ſenſes of words, and ſupport them
with good authorities; I ſhall therefore
content myſelf with offering a few general
hints, in order to regulate our choice in
the uſe of them. Now all words may be
divided into *proper words* and *tropes.* Thoſe
are called *proper words,* which are expreſſed in their proper and uſual ſenſe.
And

And tropes are such words, as are applied
to some other thing, than what they properly denote, by reason of some similitude,
relation, or contrariety between the two
things. So when a subtle artful man is
called a *fox,* the reason of the name is
founded in a similitude of qualities. If we
say, *Cicero will always live,* meaning *his
works,* the cause is transfered to the effect.
And when we are told, *Caesar conquered
the Gauls,* we understand that he did it
with the assistance of his army; where a
part is put for the whole from the relation between them. And when Cicero
calls Antony, *a fine guardian of the state,*
every one perceives, he means the contrary. But I shall explain the nature and
use of tropes more fully hereafter in their
proper place. All words must at first have
had one original and primary signification,
which, strictly speaking, may be called
their proper sense. But it sometimes happens thro length of time, that words lose
their original signification, and assume a
new one, which then becomes their proper
sense. So *hostis* in the Latin tongue at
first signified a *stranger;* but afterwards
that sense of the word was entirely laid
aside, and it was used to denote a *public*

Y   *enemy.*

enemy. And in our language it is well known, that the word *knave* antiently signified a *servant*. The reason of the change seems to be much the same, as in that of the Latin word *latro*, which first signified a *soldier*, but afterwards a *robber*. Besides, in all languages it has frequently happened, that many words have gradually varied from their first sense to others somewhat different; which may notwithstanding all of them, when rightly applied, be looked upon as proper. Nay, in process of time, it is often difficult to say, which is the original, or most proper sense. Again, sometimes two or more words may appear to have the same signification with each other, and may therefore be used indifferently; unless the beauty of the period, or some other particular reason, determine to the choice of one, rather than another. Of this kind are the words *ensis* and *gladius* in the Latin tongue, and in ours *pity* and *compassion*. And there are other words of so near an affinity to each other, or at least appear so from vulgar use, that they are commonly thought to be synonymous. Such are the words *mercy*, and *pity*; tho mercy in its strict sense is exercised towards an offender, and pity respects one in distress.

As

As this peculiar force and diftinction of words is carefully to be attended to, fo it may be known feveral ways. Thus the proper fignification of fubftantives may be feen by their application to other fubftantives. As in the inftance juft now given, a perfon is faid to fhew *mercy to a criminal*, and *pity to one in diftrefs*. And in the like manner verbs are diftinguifhed, by being joined to fome certain nouns, and not to others. So a perfon is faid *to command an inferior*, *to intreat a fuperior*, and *to defire an equal*. Adjectives alfo, which denote the properties of things, have their fignification determined by thofe fubjects, to which they moft properly relate. Thus we fay, *an honeft mind*, and *a healthful body*; *a wife man*, and *a fine houfe*. Another way of diftinguifhing the propriety of words, is by their ufe in gradations. As if one fhould fay: *Hatreds, grudges, quarrels, tumults, feditions, wars, fpring from unbridled paffions.* The proper fenfe of words may likewife be known, by obferving to what other words they are either oppofed, or ufed as equivalent: So in that paffage of Cicero, where he fais: *I cannot perceive why you fhould be angry with me; if it be becaufe I defend him, whom you ac-*

cufe;

LECT. *cuse* ; *why may not I be displeased with you,*
XXI. *for accusing him, whom I defend? You say,*
I accuse my enemy ; and I say, I defend my
[1] *Pro Sulla, freind* [1]. Here the words *accuse* and *de-*
c. 17. *fend, freind* and *enemy,* are opposed ; and
to be angry and *displeased,* are used as terms
equivalent. Lastly, the derivation of words,
contributes very much to determine their
true meaning. Thus because the word
manners, comes from the word *man,* it may
properly be applied either to that, or any
other put for it. And therefore we say,
the manners of men, and *the manners of the*
age, because the word *age* is there used for
the men of the age. But if we apply the
word *manners* to any other animal, it is a
trope. By these, and such like observations, we may perceive the proper sense
and peculiar force of words, either by their
connection with other words, distinction
from them, opposition to them, equiva-
lency with them, or derivation. And by
thus fixing their true and genuine signification, we shall easily see when they become tropes. But tho words, when taken
in their proper signification, generally convey the plainest and clearest sense ; yet
some are more forceable, sonorous, or beautiful than others. And by these considerations

rations we muſt often be determined in
our choice of them. So whether we ſay,
he got, or, *he obtained the victory*, the ſenſe
is the ſame; but the latter is more full
and ſonorous. In Latin, *timeo* ſignifies
I fear, *pertimeo* is more full and ſignificant,
and *pertimeſco* more ſonorous than either
of the former. The Latin and Greek languages have much the advantage of ours
in this reſpect, by reaſon of their compo-
ſitions; by the help of which they can
often expreſs that in one word, for which
we are obliged to put two words, and
ſometimes more. So *pertimeo* cannot be
fully expreſſed in our language by one
word; but we are forced to join one or
two particles to the verb, to convey its
juſt idea, and ſay, *I greatly*, or *very much
fear*: and yet even then, we ſcarce ſeem
to reach its full force. As to tropes, tho
generally ſpeaking they are not to be choſen, where plainneſs and perſpicuity of expreſſion is only deſigned, and proper words
may be found; yet thro the penury of all
languages, the uſe of them is often made
neceſſary. And ſome of them, eſpecially
metaphors, which are taken from the ſimilitude of things, may, when cuſtom has
rendered them familiar, be conſidered as

proper

proper words, and ufed in their ftead. Thus, whether I fay, *I fee your meaning,* or, *I underftand your meaning,* the fenfe is equally clear; tho the latter expreffion is proper, and the former metaphorical, by which the action of feeing is transfered from the eyes to the mind.

But *Perfpicuity,* as I have faid, arifes not only from a choice of *fingle words,* but likewife from the *conftruction* of them in fentences. For the meaning of all the words in a fentence, confidered by themfelves, may be very plain and evident; and yet by reafon of a diforderly placing them, or confufion of the parts, the fenfe of the whole may be very dark and obfcure. Now it is certain, that the moft natural order is the plaineft; that is, when both the words and parts of a fentence are fo difpofed, as beft agrees with their mutual relation, and dependance upon each other. And where this is changed, as is ufually done, efpecially in the antient languages, for the greater beauty and harmony of the periods; yet due regard is had by the beft writers to the evidence and perfpicuity of the expreffion.

But to fet this fubject in a clearer light, on which the perfection of language

fo

so much depends, I shall mention some few things, which cheifly occasion obscurity; and this either with respect to single words, or their construction.

AND first, all ambiguity of expression is one cause of obscurity. This sometimes arises from the different senses, in which a word is capable of being taken. So we are told, that upon Cicero's addressing himself to Octavius Caesar, when he thought himself in danger from his resentment, and reminding him of the many services he had done him; Octavius replied, *He came the last of his freinds* [1]. But there was a designed ambiguity in the word *last*, as it might either respect the time of his coming, or the opinion he had of his freindship. And this use of ambiguous words we sometimes meet with, not only in poetry, where the turn and wit of an epigram often rests upon it; but likewise in prose, either for pleasantry or ridicule. Thus Cicero calls Sextus Clodius, *the light of the senate* [2]; which is a compliment he pais to several great men, who had distinguished themselves by their public services to their country. But Sextus, who had a contrary character, was a relation of P. Clodius, whose dead body, after he had

LECT.
XXI.

[1] Appian. *De Bell. civ. Lib.* v.

[2] *Pro Milon. c.* 12.

Y 4 been

LECT.
XXI.

been killed by Milo, he carried in a tumultuous manner into the senate house, and there burnt it with the senators benches, in order to inflame the populace against Milo.   And it is in illusion to that riotous action, that Cicero, using this ambiguous expression, calls him, *the light of the senate.* In such instances therefore it is a beauty, and not the fault I am cautioning against; as the same thing may be often good or bad, as it is differently applied.   Tho even in such designed ambiguities, where one sense is aimed at, it ought to be sufficiently plain, otherwise they lose their intention. And in all serious discourses they ought carefully to be avoided.   But obscurity more frequently arises from the ambiguous construction of words, which renders it difficult to determine, in what sense they are to be taken.   Quintilian gives us this example of it : *A certain man ordered in his will, that his heir should erect for him a statue holding a spear, made of gold* [1].   A question arises here, of great consequence to the heir, from the ambiguity of the expression; whether the words *made of gold,* are to be applied to the *statue,* or the *spear :* that is, whether it was the design of the testator by this appointment, that

[1] *Inst. orat. Lib.* vii. *c.* 9.

the

the whole ftatue, or only the fpear, fhould
be made of gold. A fmall note of diftinction, differently placed between the parts
of this fentence, would clear up the doubt,
and determine the fenfe either way. For
if one comma be put after the word *ftatue*,
and another after *fpear*, the words *made of
gold*, muft be refered to the *ftatue*, as if it
had been faid, *a ftatue, made of gold, holding
a fpear*. But if there be only the firft
comma placed after *ftatue*, it will limit
the words *made of gold*, to the *fpear* only;
in the fame fenfe, as if it had been faid,
A ftatue holding a golden fpear. And
either of thefe ways of expreffion would
in this cafe have been preferable, for
avoiding the ambiguity, according to the
intention of the teftator. The antient
heathen oracles were generally delivered in
fuch ambiguous terms. Which without
doubt were fo contrived on purpofe, that
thofe, who gave out the anfwers, might
have room left for an evafion.

AGAIN, obfcurity is occafioned either
by too fhort and concife a manner of fpeaking, or by fentences too long and prolix;
either of thefe extremes have fometimes
this bad confequence. We find an inftance of the former in Pliny the elder,

where

LECT.
XXI.
where speaking of Hellebore, he sais: *They
forbid it to be given to aged persons and children, and less to women than men* [1]. The
verb is wanting in the latter part of the
sentence, *and less to women than men,* which
in such cases being usually supplied from
what went before, would here stand thus:
*and they forbid it to be given less to women
than men.* But this is directly contrary to
the sense of the writer, whose meaning is,
either that it is ordered to be given in a
less quantity to women than men, or not
so frequently to women as men. And
therefore the word *order* is here to be supplied, which being of a contrary signification to *forbid,* expressed in the former part
of the sentence, occasions the obscurity.
That long periods are often attended with
the same ill effect, must be so obvious to
every one's experience; that it would be
intirely needless to produce any examples,
in order to evince the truth of it. And
therefore I shall only observe, that the best
way of preventing this seems to be, by dividing such sentences, as excede a proper
length, into two or more, which may generally be done without much trouble.

ANOTHER cause of obscurity, not inferior to any yet mentioned, is *Parenthesis,*
when

[1] *Hist. Nat.
Lib.* xxv.
c. 5.

when it is either too long, or too frequent. This of Cicero, in his oration for
Sulla, is longer than we usually find in
him : *O immortal gods (for I must attribute
to you, what is your own: nor indeed can
I claim so much to my own abilities, as to
have been able of myself to go thro so many,
so great, such different affairs, with that expedition, in that boisterous tempest of the
state) you inflamed my mind with a desire to
save my country* [1]. But where any obscu- [1] *Cap.* 14.
rity arises from such sentences, they may
frequently be remedied by much the same
means, as was just now hinted concerning
long and prolix periods ; that is, by separating the parenthesis from the rest of the
sentence, and placing it either before or
after. So in this sentence of Cicero, the
parenthesis may stand last, in the following
manner : *O immortal gods, you inflamed my
mind with a desire to save my country : for
I must attribute to you, what is your own;
nor indeed can I claim so much to my own
abilities, as to have been able of myself to go
thro so many, so great, such different affairs, with that expedition, in that boisterous
tempest of the state.* This order of the
sentence is very plain, and less involved
than the former. But to remove the obscurity,

 fcurity, which otherwife might be occafioned by a long parenthefis, one or more
words are fometimes repeated immediately
after it, which had been mentioned juft
before. Thus Cicero in his fecond Philippic fais : *A fpear being erected before the
temple of Jupiter Stator, the goods (unhappy I, tho my tears are exhaufted, my greif
yet continues fixed in my breaft) the goods,
I fay, of Pompey the Great were expofed to*
Cap. 26. *auction by the doleful voice of a crier* [1].   In
the following fentence of the fame excel-
lent writer, there are no lefs than three
parenthefes ; which I take notice of, as a
thing very feldom to be found in him ;
and therefore rather to be obferved, than
imitated without neceffity.   Speaking of
the duty of magiftrates, and fuch who have
the management of public affairs, he fais :
*Care muft be taken, that it be not (as was
often done by our anceftors, thro the fmall-
nefs of the treafury, and continuance of the
wars) neceffary to raife taxes ; and in order
to prevent this, provifion fhould be made a-
gainft it long before hand : but if the neceffity of this fervice fhould happen to any
ftate (which I had rather fuppofe of another,
than our own ; nor am I now difcourfing of
our own, but of every ftate in general) me-*
                                                      thods

*thods must be used to convince all persons
(if they would be secure) that they ought
to submit to necessity* [1]. Every one will
readily perceive, that the sense of this period is not altogether so clear, nor the run
of it so free and easy, as it would otherwise have been without the parentheses.
But even two of these might be avoided,
by a small change in the disposition of the
members, in the following manner : *Care
must be taken, that it be not necessary to
raise taxes, as was often done by our an-
cestors, thro the smallness of the treasury,
and continuance of the wars ; and in order
to prevent this, provision should be made
against it long before hand : but if the necessity of this service should happen to any
state (which I would rather suppose of another, than our own ; nor am I now dif-
coursing of our own, but of every state in general) methods must be used to convince all
persons, that they ought to submit to necessity, if they would be secure.* The words
are here exactly the same as before, and
no other alteration made, but that two of
the members, which before were included
in others, are now placed after them. I
have been the longer upon this head, because it is what many persons are too apt
to

LECT.
XXI.
to fall into, by involving several sentences, or parts of sentences, one within another, instead of separating them, and placing one after another, in a proper dependance and connexion, as might be done by due care and attention.

THESE are the principal things, which occasion obscurity in a discourse, with respect to the language. There have been some persons, who have affected a dark and obscure way of speaking. We are told concerning Tiberius the emperor, that, *He was thought to speak better off hand (as we say) than when he made a studied and* [1] *set discourse* [1]. But this was not occasioned from his want of skill, but, as the historian sais, from an affected obscurity in his stile. And Heraclitus was called the *dark philosopher* upon that account [2]. And Quintilian mentions a certain rhetorician of this make, *Who used to order his scholars to cloud their discourses.* And his highest applause was: *Bravely said, I did not understand it myself* [3]. It is hard to guess what such persons can propose to themselves by this conduct; unless they imagine their discourses will be thought to have the more in them, the less they are understood. But the design of language is to communicate our thoughts

[1] Suet. *in Vit. c. 70.*

[2] Clem. *Strom.* v.

[3] *Inst. orat. Lib.* viii. c. 2.

thoughts to others, and the plainer it is, the better this defign is anfwered. And therefore Quintilian very prudently advifes perfons not only to endeavour, *that their hearers may underftand them, but as far as may be, that it fhould be impoffible for them not to underftand them* [1].

[1] *Ubi fupra.*

LEC-

LECTURE XXII.

Of Composition, and particularly of Period.

THE firſt part of *Elocution*, which conſiſts in *Elegance*, I finiſhed in my laſt diſcourſe; and ſhall now procede to the ſecond, which is *Compoſition*.

Now *Compoſition*, in the ſenſe it is here uſed, gives rules for the ſtructure of ſentences, with the ſeveral members, words, and ſyllables, of which they conſiſt, in ſuch a manner, as may beſt contribute to the force, beauty, and evidence of the whole. Some have not only neglected this, but pleaded againſt it, that ſuch an attendance to rules of art in the ſtructure and formation of ſentences rather weakens and enervates the ſtile; which is more ſtrong and natural, when every thing is expreſſed in the manner it firſt occurs to the mind. But to this Quintilian very well replies: *If that only is to be eſteemed natural, which firſt ſprang from nature, before it was cultivated; then the whole art of oratory is unnatural. And beſides, if what nature at firſt dictates, is not to be improved by ſtudy and induſtry, mankind muſt be deprived not only*

only of many pleasures, but likewise conveniences of life. But if all these are found suitable to nature; then that seems to be most natural, which is most agreable to reason; and that is most agreable to reason, which is best in its kind [1]. So that nature and art are not opposite to each other, and different in kind, but only in degree, as art is nature improved. Nor is it true, that rough and harsh language is more strong and nervous; than when the composition is smooth and harmonious. A stream, which runs among stones and rocks, makes more noise, from the opposition it meets with in its course; but that, which has not those impediments, flows with greater force and strength. So harsh and jarring sounds are disagreable to the ear, which does not give them that easy admittance to the mind, as those, which are more pleasant and melodious. Besides harmonious numbers do not only give delight; but oftentimes impress the mind with an irresistable force, by the powerful influence they have upon the passions. This is evident from music, whose sounds, not being attended with rational ideas, cannot affect the understanding, and yet raise in the hearers a variety of emotions.

[1] *Inst. orat. Lib.* ix. *c.* 4.

Z   But

L E C T.
XXII.
But poetry is still a greater instance of it,
which, by reason of its numbers joined to
fine thoughts, affords us both a rational
and delightful entertainment. But nothing
more is necessary to shew the advantage
of this part of elocution, and how necessary it is for an orator, than to take a
period well wrought up, and alter the form
of it; by which it may be easily seen,
how differently the mind will be affected
by such an alteration. Cicero has shewn
this from several instances, in his book
¹ Cap. 70. *Of a perfect orator* ¹. But since they cannot so well be expressed in a translation,
let us try it by one example in our own
language, taken from a very polite writer,
thus addressing his patron: *You have,* said
he, *acted in so much consistency with your-*
self, and promoted the interests of your coun-
try in so uniform a manner; that even those,
who would misrepresent your generous designs
for the public good, cannot but approve the
steadiness and intrepidity, with which you
² Spectat. *pursue them* ². I think this may be justly
Vol. v. esteemed an handsome period. It begins
pref. with ease, rises gradually till the voice is
inflected, then sinks again, and ends with
a just cadency. And perhaps there is not
a word in it, whose situation could be altered

tered to an advantage. Let us now but
fhift the place of one word in the laft
member, and we fhall fpoil the beauty of
the whole fentence. For, if inftead of
faying, as it now ftands, *cannot but approve*
the fteadinefs and intrepidity, with which
you purfue them; we put it thus, *cannot*
but approve the fteadinefs and intrepidity,
which you purfue them with; the cadency
will be flat and languid, and the harmony
of the period entirely loft. Let us try it
again by altering the place of the two laft
members, which at prefent ftand in this
order, *that even thofe, who would mifre-*
prefent your generous defigns for the public
good, cannot but approve the fteadinefs and
intrepidity, with which you purfue them.
Now if the former member be thrown
laft, they will run thus, *that even thofe*
cannot but approve the fteadinefs and intre-
pidity, with which you purfue them, who
would mifreprefent your generous defigns for
the public good. Here the fenfe is much
obfcured by the inverfion of the relative
them, which ought to refer to fomething
that went before, and not to the words
generous defigns, which in this fituation of
the members are placed after it. And
Perfpicuity, as I have fhewn already, is to

Z 2 be

L E C T. be always carefully regarded, as the cheif
   XXII.
          and moſt neceſſary property of language.
It may perhaps be thought, that this is a
thing in itſelf ſo very plain and obvious,
that no one can well miſs of falling into
that manner, which is beſt. But ſurely if
it was ſo, the contrary would not ſo often
appear both in ſpeaking and writing.

COMPOSITION conſiſts of four parts;
which rhetoricians call *Period, Order, Juncture*, and *Number*. The firſt of theſe treats
on the ſtructure of ſentences; the ſecond
of the parts of ſentences, which are words
and members; and the two laſt of the
parts of words, which are letters and ſyllables. For all articulate ſounds, and even
the moſt minute parts of language, come
under the cognizance of oratory. I ſhall
begin with the firſt of theſe, which relates
to ſentences.

BUT before I enter upon this, it may
not be improper to conſider a little the
nature of a ſentence in general, with the
different kinds of it, which are either ſimple
or compound. Now in every ſentence,
or propoſition, ſomething is ſaid of ſomething. That of which ſomething is ſaid,
logicians call the *ſubject*, and that, which
is ſaid of it, the *predicate :* but in gram-
                                        matical

matical terms, the former is *a noun fub-*
ftantive of the nominative cafe, and the
latter *a finite verb.* Thefe two parts may
of themfelves conftitute a fentence. As
when we fay, *The fun fhines,* or, *The clock*
ftrikes, the words *fun* and *clock* are the
fubject in thefe expreffions, *fhines* and
ftrikes the predicate. But moft commonly
they are accompanied with other words,
which in grammatical conftruction are faid
either to be connected with, or to depend
upon them ; but in a logical confideration
they denote fome property, or circumftance
relating to them. As in the following
fentence : *A good man loves virtue for it-*
felf. The fubject of this fentence is *a*
good man; and the predicate, or thing affirmed of him, that he *loves virtue for*
itfelf. But the two principal or neceffary
words, on which all the reft depend, are
man and *loves.* Now a fimple fentence
confifts of one fuch noun and verb, with
whatever elfe is joined to either, or both
of them. And a compound fentence contains two or more of them, and may be
divided into fo many diftinct propofitions,
as there are fuch nouns and verbs, either
expreffed or underftood. So in the following fentence : *Compliance gains freinds,*

Z 3   *but*

LECT.
XXII.

but truth procures hatred ⁵, there are two members, each of which contains in it an entire propofition. For, *Compliance gains freinds,* is one complete fentence; and, *Truth procures hatred,* is another; which are connected into one compound fentence by the particle *but.* Moreover it frequently happens, that compound fentences are made up of fuch parts or members, fome if not all of which are themfelves compounded, and contain in them two or more fimple members. Such is that of Salluft: *Ambition has betrayed many perfons into deceit; to fay one thing, and to mean another; to found freindfhip and enmity, not upon reafon, but intereft; and to be more careful to*
appear honeft, than really to be fo ². This fentence confifts of four members, the three laft of which confifting of oppofite parts are all compounded; as will appear by exprefling them at length in the following manner: *Ambition has betrayed many perfons into deceit; it* [that is ambition] *has betrayed them to fay one thing, and to mean another; it has betrayed them to found freindfhip and enmity, not upon reafon, but intereft; and it has betrayed them to be more careful to appear honeft, than really to be fo.* The three laft of thefe members, begining

with

with the words *it betrays,* are all of them
compounded, and confist of two oppofite
members; which might each of them be
expreffed at length in the fame manner,
by fupplying the ellipfis. As : *Ambition
has betrayed many perfons to fay one thing,
and it has betrayed them to mean another.*
And fo of the reft. From this inftance
we fee, how much is left to be fupplied
by the mind in all difcourfe ; which if expreffed, would both deftroy its harmony,
and render it exceding tedious. But ftill
regard muft be had to that, which is omitted, fo as to render what is faid confiftent
with it; otherwife there can be no propriety in what is fpoken. Nor can the
members of a fentence be diftinguifhed,
and duly ranged in their proper order,
without this. But to procede, fome fentences confift either wholly, or in part, of
fuch members, as contain in them two or
more compound ones, which may therefore for diftinction's fake be called de-
compound members. Of this kind is that
of Cicero, in his *defence of* Milo : *Great
is the force of confcience, great either way :
that thofe perfons are not afraid, who have
committed no offence ; and thofe, who have
offended, always think punifhment prefent be-*

Z 4   *fore*

fore their eyes [1]. The latter member of this fentence, which begins with the word

[1] *Cap.* 23.

that, contains in it two compound members, which reprefent the different ftate of mind between innocent and guilty perfons. And it is in the proper diftinction, and feparation of the members in fuch complex fentences, that the art of pointing cheifly confifts. For the principal ufe of a comma is to divide the fimple members, a femicolon the compound ones, a colon fuch as are decompounded, and a period the whole from the following fentence. I mention this the rather, to fhew the different acceptation of thefe terms by grammarians, from that of the antient writers upon oratory. For thefe latter apply them to the fenfe, and not to any points of diftinction. A very fhort member, whether fimple or compound, with them is a comma ; and a longer a colon ; for they have no fuch term, as a femicolon. Befides they call a very fhort fentence, whether fimple or compound, a comma ; and one of fomewhat a greater length, a colon. And therefore, if a perfon expreffed himfelf either of thefe ways in any confiderable number of fentences together, he was faid to fpeak by commas, or colons. But a fentence

con-

containing more words, than will confift with either of thefe terms, they call a fimple period; the leaft compound period with them requiring the length of two colons. However this way of denominating fentences, and the parts of them, rather from their length, than the nature of them, appearing not fo fuitable, I have chofen rather to make ufe of the terms fimple and compound members; and to call all thofe compound periods, which contain two or more members, whether fimple or compounded.

But I procede to the ftruЯure of fentences, which with refpeЯ to their form or compofition, are diftinguifhed into two forts, called by Cicero *traЯa*, ftrait or di-rect; and *contorta*, bent or winding [1]. By the former are meant fuch, whofe mem-bers follow each other in a direЯ order, without any inflexion; and by the latter thofe, which ftriЯtly fpeaking are called periods. For περιοδ⊙. in Greek fignifies a *circuit* or *circle*. And fo the Latins call it *circuitus* and *ambitus*. By which they both mean a fentence confifting of corre-fpondent parts, fo framed, that the voice in pronouncing them may have a proper elevation and cadency, and diftinguifh them

by

[1] *Orat. c. 20.*

by its inflexion. And as the latter part returns back, and unites with the former, the period, like a circle, furrounds and inclofes the whole fenfe. This elevation of the voice in the former part of the period, is by the Greeks called, πρότασις, and by the Latins *propofitio*; and the depreffion of it in the latter part, by the one ἀπόδοσις, and by the other *redditio*.

Now as fimple fentences have not thefe correfpondent parts, which require any inflexion of the voice; nor a circular form, by reafon of their brevity, they are not properly periods, in the ftrict fenfe of the word: tho in common fpeech the words fentence and period are often ufed as equivalent terms. Thus, if I fay: *Generous minds are incited to the performance of noble exploits from motives of glory:* here is no diftinction of parts, nor inflexion of the voice in this fentence. And indeed there is not any thing, which relates to the ftructure of thefe fentences, but what will more properly be taken notice of in the fecond part of *Compofition*, which is *order*.

And as to thofe compound fentences, whofe members follow each other in a direct order, without any inflexion, there is little art required in their compofition.

I fhall produce one example of this kind
from Cicero: *Natural reafon inclines men
to mutual converfe and fociety; and implants
in them a ftrong affeƈtion for thofe, who
fpring from them; and excites them to form
communities, and join in public affemblies;
and for thefe ends to endeavour to procure
both the neceffaries and conveniences of life;
and that not for themfelves only, but likewife their wives, children, and others, who
are dear to them, and have a right to their
affiftance* [1]. Here are five fhort members
in this fentence, placed in a feries, without
any inflexion of the parts, or orbit of the
whole. And as fuch fentences have no
other boundary, but the conclufion of the
fenfe, fuited to the breath of the fpeaker;
he may either contraƈt, or lengthen them
at pleafure, without offending the ear. So
fhould the fentence laft mentioned conclude with the firft member, in this manner: *Natural reafon inclines men to mutual
converfe and fociety:* the fenfe would be
perfeƈt, and the ear fatisfied. The cafe
would be the fame at the end of the fecond member, thus: *Natural reafon inclines men to mutual converfe and fociety;
and implants in them a ftrong affeƈtion for
thofe, who fpring from them.* And the like
may

[1] *Off:
Lib.* i.
c. 4.

may be faid of the reft. Since fuch fentences therefore may be thus limited at pleafure, it feems more convenient both for the fpeaker and hearers to confine them to a moderate length.

But becaufe the principal art, relating to this part of compofition, lies in the frame and ftructure of fuch compound fentences, as are properly called periods; I fhall treat upon thefe fomewhat more largely. In the formation of thefe periods, two things are cheifly to be regarded, their length and cadency. As the length ought to be fuited to the breath of the fpeaker, the antient rhetoricians fcarce admit of more than four colons; by which we may here underftand compound members of a moderate fize, which will, I beleive, upon obfervation be generally found a fuitable and proportionate length [1]. For to extend them farther, than the voice can well manage, muft be painful to the fpeaker, and of confequence unpleafant to the hearers. As to the cadency, what Cicero has obferved, is found true by experience, that the ears judge what is full, and what is deficient; and direct us to fill up our periods, that nothing be wanting, of what they expect. When the voice is raifed at

the

[1] Cic. *Orat.* c. 66.

the begining of a fentence, they are in
fufpenfe till it be finifhed; and are pleafed
with a full and juft cadency, but are fenfible of any defect, and are difpleafed with
redundancy. Therefore care muft be taken,
that periods be neither deficient, and as it
were maimed, that is, that they do not
drop before their time, and defraud the
ears, of what feemed to be promifed them;
nor, on the other hand, offend them by
too long and immoderate excurfions [1]. This
rife and cadency of the voice in pronunciation, depend on the nature and fituation
of the members, as I fhall endeavour to
fhew by particular inftances; in the explication of which, by the word *members,* are
to be underftood fuch as are compounded.
In a period of two members, the turn of
the voice begins with the latter member.
Of this kind is the following fentence of
Cicero: *If impudence prevailed as much in
the forum and courts of juftice, as infolence
does in the country and places of lefs refort;
Aulus Caecina would fubmit as much to the
impudence of Sextus Ebutius in this caufe,
as he did before to his infolence when affaulted by him* [2]. Here the cadency begins
at the words *Aulus Caecina.* If a fentence
confift of three members, the inflexion is
                                                    beft

[1] See Cic.
*De clar.
orat. c.* 8.
*& Orat.
c.* 50,
& 53.

[2] *Pro Cae-
cin. c.* 1.

beſt made at the end of the ſecond member; for if it begin immediately after the
firſt, the voice will either be apt to ſink
too low, and not be heard, before it reach
the end; or elſe be precipitated, in order
to prevent it. Cicero begins his oration
for Milo with a ſentence of this form:
Altho I fear, it may be a ſhame to be diſ-
mayed at the entrance of my diſcourſe in de-
fence of a moſt valiant man; and that it no
ways becomes me, while Milo is more con-
cerned for the ſafety of the ſtate than for
himſelf, not to ſhew the ſame greatneſs of
mind in his behalf: yet *this new form of*
proſecution terrifies my eyes, which, whatever
way they turn, want the antient cuſtom of
the forum, and former manner of trials.
Here the cadency begining at the third
member with the word *yet,* makes a proper
diviſion of the ſentence, and eaſy for the
ſpeaker. But a period of four members
is reckoned the moſt complete and perfect,
where the inflexion begins at the middle,
that is, with the third member. Nor is it
the ſame caſe here, as if in a ſentence of
three members, the cadency be made at the
ſecond. For in proportion to the time of
raiſing the voice, may the ſpace be allowed
for its ſinking. The following ſentence
of

of Cicero gives us an inftance of this,
where he fpeaks to his fon : *Altho, fon
Mark, having now been an hearer of Cra-
tippus for a year, and this at Athens, you
ought to abound in the precepts and doctrines
of philofophy, by reafon of the great character both of your inftructor, and the city;
one of which can furnifh you with knowledge, and the other with examples :* yet,
*as I always to my advantage joined the La-
tin tongue with the Greek, and have done
it not only in oratory, but likewife in philofophy ; I think you ought to do the fame,
that you may be equally converfant in both
languages* [1]. The turn in this period begins at the word *yet,* which ftanding near
the middle, the voice is raifed to that
pitch in pronouncing the former part, as
to admit of a gradual cadency, without
being loft, before the conclufion of the
fentence. But where the fenfe does not
fuit with this divifion at the entrance upon
the third member, it is beft made at the
fourth. Such is the following fentence
of Cicero : *If I have any genius, which
I am fenfible how fmall it is ; or any readinefs in fpeaking, wherein I do not deny, but
I have been much converfant ; or any fkill*

[1] *De Off.
Lib.* i.
c. 1.

in

in oratory, from an acquaintance with the best arts, to which I confefs I have been always inclined : no one *has a better right to demand of me the fruit of all thefe things, than this Aulus Licinius* [1]. The cadency of this fentence does not begin, till the words *no one*; yet it ends handfomly, and without difappointing the ear. Tho indeed the three firft members having each of them an inflexion, check the elevation of the voice, and by that variety in the pronunciation add to the harmony of the fentence. An equality of the members fhould likewife be attended to in the compofition of a period, the better to adjuft their rife and cadency. And for this reafon in fentences of three members, where the cadency begins with the third; or in thofe of four members, where it begins at the fourth; it promotes the harmony, to make the laft member longeft. This is properly the nature of rhetorical periods, which when rightly formed have both an equal beauty and dignity in their compofition.

But, as all difcourfe is made up of diftinct fentences, and whenever we exprefs our thoughts, it is in fome of the forms
above

[1] *Pro Archia, c. 1.*

above mentioned; fo the ufe of them is not promifcuous, but fuited to anfwer different defigns in fpeaking. And in this view they are confidered, and made ufe of by the orator, as will be fhewn hereafter.

LEC-

LECTURE XXIII.

Of Order.

HAVING already difcourfed upon the different forms and ftructure of fentences, I am next to confider the conftruction of the parts, of which they confift. This rhetoricians call *Order*. And by this they mean the placing each word, and member of a fentence, in fuch a manner, as will moft contribute to the force, beauty, or evidence of the whole. But regard muft always be had to the genius and cuftom of different languages. For that order is agreable to one language, which will not fuit with another; as I fhall have occafion to fhew in the feries of this difcourfe.

Now there are two kinds of *Order*, one of which may be called *natural*, and the other *artificial*. And each of thefe may be confidered with refpect to the parts either of fimple, or compound fentences.

As to fimple fentences, we may call that order *natural*, when all the words in a fentence are fo placed, as they are connected with, or follow each other, in a

gram-

grammatical conſtruction. And it may properly enough admit of this name, as it is founded in the nature of a propoſition; and the relation of the ſeveral words, of which it conſiſts, to each other. This I explained in my laſt diſcourſe, and illuſtrated by proper examples; and ſhall therefore only give one inſtance of it here, to introduce the ſubject I am now upon. And it is this: *The fame of Iſocrates excited Ariſtotle to the profeſſion of oratory.* Here theſe words, *the fame of Iſocrates,* contain the ſubject of this ſentence, with what relates to it; and all thoſe which follow, *excited Ariſtotle to the profeſſion of oratory,* make up the predicate, and its dependants. And in both parts each word grammatically conſidered ſtands in its pro‑ per order of conſtruction. And this ſeems agreable to the natural way of conveying our thoughts, which leads us firſt to expreſs the ſubject, or thing, of which ſome other thing is ſaid, before the predicate, or that which is ſaid concerning it; and with reſpect to both, as every idea ſuccedes another in the order of our conceptions, to range it in the ſame order, when we communicate them to others. Our language in the general keeps pretty

much

much to this method. But in one thing particularly it recedes from it; and that is, in placing adjectives, which denote the properties of things, before their fubftantives or fubjects, whofe properties they are. As when it is faid: *Evil communication corrupts good manners.* And this we always do, except fomething follows, which depends upon the adjective. So we fay: *He was a man eminent for his virtue*, not, *an eminent man.*

ARTIFICIAL order, as it refpects fimple fentences, has little or no regard to the natural conftruction of words; but difpofes them in fuch a manner, as will be moft agreable to the ear, and beft anfwer the defign of the fpeaker. The Latins take a much greater liberty in this refpect, than we do, or the nature of our language will permit. Quintilian fais, it is beft for the verb to ftand laft, when there is no particular reafon to the contrary. And he gives this reafon for it, *becaufe the force of* ¹ *In/t.orat.* *the fentence lies in the verb* ¹. So that ac-
Lib. ix. *c.* 4.
cording to him, they feem to have had this view in puting the verb at the end; that as the whole fentence is imperfect without the verb, the mind being thus held in fufpence might receive the deeper impreffion

from

from it at laſt. They likewiſe ſeparate
ſuch words, as have an immediate relation
between them, or dependance one upon
another; and place any of them firſt or
laſt, as they pleaſe. In ſhort, their order
ſeems in a manner arbitrary, if it does not
break in upon perſpicuity, to which they
uſually attend. But moſt of theſe things
are unſuitable to the genius of our language. One might ſay indeed: *Convince
him he cannot*, inſtead of ſaying: *He cannot convince him.* Or: *With my own eyes
I ſaw it*, for, *I ſaw it with my own eyes.*
And again: *In proportion to the increaſe
of luxury the Roman ſtate declined*, for, *The
Roman ſtate declined in proportion to the
increaſe of luxury.* But the inverſion of
the words in the former order of theſe
expreſſions, doth not ſound ſo kindly to an
Engliſh ear, which is not accuſtomed to
ſuch a manner of ſpeaking.

As to compound ſentences, that is, ſuch
as conſiſt of two or more members, either
ſimple or compounded; what relates to
the words in each member ſeparately, is
the ſame, as in ſimple ſentences. But with
regard to the diſpoſition of the ſeveral
members, that may be called the *natural*
order, which ſo places them, as they mu-

tually

tually depend on each other. Thus the antecedent member naturally precedes the relative. As in this expreſſion: *Men are apt to forgive themſelves, what they blame in others.* In hypothetical ſentences the conditional member naturally ſtands firſt. Thus: *If Socrates be a rational creature, he is a man.* That member, which expreſſes the effect of an action, naturally comes laſt. As: *Tho you offer never ſo good reaſons, you will not prevail with him.* The like may be ſaid of time, with regard to things done in it. As: *The Roman eloquence ſoon declined, when Cicero was dead.* And to name no more, the reaſon of a thing naturally follows that, of which it is the reaſon. As thus: *All the pleaſures of life muſt be uncertain, ſince life itſelf is not ſecure*

WHEN this order is inverted, it may be ſtiled *artificial.* So to keep to the inſtances already given, the two members in the firſt ſentence may be thus inverted: *What they blame in others, men are apt to forgive themſelves.* In the ſecond in this manner: *Socrates is a man, if he be a rational creature.* In the third thus: *You will not prevail with him, tho you offer never ſo good reaſons.* And ſo in the reſt. As: *When Cicero*

Cicero was dead, the Roman eloquence soon declined. And : *Since life itself is not secure, all the pleasures of life must be uncertain.* The variety of inversions in a sentence may generally be greater or less, in proportion to the number of its members. In the following sentence of Cicero, the natural order seems to be this : *If that greatness of mind be void of justice, which shews itself in dangers and labors, it is blameable.* Which may be varied by changing the place of the first and third member, in the following manner : *That greatness of mind is blameable, which shews itself in dangers and labors, if it want justice.* Or by altering the place of all the three members thus : *That greatness of mind is blameable, if it be void of justice, which shews itself in dangers and labors.* But oftentimes one member may be included in another, as in the instance here given : *If that greatness of mind, which shews itself in dangers and labors, be void of justice, it is blameable.* Here the relative member is included in the conditional, which is placed first, and the antecedent member follows both. But in Cicero it stands thus : *That greatness of mind, which shews itself in dangers and labors, if it want justice, is blameable* [1].

[1] *De Off. Lib.* i. *c.* 19.

Where

Where the relative and conditional members are both included in the antecedent member. The Latin tongue commonly admits of a much greater variety in the tranſpoſition of members, as well as in that of ſingle words, than ſuits with our idiom. In the following ſentence the natural order is much preferable, as it beſt ſuits with the proper elevation and cadency of the voice in its pronunciation : *I am willing to remit all that is paſt, provided it may be done with ſafety.* But ſhould we invert the members, and ſay : *Provided it may be done with ſafety, I am willing to remit all that is paſt :* the harmony of the cadency would be loſt. And if the latter member be included in the former, the alteration will ſtill be worſe. As : *I am willing, provided it may be done with ſafety, to forgive all that is paſt.* Here the inflection of the voice falls upon the ſame member as before, and deſtroys the beauty of the period by its elevation afterwards. Some ſentences admit of no involution of their members. Such are thoſe, whoſe members are connected by conjunctive or disjunctive particles. As : *Virtue furniſhes the mind with the trueſt pleaſure in proſperity, and affords it the greateſt comfort in adverſity.* And :

*A wise man is neither elated by prosperity,
nor depressed by adversity.* And the like
may be said of those, where the latter
member begins with some illative or red-
ditive particle. As in these instances: *The
cheif thing to be regarded in life is virtue,
for all other things are vain and uncertain.*
And: *Tho fortune is always inconstant, yet
she has many votaries.* Neither of the members in any of these ways of expression,
and some others, which might be named,
can be included one in the other. In all
the examples hitherto given, the sentences
consist only of simple members; and indeed compound members are not so often
inverted, nor included one in another, by
reason of their length. However I shall
here produce one instance of each: *Whoever considers the uncertainty of human affairs, and how frequently the greatest hopes
are frustrated; he will see just reason to be
always on his guard, and not place too much
dependance upon things so precarious.* This
sentence consists of two compound members, which here stand in their natural
order, but may be thus inverted: *He will
see just reason to be always on his guard, and
not place too much dependance on things so
precarious; whoever considers the uncertainty*

of

*of human affairs, and how often the greatest
hopes are frustrated.* In the following sentence one compound member is included
in another : *Let us not conclude, while dangers are at a distance, and do not immediately
approach us, that we are secure ; unless we
use all necessary precaution to prevent them.*
Here the natural order would be : *While
dangers are at a distance, and do not immediately approach us ; let us not conclude, that
we are secure ; unless we use all necessary
precaution to prevent them.*

B U T there are some other considerations
relating to order, which being taken from
the nature of things, equally suit all languages. So in amplifying there should be
a constant gradation from a less to a greater. As when Cicero sais : *Ambition creates
hatred, shyness, discords, seditions, and wars* [1].
On the contrary, in extenuating we should
descend from a greater to a less. As if
speaking of the antient laws of Rome one
should say : *They were so far from suffering
a Roman citizen to be put to death, that they
would not allow him to be whipt, or even to
be bound* [2]. In constituting any whole we
put the parts first. As : *Invention, disposition, elocution, and pronunciation, make up
the art of oratory.* But in separating any
whole

[1] *De fin.
Lib.* 1.
c. 13.

[2] *In Verr.
c.* 66.

whole the parts follow. As: *The art of oratory may be divided into these four parts; invention, disposition, elocution, and pronunciation.* In every enumeration care muſt be taken not to mix the whole with the parts; but if it be mentioned at all, it muſt either be put firſt, or laſt. So it would be wrong to ſay: *He was a man of the greateſt prudence, virtue, juſtice, and modeſty.* For the word *virtue* here contains in it the other three, and therefore ſhould not be inſerted among them.

THESE are the principal things neceſſary to be obſerved with regard to order. There are others, which might be mentioned; but they will readily offer themſelves to thoſe, who attend to this ſubject. And there are ſome ſo variable and uncertain, that they are ſcarce reducible to any fixed rules; and may therefore be more eaſily acquired by uſe and obſervation. Variety is always neceſſary, for the moſt accurate and exact compoſition, if it return too often, will be unpleaſant. And therefore, notwithſtanding Quintilian recommends it as beſt in the Latin tongue to end a ſentence with the verb; yet it would be wrong, and contrary to the uſage of the beſt writers, always to keep to this, or indeed

deed too frequently. Befides, the fame accuracy is not at all times neceffary; but
regard muft be had to the nature of the
difcourfe, as I fhall have occafion to fhew
hereafter.

IN treating upon this fubject I have been
more particular in obferving the analogy
between our language, and the Latin; becaufe there feems to me no better way of
difcovering the genius, and peculiar properties of any language, than by comparing it
with others. And we cannot but perceive, from what has been faid, that our
compofition is in this part of it much more
limited and confined, than the Latin. The
natural order is certainly more plain and
eafy; but yet it muft be owned, that the
other has its advantages, and thofe very
confiderable. The language both of the
Greeks and Romans has more ftrength, as
well as harmony, than any modern tongue;
which is owing in a good meafure to this
liberty in their compofition. For by giving
their periods the fineft turn, and placing
the moft fignificant words, where they may
ftrike the mind with the greateft force; at
the fame time they both delight the ear,
and excite the attention. Soon after learning began to revive in Europe, and to

I

difpel

difpel thofe clouds of ignorance, which had
overfpread it for feveral ages before, the
ftudy of the antient languages was very
much purfued, as the neceffary key to all
ufeful knowledge. At which time many
learned men began to cultivate the language of their own country, both in foreign parts, and here in England. And
fome among us endeavoured to reduce our
tongue, as near as they could, to the Latin,
as in other things, fo likewife in the compofition of fentences. However this did
not meet with the defired fuccefs, but rendered their ftile very harfh and ftiff, and
often obfcure; as appears by the works of
fome eminent writers in that age. Nor
have fome later attempts of that kind been
able to reconcile it to an Englifh ear. And
indeed our language is not fuited to all the
varieties in this refpect, which the Latin
tongue admits of from the different terminations of the declinable words. I will illuftrate this by one plain inftance. In Latin
thefe three forms of expreffion, *Ariftoteles
docuit rhetoricam*, and, *Rhetoricam docuit Ariftoteles*, and, *Docuit Ariftoteles rhetoricam*,
have all one fenfe; the fame, as when I
fay in Englifh, *Ariftotle taught rhetoric*.
But with us, if the words are placed in
the

the fecond form, *Rhetoric taught Ariftotle*;
the fenfe is abfurd. And in the laft, *Taught
Ariftotle rhetoric*, they make only an imperfect fentence without a fubject. But
now in the Latin, the word *Ariftoteles* being
limited to the fubject, and *rhetoricam* to
the predicate, by their terminations, the
fenfe remains the fame, in whatever order
the words are placed. So great is the advantage of a language to be thus formed.

UPON the whole therefore; in Englifh
the nearer we keep to the natural or grammatical order, it is generally beft; but in
Latin we are to follow the ufe of the beft
writers; a joint regard being always had
to the judgement of the ear, and perfpicuity of the fenfe, in both languages.

L E C-

LECTURE XXIV.

Of Juncture and Number.

QUINTILIAN speaking of compo- LECT.
sition, represents a discourse, as very XXIV.
happy in that respect, when the *Order,*
Juncture, and *Number,* are all just and
proper [1]. The first of these, which gives [1] *Inst. orat.*
rules for the due placing of the words, and *Lib.* ix.
members of a sentence, I made the subject *c.* 4.
of my last lecture. The other two relate
to letters and syllables, the former treating
of their connection, and the latter of their
quantity. I propose therefore to give some
account of both these in my present discourse, and shall begin with *Juncture.*

BUT before I enter upon this, it will
be proper to take notice of some conditions,
which are necessary to render the sounds of
words and syllables agreable in their pronunciation; as likewise of the force and
power of the different sorts of letters, which
compose them.

AND with regard to sounds, it is requisite in the first place, they should be moderate; that is, soft, and yet clear and
distinct. For harsh and rough sounds grate

upon

upon the ears, and by that means give
them offence; and if they are too low or
confufed, they difpleafe, by not being fully
and clearly perceived. And the cafe is the
fame with refpect to the other fenfes,
which feel the moft agreable fenfations
from fuch things, as act upon them with
moderation. Sweet things are foft to the
tongue, and fo create a pleafure; whereas
four things give pain, by being too pungent; and thofe things, whofe parts are
too blunt to excite a fenfation, are therefore infipid. So likewife moderate light is
moft agreable to the eyes; and that which
is either too ftrong, or too feeble, is offenfive. And the like may be faid of the reft
of the fenfes. Again, founds muft have a
certain equality and proportion, to render
them agreable. Unequal founds, that ftrike
the organ ftrongly or weakly, fwiftly or
flowly, by frequent and fudden changes
from one to the other, without a due proportion, can never be grateful. Laftly, a
variety is requifite, in conjunction with
their proportion or fymmetry. This is a
neceffary ingredient of pleafure, for fimilitude and a conftant return of the fame
thing foon cloys. And it is this conjunction
of a proportionate equality with variety,
which

which conſtitutes all harmony. Theſe conditions are indeed neceſſary in ſounds of
all kinds, to render them pleaſant and delightful. But my buſineſs is to conſider
them only, as they relate to diſcourſe.
There is a natural ſympathy between the
ears of the hearer, and the voice of the
ſpeaker; inſomuch that whatever is difficult to pronounce, is painful to hear. We
find this very evidently in thoſe, who have
an impediment or heſitation in their ſpeech.
When they attempt to ſpeak, it gives an
uneaſineſs to thoſe about them. From
whence it is plain, that no diſcourſe can
be attended to with pleaſure, which is not
ſo compoſed, as to be ſpoken with eaſe.

As to the letters, ſome have a ſmoother,
and others a harſher ſound. All the vowels
have a ſofter pronunciation, than the conſonants; for which reaſon it is neceſſary
in the formation of words, that the roughneſs of the latter ſhould be duly attem-
pered with a juſt proportion of the former.
But tho all the vowels are ſofter than the
conſonants, yet they differ conſiderably from
each other in that reſpect. *A, o,* and *u,*
have generally a much ſtronger and broader
ſound, than *e,* and *i.* As to the conſonants, thoſe are hardeſt, which end with

VOL. I.   B b   the

the found of the vowel, and are therefore called mutes, as *b, c, d, g, k, p, q,* and *t*; of which *c, k,* and *q,* may be confidered as the fame letter. The other fingle confonants, which begin with the found of the vowel, being fofter, are for that reafon called half vowels, as *f, h, l, m, n, r,* and *s*. *X* and *z* are double confonants, the former of which has the force of *cs,* and the latter of *ds.* And fome letters are both vowels and confonants in a different fituation, as *i, u, w,* and *y*. Befides, moft of the letters are very differently pronounced, and have a variety of founds, harder or fofter, fuller or fmaller, longer or fhorter, in different words. Now there are feveral organs of fpeech, whofe action is not only different, but fometimes contrary, in pronouncing the letters, and their various combinations, both in the forming of feparate words, and their connection in fentences. Thus the lips are drawn backward in pronouncing the three firft vowels, *a, e,* and *i*; and pufhed forward in the two laft, *o,* and *u*. *P,* and *b,* are called labials, becaufe they principally require the action of the lips, which are firft clofed, and then opened again, in their pronunciation. *C,* and *g,* are termed dentals, from the agency of
the

the teeth; and *t*, and *d*, linguals, from
that of the tongue; but they all four draw
back the lips, when they are pronounced.
Besides, *p*, *c*, and *t*, require less force of
the organ in sounding them; than *b*, *g*,
and *d*. Now it is the different mixture of
the letters and syllables in the make of
the words, suited to the action of the several organs of speech, that in a good measure renders the harmony of one language
greater than another. The English tongue
abounds with consonants, and therefore
cannot but seem harsh and ruged to those,
whose ears have been accustomed to softer
sounds. Indeed use makes this less ob-
servable to us, unless when we compare
it with other languages, which are smoother
(as those are in the more southern climates)
and then we soon perceive the difference.
Tho of late years, it must be owned, that
our tongue has in this respect, as well as
others, been very much improved and po-
lished by persons of the finest taste, and
most exact judgement. But in order to
render the sound of words more smooth
and easy, it has been customary in all
languages to take out, and put in letters,
or to substitute one in the place of another. And the more any language has

been

been cultivated, the more commonly has this been practised. And therefore, as the Greeks seem to have been most careful to improve and perfect their language, they have taken the greatest liberties in this respect. They often put one vowel for another, or unite them into diphthongs ; and in like manner, with regard to the consonants, they frequently change, insert, or remove them. And this they do both in the inflexion of their simple words, and the formation of such as are compounded. By which means they not only increase the variety of sounds in the pronunciation of their words, but likewise promote their harmony. Examples of all these things might easily be given from their writers, were they suitable to an English discourse. The Latins copied after them in some measure, but not to the same degree, nor will their language admit of it. But it is doubtless from a regard to the sound, which makes them say *abstineo* for *ab-tineo*, and *prodes* for *proes*, by inserting a letter ; and by droping one to say *coheres* for *conheres* ; as also to alter *abfero* into *aufero*, *adlego* to *allego* ; with many other instances of the like nature. We take the same method likewise in some cases. As when

when we say *mirrour* for *mirour* to strengthen
the found, *can't* for *cannot* to eafe it, and
knives for *knifes* to foften it. And the
French do this more than we. But this
is not properly the fubject, I now propofe
to treat on ; tho it may help to illuftrate,
and fhew the ufe of it. For an orator
muft take the words of a language, as he
finds them ; tho he may place them in
fuch a manner, as will render the pronunciation moft eafy and pleafant, and beft
promote the harmony of the fentence ;
which, fo far as it relates to letters and
fyllables, is what rhetoricians call *Juncture*.

Now the method of doing this confifts
in three things ; a due attendance to the
nature of the vowels, confonants, and fyllables in the connexion of words, with regard to the found : each of which I fhall
confider diftinctly.

As to the firft, when a word ends with
a vowel, and the next begins either with
a different vowel, or the fame repeated, it
ufually renders the pronunciation hollow
and unpleafant. For, as Quintilian has
juftly obferved : *This makes a chafm in the
fentence, and ftops the courfe of it* [1]. For [1] *Inft. orat.*
there muft be fome paufe, in order to *Lib.* ix.
c. 4.

B b 3 pro-

pronounce them both, or otherwife the found of one will be loft. So, for inftance, in pronouncing thefe words, *the other day,* unlefs you ftop a little after the word *the,* the found of *e* will not be heard. And if it is dropt, it will occafion a rougher found, from the afpiration of *th* twice repeated fo near together, as *th' other day.* Therefore to prevent both thefe inconveniences, we ufually fay, *t'other day.* But the different confonants, which together with the vowels make up thofe fyllables, often caufe a confiderable difference in the pronunciation, fo as to render it more or lefs agreable. As, if I fay, *he over did it,* the words *he over* have not fo harfh a found, as *the other;* tho ftill they require fome paufe to keep them diftinct. Befides fome vowels meet more amicably, and admit of a fofter pronunciation, than others. Thofe which have the weakeft and fmalleft found, follow beft; becaufe they occafion the leaft alteration of the organ in forming the two founds. Such are *e* and *i;* and therefore without any chafm in the found, or hefitation of the voice, we fay, *he is.* But where the action of the organ is greater, and the found ftronger, the pronunciation is more difficult: as when we fay, *tho all.*

For

For here is a contrary motion of the lips,
which are firſt put forward in ſounding
the *o*, and then drawn backward to pronounce the *a*; and therefore the ſound is
much ſofter to ſay, *tho every*, where their
action is leſs. And the like ill effect commonly happens from the repetition of the
ſame vowel: as if I ſay, *go on*, or, *you uſually act thus*. There is a conſiderable difference between theſe two expreſſions, in
repeating the ſound of the vowel, and
where either of them is doubled in a ſingle
word. For then the ſame ſound only is
protracted by one continued motion of the
organ; as in the words *good*, and *deem*.
But here the ſound is repeated again by
a new action of the organ, which, if precipitated, obſcures the ſound of one of the
vowels, and, if too much retarded, makes
a chaſm in the pronunciation; either of
which is unpleaſant to the ear.

BUT as the coalition of two vowels occaſions an hollow and obſcure ſound, ſo
the meeting of ſome conſonants renders it
very harſh and rough. Thus the words
king Xerxes, and *public good*, when ſo
placed, have not only a roughneſs, but
likewiſe a difficulty in their pronunciation,
from the contrary action of the lips; which

in

in the former are first drawn back and then forward, but in the latter the contrary way, and in both of them with some confiderable force. But this may very eafily be avoided, by faying, with a little alteration in the words, *Xerxes the king*, and *the good of the public*. So likewife the words *ill company* have a fofter found, than *bad company*, for the fame reafon. To multiply inftances of this kind feems unneceffary, which fo frequently occur in all difcourfe.

THE repetition of the fame fyllable, at the end and begining of words, is the laft thing to be confidered. And a little obfervation will convince us, that where this happens, it generally renders the found either confufed, or unpleafant. Cicero was often rallied on account of this verfe :

ᵡ Quint.
Inft. orat.
Lib. ix.
c. 4.

O fortunatam natam me confule Romam ᵡ.
Every one will eafily perceive a difagreeable found in the following expreffion : *A man many times does that unadvifedly, of which he afterwards repents.* The chime of the words *man many* both feems affected, and difpleafes the ear. But this will foon be remedied, if we feparate thofe two words, and fay, *A man does that many times unadvifedly*.

FROM

FROM the short account here given of this part of compofition it is eafy to perceive, what things are neceffary to render it moft complete and accurate; which are thefe following. If a word end with a vowel, the next ought to begin with a confonant; or fuch a vowel, whofe found may agree well with the former. But if a word conclude with a confonant, either a vowel fhould follow; or fuch a confonant, whofe pronunciation will fuit with it. And laftly, the fame fyllable ought not to be repeated at the end of one word, and the begining of the next. It has been obferved by fome critics, that the following verfe at the begining of Virgil's *Eneid*, has all thefe properties.

Arma virumque cano, Trojae qui primus
  ab oris.

Where any word in this verfe ends with a vowel, the next begins with a confonant; and where any one ends with a confonant, the next begins with a vowel; and there is no repetition of the fame found throughout the whole. But this is what rarely happens, efpecially in our language, which abounds with confonants. And what Quintilian fais of the coalition of vowels, in treating upon this fubject, feems applicable
cable

cable to the whole. *This, fais he, is a thing not much to be dreaded, and I know not whether the neglect of it, or too great a concern about it, be worse. It neceſſarily checks the vigor of the mind, and diverts it from matters of greater importance. And therefore, as it ſhews negligence to permit it; ſo to be in conſtant fear of it diſcovers a low genius* [1]. This was the opinion of that judicious writer. And as theſe things cannot always be attended to, it may be ſufficient to avoid them, where they prove very offenſive to the ear, and it may be done without ſome greater inconvenience. So in this ſentence, *Honeſty is the beſt policy*, the coalition of *t* and *p* in the two laſt words *beſt policy* produce a roughneſs in their pronunciation; but as the expreſſion is ſtrong, and cannot perhaps be well altered for the better, the ſound here ought to give way to the ſenſe.

[1] *Inſt. orat.
Lib.* ix.
c. 4.

I come now to the fourth and laſt part of *Compoſition*, which is called *Number*. And this reſpects the quantity of ſyllables, as *Juncture* does their quality. In the Greek and Roman languages every ſyllable has its diſtinct quantity; and is either long, ſhort, or common: two or more of which joined together in a certain order

make

make a foot; and a determinate number
of thefe in a different order conftitute their
feveral forts of metre. This variety of
founds gives a much greater harmony to
their poetry; than what can arife only
from the feat of the accent, and the fimilitude of found at the end of two verfes,
which cheifly regulate our metre. And
altho their profe was not fo confined with
regard to the feet, either as to the kind or
place of them, as their metrical compofitions; yet it had a fort of meafure, more
efpecially in the rife and cadency of their
periods. This they call *rhetorical number*.
And accordingly the antient writers upon
this art acquaint us, what feet are beft
fuited to the begining, middle, or conclufion of a fentence. Such rules are not applicable to our language, which has not
that accurate diftinction of quantity in its
fyllables. For we are apt to confound accent with quantity, and pronounce thofe
fyllables longeft, on which we lay the accent, tho in their nature they are not fo.
As in the word *ádmirable*, where none but
the firft fyllable *ad* is pronounced long;
tho that is only rendered fo by pofition,
and the two following are fo by nature.
And again, in the word *ávarice*, we found
the

LECT.
XXIV. the firſt *a* long for the ſame reaſon, and the
ſecond ſhort; contrary to the nature of
both thoſe vowels. However I ſhall offer
a few things, that may be of ſome uſe to
modulate our periods, and adjuſt their cadency.

A GREAT number of monoſyllables do
not ſtand well together. For as there ought
to be a greater diſtance in the pronunciation between one word and another, than
between the ſyllables of the ſame word;
ſuch pauſes, tho ſhort, yet when too frequent, make the ſound rough and uneven,
and by that means ſpoil its harmony. And
this may ſeem more neceſſary to be attended to, becauſe the Engliſh language
abounds ſo much with monoſyllables. On
the contrary, a continuation of many long
words makes a ſentence move too ſlow
and heavily. And therefore ſuch periods
generally run beſt, which have a proper
mixture of words of a different length. Beſides, as every word has its accent, which
with us ſtands for quantity; a number either of monoſyllables, or long words, coming together ſo far abates the harmony,
as it leſſens the variety.

AGAIN, ſeveral words of the ſame ending
do not ſtand well together, eſpecially where
the

the accent falls upon the same syllable in
each of them. For this creates too great
a jingle by the similitude of sound; and is
apt to displease, from an appearance of affectation. Of this kind is the following
sentence: *Nothing is more wélcome, delight-*
some, or whólesome, than rest to a wearied
man. In such expressions therefore, if the
order of the words cannot well be altered;
some other word should be substituted in
the room of one of them at least, to diver-
sify the sound. So in the example here
given, the sound might be varied by saying:
Nothing is more wélcome, pleásant, or whóle-
some.

BUT to add no more, if a sentence end
with a monosyllable, it is apt to hurt the
cadency, and disappoint the ear; whereas
words of a moderate length carry a greater
force with them, by the fulness of their
sound, and afford the ear what it expected.
And there is one sort of monosyllables
more especially, which never stands well at
the conclusion of a period, tho we frequently find it there; and that is the signs
of cases. Thus we say: *Avarice is a crime,*
which wise men are too often guilty óf. But
the cadency would doubtless be more agreable, if it was altered thus: *Avarice is a*
crime,

crime, of which wife men are too often guilty.
Every one muſt perceive, when the accent
falls upon the laſt ſyllable in the ſentence,
as it does, if it end with *of*, the ſound is
not ſo pleaſant, as when it reſts upon the
preceding ſyllable in the word *guilty*. Nor
are very long words well ſuited, either to
the begining or concluſion of a period; for
they retard the pronunciation at firſt, and
fall too heavy at the end.

THESE obſervations may ſuffice for our
conduct, in what relates to number, ſo far
as it agrees with the genius of our language. But this, and all the parts of compoſition, ſhould be ſo managed, as may beſt
ſuit the nature of the ſubject, and deſign
of the ſpeaker. Long and full periods, a
juſt order, ſmooth connection, and flowing
numbers, are not always requiſite. Nay
ſometimes the neglect of accuracy is itſelf a
beauty. And even harſh and rough ſounds,
when moſt expreſſive of thoſe ideas, they
are deſigned to convey, ought to be choſen.
But of theſe things I ſhall have occaſion to
ſpeak more largely hereafter, in their proper
place.

L E C-

LECTURE XXV.

Of Dignity, and particularly of Tropes.

HAVING finished the two first parts LECT.
of *Elocution*, I now procede to the XXV.
third and laſt part, which is called *Dignity*,
and conſiſts in the right uſe of *Tropes* and
Figures. It is not ſufficient for an orator
to expreſs himſelf with propriety and clearneſs, or in ſmooth and harmonious periods;
but his language muſt likewiſe be ſuited
to the nature and importance of the ſubject. And therefore as *Elegance* gives rules
for the firſt of theſe, and *Compoſition* for
the ſecond; ſo does *Dignity* for the laſt of
them. It is very evident, that different
ſubjects require a different ſtile and manner of expreſſion; ſince, as Quintilian ſais,
*What is magnificent in one diſcourſe, would
be turgid in another; and thoſe expreſſions,
which appear low upon a ſublime ſubject,
would ſuit leſſer matters; and as in a florid
harangue a mean word is remarkable, and
like a blemiſh, ſo any thing lofty and bright
upon a trivial argument is diſproportionate,
and like a tumour upon an even ſurface* [1]. [1] *Inſt. orat.*
Now this variety in the manner of ex- *Lib.* viii.
c. 3.

p700reſſion

preſſion ariſes in a great meaſure from *Tropes* and *Figures*, which not only inliven and beautify a diſcourſe, but give it likewiſe force and grandeur; for which reaſon this part of elocution ſeems to have been called *Dignity*.

Tropes and *Figures* are diſtinguiſhed from each other in ſeveral reſpects. *Tropes* moſtly affect ſingle words, but *Figures* whole ſentences. A *Trope* conveys two ideas to the mind by means of one word, but a *Figure* throws the ſentence into a different form from the common, and uſual manner of expreſſion. Beſides, *Tropes* are cheifly deſigned to repreſent our thoughts, but *Figures* our paſſions. In treating upon this ſubject, I ſhall begin with *Tropes*. And that I may procede in the moſt regular and eaſy method, I ſhall firſt conſider the nature of *Tropes* in general, with the ſeveral kinds or ſpecies of them; then aſſign the reaſons, which have occaſioned their uſe; and laſtly, lay down ſome directions, proper to be obſerved in the choice of them.

A trope then, as it has been uſually defined, is, *the change of a word from its proper ſignification to ſome other with advantage* [1]. The words *with advantage* are added

[1] Quint. *Inſt. orat. Lib.* viii. *c.* 5.

added in the definition, becaufe a *Trope* ought not to be chofen; unlefs there is fome good reafon for ufing it rather than the proper word. But in what manner, or how far, it can be faid of all *Tropes* in general, that they change the proper fignification of words, will beft appear by confidering the nature of each kind of them feparately. Now in every *Trope* a reference is had to two things, which occafions two ideas, one of the thing expreffed, and another of that thing, to which it has a refpect, and is fupplied by the mind. For all *Tropes* are taken either from things internally related, as the whole and a part; or externally, as caufe and effect, fubject and adjunct; or from fome fimilitude, that is found between them; or from a contrariety. The firft of thefe is called *Synecdoche*, the fecond *Metonymy*, the third *Metaphor*, and the laft *Irony*. I will endeavour to illuftrate this by examples. When I fay, *Hannibal beat the Romans*, the meaning is, that Hannibal and his army did this. So that altho in fome fenfe a part may here be faid to ftand for the whole, which makes it a *Synecdoche*; yet ftrictly fpeaking the word *Hannibal* does not alter its fenfe, but there is an ellipfis in the expreffion, Hannibal being put for himfelf and his army. But if I fay, *Cicero fhould be read by all lovers of eloquence*, here indeed the word *Cicero* appears to be changed from its proper fenfe, and to fignify the books of Cicero, which is a *Metonymy*, the author being put for his works ; and therefore fuch expreffions need not be deemed elliptical. Again, if any one fpeaking of a fubtle and crafty man, fhould fay, *He is a fox*, the meaning is, he is like a fox, which is a *Metaphor*, where the word *fox* retains its proper fenfe, and denotes that animal, to which the man is compared on account of his craft. Laftly, if a perfon fay to another, *Well done*, meaning that the thing was ill done, the word *well* keeps its own fenfe, but from the manner of its pronunciation, or fome other circumftance attending the expreffion, it will be evident, that the contrary is intended, which is called an *Irony*. From thefe inftances it may appear, in what latitude we muft underftand the common definition of a *Trope*, which makes it to confift in the change of a word from its proper fenfe into fome other. But tho in reality there are but four kinds of *Tropes*, which are diftinguifhed by fo many different refpects, which things bear

bear one to another; yet as thefe feveral refpects are found in a variety of fubjects, and attended with different circumftances, the names of *Tropes* have from hence been greatly multiplied; which however may all be refered to fome or other of thofe already mentioned, as will be fhewn, when I come to treat of them in their order. And for diftinction fake I fhall call the former *primary* and the latter *fecondary* *Tropes.*

I NOW procede to confider the reafons, which have occafioned the introduction of *Tropes.* And thefe, as Quintilian obferves, are three; *Neceffity*, *Emphafis*, and *Beauty.*

TROPES were firft introduced from *Neceffity*, becaufe no language contains a fufficient number of proper words, to exprefs all the different conceptions of our minds. The mind confiders the fame thing various ways, views it in different lights, compares it with other things, and obferves their feveral relations and affections, wherein they agree, and in what they differ. From all which reflections it is furnifhed with almoft an infinite number of ideas; which cannot all of them be diftinguifhed and expreffed by proper words, fince new ones occur daily. And were this poffible, yet would it be

C c 2 im-

impracticable ; becaufe the multitude of
words muſt be fo vaſtly great, that the memory could not retain them, and be able
to recall them as occaſion required. *Tropes*
have in a good meaſure redreſſed both theſe
inconveniences ; for by means of them the
mind is not burdened with a numberleſs
ſtock of different words, and yet nothing
ſeems to want a name. Thus ſometimes,
where a word is wanting to expreſs any
particular thing, it is clearly enough repreſented by the name of ſome other thing,
by reaſon of the ſimilitude between them.
At other times the cauſe is ſignified by the
effect, the ſubject by the adjunct ; or the
contrary. And the whole is often underſtood by a part, or a part by the whole.
And thus by the uſe of *Tropes* the mind is
helped to conceive of ſomething not expreſſed, from that which is expreſſed. It is
much the ſame caſe, as when we have occaſion to ſpeak of a perſon, whoſe name
we are either unacquainted with, or have
forgot ; for by deſcribing his perſon, abode,
or ſome other circumſtances relating to
him, thoſe we converſe with as well underſtand whom we mean, as if we mentioned his name. So the ſhepherd in Virgil, when he could not think of the name
                                          of

of Archimedes, defcribes him by his
works :

> *And what's his name, who form'd the*
> *fphere,*
> *And fhew'd the feafons of the fliding year* [1]?

[1] *Ed.* iii. *v.* 40.

Befides, it fometimes happens in a difcourfe, that thofe things are neceffary to be faid, which, if expreffed in their proper terms, would be offenfive; but being clothed with metaphors, may be conveyed to the mind with decency.

A SECOND reafon above mentioned for the ufe of *Tropes* was, *Emphafis.* *Tropes* do many times exprefs things with greater force and evidence, than can be done by proper words. We receive much the greateft part of our knowledge by our fenfes. And fimilitudes taken from fenfible things, as in metaphors, very much affift the mind in its reflections upon thofe things, which do not come under the cognizance of the fenfes. For it is certain, that we are fooner, and more ftrongly affected with fenfible objects; than with fuch things, of which we can have no ideas but from the internal operations of our own minds. Nay fometimes one bright and lively *Trope* fhall convey a fuller, and more juft idea of a thing, than a large periphrafis. So when

C c 3

Virgil

Virgil calls the Scipios, *two thunderbolts of war* [1], he gives us a more lively image of the rapid force, and fpeedy fuccefs of their arms, than could have been conveyed by a long defcription in plain words. And in many cafes the tropical ufe of words is fo emphatical, and fuited to the idea we defign to excite; that in this refpect it may be juftly efteemed the moft proper. So, *incenfed with anger, inflamed with defire, fallen into an error,* are all metaphorical expreffions, ufed in a way of fimilitude; and yet perhaps no proper words can be made ufe of, which will convey a more lively image of the thing, we defign to reprefent by them.

BUT *Beauty* and ornament, as was obferved before, has been another caufe of the ufe of *Tropes.* Some fubjects require a more florid and elegant drefs, than others. When we defcribe or applaud, ornaments of fpeech, and a gaiety of expreffion, are requifite. And it is the bufinefs of an orator to entertain his hearers, at the fame time that he inftructs them. Now Cicero, who was an admirable judge of the force and power of eloquence, has obferved, that tropical expreffions give the mind the greateft delight and entertainment. *I have often wondered,*

wondered, fais he, *why tropes fhould give greater pleafure, than proper words.* I ima-gine the reafon muft be, either that there is an appearance of wit in neglecting what is at hand, and making choice of fomething at a diftance; or that the hearer is furnifhed with a different thought, without being led into a miftake, which affords a very agreable plea-fure; or that a whole fimilitude is conveyed to the mind by a fingle word; or that parti-cularly in the beft and moft lively metaphor, the image is prefented to our fight, which is the quickeft of our fenfes [1]. And therefore he fuppofes, that, *as garments were firft in-vented from neceffity, to fecure us from the injuries of the weather; but improved after-wards for ornament and diftinction; fo the poverty of language firft introduced tropes, which were afterwards increafed for delight* [2].

[1] *De orat. Lib.* iii. *c.* 39.

[2] *Ibid. c.* 38.

Befides, a variety of expreffion is pleafing in a difcourfe. It is many times neceffary, that the fame things fhould be repeated. And if this be done in the fame words, it will grow tirefome to the hearers, and fink their efteem of the fpeaker's ability. There-fore to prevent this, it is proper the ex-preffion fhould be varied, that altho the fenfe be the fame, it may give the mind a new pleafure by its different drefs.

I

I come now in the laſt place to lay down ſome directions, proper to be obſerved in the choice of *Tropes*.

And firſt, as every *Trope* gives us two ideas, one of the word expreſſed, and another, which by means of that the mind connects with it; it is neceſſary, that the relation between theſe two appear very plain and evident. For an obſcure *Trope* is always faulty, unleſs where ſome particular reaſon makes it neceſſary. And therefore *Tropes* ought not to be too far fetched, left that ſhould render them dark. For which reaſon Cicero ſais, he ſhould not chooſe to call any thing deſtructive to a perſon's fortune, *the Syrtis of his patrimony, but rather the rock of it*; nor, *the Charybdis of his eſtate, but the gulph of it* [1]. For thoſe, who either did not know, that the Syrtes were two quickſands upon the coaſt of Africa, or that Charybdis was a gulph in the ſtreight of Sicily, both of them very deſtructive to mariners, would be at a loſs to underſtand the meaning of the metaphor. Beſides, metaphors taken from things we have ſeen, affect the mind more forceably; than thoſe, which are taken from ſuch things, of which we have only heard. Now there is ſcarce any one, who has not
ſeen

[1] *Ibid. c.* 41.

seen a rock, or a gulph ; but there are very few perfons comparatively, who have been either at Charybdis, or the Syrtes. It is neceffary therefore in a good *Trope*, not only that there be a near affinity between the two ideas, but likewife, that this affinity be very obvious, and generally known ; fo that the word be no fooner pronounced, but both images do immediately prefent themfelves to the mind.

AGAIN, as a *Trope* ought to be very plain and evident, fo likewife fhould it bear a due proportion to the thing it is defigned to reprefent, fo as neither to highten, nor diminifh the juft idea of it. Indeed fome-times, when we fpeak of things indefinitely, we fay too much, left we fhould feem to fay too little. And this manner of fpea-king is called an *Hyperbole*, which is not uncommon in the facred writings. So, for inftance, *Saul* and *Jonathan* are faid to be, *fwifter than eagles, and ftronger than lions* [1]. But even in this way of expreffion a pro-portion is to be obferved. For fome very confiderable, and unufual excefs of the thing in its kind is at leaft defigned by it; which perhaps cannot, or however is not neceffary to be defined. And therefore Quintilian blames Cato for calling the top of an hill

[1] 2 *Sam.* i. 23.

a

*¹ Inſt. orat.
Lib.* viii.
c. 3.
*& Gell.
Lib.* iii.
c. 8.
*² De rhe-
tor. Lib.* iii.
c. 2. §. 3

a *wart* ¹. Becauſe the proportion between the two ideas is no ways adequate. And ſo on the contrary, Ariſtotle cenſures Euripides for calling *rowing, the empire of the oar* ². Poets indeed are allowed a greater liberty in this reſpect. But an orator ſhould be modeſt in his expreſſions, and take care, that he neither ſo highten, nor diminiſh the natural ideas of things by *Tropes,* as to lead his hearers into miſtakes.

BUT further, as a moderate uſe of *Tropes,* juſtly applied, beautifies and inlivens a diſcourſe ; ſo an exceſs of them cauſes obſcurity, by runing it into abſtruſe allegories and riddles. *Tropes* are not the common and ordinary dreſs of our thoughts, but a foreign habit. And therefore he, who fills his diſcourſe with a continued ſeries of them, ſeems to act like one, who appears in public in a ſtrange dreſs ; which no man of character would chooſe to do.

MOREOVER, as one uſe of *Tropes* is pleaſure and entertainment, we ſhould endeavour to make choice of ſuch, as are ſmooth and eaſy. But if at any time we think it neceſſary to uſe a harſh *Trope,* it is proper to ſoften it by ſome precaution. For, as Cicero very handſomly ſais : *A trope ſhould be modeſt, ſince it ſtands in a place, which does*

does not belong to it : for which reason it should seem to come thither by permission, and not by force. And therefore, when he thought it harsh to say, *The death of Cato made the senate an orphan,* he guards the expression by saying, *The death of Cato has (if I may be allowed to say so) rendered the senate an orphan* [1].

AND to add no more, care should be taken how we transfer *Tropes* from one language into another. For as they are frequently taken not only from natural things, or such notions, as are common to the generality of mankind, but likewise from the manners, customs, and occurrences of particular nations; so they may be very plain and obvious to those, among whom they took their rise, but altogether unintelligible to others, who are unacquainted with the reason of them. It was customary for the Roman soldiers to carry their money in their girdles; hence it was the same thing with them to say, *a person had lost his girdle* [2], as that, *he had lost his money.* And because the Romans wore the *toga,* which was a long gown, in time of peace, and a different garb, when ingaged in war, their writers sometimes use the word *toga* to signify peace. But as neither

of

[1] *De orat. Lib.* iii. *c.* 41.

[2] Hor. *Lib.* ii. *ep.* 2.

of thefe cuftoms is in ufe among us, fo
neither would the *Tropes* fuit our language,
or be generally underftood by us. And
even in fuch *Tropes*, as are taken from the
common nature of things, languages very
much differ. There is a very beautiful
Trope in the account of St. Paul's fhip-
wreck, where it is faid : *The ſhip was
caught, and could not bear up into the wind.*
The original word, that we tranflate *bear*
up, is ἀντοφθαλμᾶν [1], and properly fignifies,
to look, or keep its eyes againſt it; which is
a very ftrong and lively image, taken from
animate beings, and when applied to men
often fignifies, *to withſtand*, or *reſiſt*: as,
ἀντοφθαλμᾶν πολεμίῳ, *to reſiſt an enemy*:
and Plutarch fais of Demofthenes, that he
could not ἀντοφθαλμᾶν τῷ ἀργυρίῳ [2], *look*
againſt, or, *reſiſt the power of money.* Nothing is more common with Latin writers,
than to call men of a public fpirit, and
true patriots, *lumina et ornamenta reipubli-
cae*, that is, *the lights and ornaments of the
ſtate.* And we have borrowed from them
the ufe of both thefe metaphors. But becaufe *Tropes* and *Figures* illuftrate and
highten the ftile, they call them alfo, *lumina orationis*, or, *the lights of a diſcourſe*;
which I do not know that we have yet
adopted

[1] *Acts* xxvii. 15.
[2] *In vit.*

adopted into our language. It fometimes happens, that only the tropical fenfe of a word is taken from one language into another, and not the proper fignification of the fame word. So *fcrupulus* in Latin properly fignifies, *a little ftone, which getting into the fhoe, hurts a perfon as he walks*; hence it is applied to the mind, and ufed to exprefs, *a doubt, or uneafy thought, that gives it pain.* We have borrowed this latter fenfe of the word, but not the former.

I SHOULD now procede to treat more particularly on the feveral kinds of *Tropes*, but this will be the fubject of fome following difcourfes.

L E C-

LECTURE XXVI.

Of a Metaphor.

IN my laſt diſcourſe, I obſerved, that all *Tropes* may be reduced to four ſpecies, which are taken from the different reſpects, things bear one to another. For in every *Trope* a reference is had to two things; and where thoſe things have a natural and internal relation, as the whole and a part, it is called a *Synecdoche*; where the relation is external, as between the cauſe and effect, ſubject and adjunct, it is a *Metonymy*; where they have only ſome ſimilitude, as rational and brute animals, and their properties, it is a *Metaphor*; and where they are oppoſite to each other, as virtue and vice, it is called an *Irony*. And this ſeems to be the natural order of placing them, if regard be had to the riſe and foundation of them. But if we conſider their uſe and beauty in language, a *Metaphor* ought to ſtand firſt, a *Metonymy* next, then a *Synecdoche*, and an *Irony* laſt. And this is the uſual order, in which they are placed. Cicero, ſpeaking of a *Metaphor*, calls it, *the moſt florid manner of expreſſion, and brighteſt ornament of lan-*

language, that confifts in fingle words [1].
Wherefore both in compliance with cuftom, and by reafon of the juft preeminence
of this *Trope*, I fhall begin with it, and
make it the fubject of my prefent difcourfe.

[1] *De Orat.
Lib.* iii.
c. 41.

AND here I fhall endeavour firft to explain the nature of this *Trope*, then confider
the feveral kinds of it, and laftly, offer
fome confiderations relating to the choice
of *Metaphors*.

Now a *Metaphor*, as ufually defined, is:
*A trope, which changes words from their
proper fignification to another different from
it, by reafon of fome fimilitude between them* [2].
But that a word, when ufed metaphorically, does not alter its fignification, but
retains its proper fenfe, was fhewn in my
laft difcourfe. However, it may not be
amifs to explain this matter more fully, and
fet it in a clearer light. Every *Metaphor*
then is nothing elfe but a fhort fimilitude.
Cicero calls it, *a fimilitude reduced to a fingle
word* [3]. And Quintilian to the fame purpofe fais, that, *a metaphor is a fhort fimilitude, and differs from it only in this; that
the former is compared to the thing, we defign
to exprefs, and the latter is put for it. It is
a fimilitude, when I fay of a man, he has
acted like a lion ; and a metaphor, when I
fay,*

[2] Voff. *Inft.
orat. Lib.*
iv. *c.* 6.
§. 1.

[3] *De Orat.
Lib.* iii.
c. 39.

LECT.
XXVI.

say, he is a lion [1]. Thus far Quintilian.
Now in every fimilitude three things are
requifite, two things, that are compared together, and a third, in which the fimilitude
or likenefs between them confifts. And
therefore to keep to this example, when
Horace calls a Roman foldier *a lion* [2], if the
word *lion* did not retain its proper fenfe,
there could be no fimilitude; becaufe there
would not be two things to be compared
together with refpect to a third, which is
neceffary in every fimilitude, and was defigned by this expreffion. The fenfe of
which is plainly this : *That as a lion feizes
his prey with the greateft fiercenefs, fo a Roman foldier with like rage and fury attacked
his enemies.* In the fame manner, when Cicero calls Pifo, *the vulture of the province* [3],
his meaning is, *that he was like a vulture,*
or, *acted in fuch a manner, as a vulture acts,*
that is, *rapacioufly.* So that the real difference between a metaphor and a fimilitude
confifts in this ; that a metaphor has not
thofe figns of comparifon, which are expreffed in a fimilitude. But fome perfons
have run into miftakes in reafoning from
tropes of this kind. For they have fo argued from metaphorical words, as if all the
affections and properties of the things expreffed

[1] *Inft. orat. Lib.* viii. *c.* 6.

[2] *Carm.* iii. 2, 11.

[3] *In Pifon. c.* 16.

preffed by them, might be attributed to
thofe other things, to which they are applied, and by that means have ftrained the
comparifon (which has ufually but one particular view) in order to make it tally in
other refpects, where there is not that fimilitude of ideas. I will endeavour to make
this more evident by another example from
Cicero, where he calls M. Antony, *the torch
of the ftate* [1]. The fimilitude between Antony and a torch lay in this: *That as a
torch burns and deftroys every thing within
its reach; fo Antony brought devaftation and
ruin, wherever he came.* Now a torch has
not only a property to burn, but alfo to
give light; but the fimilitude would not
hold in this refpect, nor was it at all defigned. For Cicero never calls a wicked,
profligate man, as Antony was, *the light of
the ftate*; tho he often gives that character
to good and virtuous men [2], who by their
examples do, as it were, inlighten others,
and fhew them the way to be happy themfelves, and ufeful to others. But tho metaphors are ufually taken from a fimilitude
between two things, as in the inftances
here mentioned; yet fometimes they are
founded in the fimilitude, which two things
bear to two others in fome particular re-

[1] *Philipp.*
vii. *c.* 1.

[2] *Pro Sulla,*
c. 2.

D d   fpect,

LECT.
XXVI.
spect, by means whereof what properly belongs to one of them is transfered to the
other : the former of which are called simple metaphors, and the latter analogous.
Hence the rudder of a ship may be called
its reins ; for what the reins are to a horse,
that the rudder is to a ship, in guiding and
directing it. So that here is a double similitude, one between a ship and an horse,
and another between the rudder of the former, and reins of the latter ; and from the
analogy between the use of the rudder to
the one, and reins to the other, the reins,
which belong properly to the horse, are applied to the ship. Again, some metaphors
are reciprocal, in which the similitude holds
either way. Thus to steer and to govern
are used reciprocally both of a ship and a
state ; the proper expressions being, *to steer
a ship*, and *govern a state*, and the contrary
metaphorical. But tho we say, *the foot of
a mountain*, borrowing the similitude from
animals, yet we do not say on the contrary,
the bottom of an animal, meaning his feet,
and therefore that metaphor is not reciprocal. From this account therefore of the nature of a metaphor, it may be said to be :
*The application of a word by way of similitude
to some other thing, than what it properly signifies.*

nifies. And the plainer this fimilitude appears, the greater beauty there is in the
Trope.

THE ufe of metaphors is very extenfive,
as large as univerfal nature. For there are
fcarce any two things, which have not
fome fimilitude between them. However,
they may all be reduced to four kinds,
which was the fecond thing propofed to be
confidered.

THE firft kind of metaphors therefore
may be taken from fimilitudes between
animate beings. As where thofe things,
which properly relate to brutes, are accommodated to men; or thofe, which belong
to men, are applied to brutes. Of the former fort is that joke of Cicero: *My brother
being afked by Philip, why he barked fo: anfwered, becaufe he faw a theif*[1]. Here
barking, the property of a dog, is applied
to a man. And the reply does not feem
to carry more feverity, or harfhnefs with it,
than the queftion. By the latter fort we
fay, *a crafty fox,* and *a generous horfe,*
which are affections, that properly relate to
men. And to this kind of metaphors may
thofe likewife be refered, when that, which
properly belongs to the fenfes, is applied to
the mind. Thus we often fay, *that we fee*

[1] *De Orat.
Lib.* ii.
c. 54.

D d 2

a

a thing, when we mean, *that we underſtand*, or *apprehend it*. And in the ſame ſenſe we ſay, *that we hear ſuch a thing*, or *perſon*. And by the like manner of expreſſion, a perſon is ſaid, *to ſmell out a thing*. And thoſe, who have a genius or diſpoſition for any art or ſcience, are ſaid, *to have a taſte for it*. And ſuch, who have entered upon the ſtudy of it, are ſaid, *to have a touch of it*. Theſe are common ways of ſpeaking in moſt languages, and very expreſſive of what is intended by them. And we may alſo bring thoſe metaphors under this head, by which the properties and affections of men are attributed to the deity: as, when God is ſaid *to hear, ſee, be angry, repent*, and the like; which are forms of expreſſion very frequent in the ſacred writings.

A SECOND kind of metaphors lies between inanimate things, whether natural or artificial, which bear ſome ſimilitude to each other. And this head is very extenſive. Thus we ſay, *floods of fire*, and *clouds of ſmoke*, for large quantities. And ſo likewiſe, *to inflame an account*, that is, to highten or increaſe it; with innumerable others of the like ſort. In the two firſt of theſe inſtances, the terms proper to one element are applied to another; and as thoſe elements

ments

ments of fire and water are oppofite to each
other, they fhew the extenfivenefs of this
trope, that there are no things in nature fo
contrary, but may come within the limits
of it, and be accommodated to each other
in a way of fimilitude. In the laft example,
a natural action is applied to what is artificial.

A THIRD fort of metaphors is, when
inanimate things are applied to animals, on
the account of fome like properties between
them. Thus Homer calls Ajax, *the bul-
wark of the Greeks* [1], on account of his va-
lour, which like a wall defended them from
the Trojans. And nothing is more common with Cicero, than to brand ill men
with the character of being, *the peft of the
ftate* [2], by reafon of the mifcheif, which they
bring to the public. So likewife he calls
Zeno the philofopher, *an acute man* [3], for
his great difcernment, and quick perception
of things, fetching the allufion from metals,
when brought to an edge, or a point. As
on the contrary, old Chremes in Terence
calls himfelf a *ftone*, for want of apprehenfion [4]. And we fay, *a gay perfon*, and *a
bright genius*, by this kind of metaphor.

THE fourth and laft kind of metaphors
is that, by which the actions, and other at-

[1] *Iliad* γ. 229.

[2] *Pro Mi-lon. c.* 25, 33.

[3] *Ad fam. Lib.* ix. *ep.* 22.

[4] *Heaut. Act.* V. *Sc.* I. *v.* 43

D d 3   tributes

LECT. tributes of animals are accommodated to
XXVI. inanimate things.　Thus Cicero ſpeaking
of Clodius ſais : *The very altars, when they
ſaw that monſter fall, ſeemed to move them-*
ſelves, and aſſert their right againſt him [1].
Here the words, *ſaw, move,* and *aſſert,* are
all metaphors, taken from the properties of
animals.　And Virgil, when he would repreſent the impetuous force and rapidity of
the river Araxes, ſais, *it diſdained a bridge* [2].
And it is a very uſual epithet, which Homer gives to words, to call them πτεροέντα [3],
or *winged,* to intimate the ſwiftneſs of
ſpeech.

　　LASTLY, as to the choice of metaphors,
thoſe are eſteemed the fineſt and ſtrongeſt,
which *give life and action to inanimate
things* [4].　The reaſon of which is, becauſe
they do as it were invigorate all nature, introduce new forms of beings, and repreſent
their images to the ſight, which of all the
ſenſes is the quickeſt, moſt active, and yet
moſt unwearied.　What can be more moving, or in ſtronger terms expreſs the villainy of Clodius, than when Cicero ſais :
*The very altars of the gods ſeemed to exult at
his death* [5].　And the ſame great orator
particularly commends thoſe metaphors, for
their ſprightlineſs and vivacity, which are
　　　　　　　　　　　　　　　　　　taken

[1] *Pro Mi-
lon. c.* 31.

[2] *Aen.
Lib.* viii.
v. 728.

[3] *Iliad.* α.
201.

[4] Quint.
*Inſt. orat.
Lib.* viii.
c. 6.

[5] *Pro Mi-
lon. c.* 31.

taken from the fenfe of feeing [1], as when we
fay, *a bright thought*, or, *a gay expreffion*.

However, care muſt be taken not to
venture upon too bold and daring metaphors. Poets indeed claim greater liberty
in this reſpeſt, whoſe view is often to amuſe,
terrify, or delight, by hightening the juſt
and natural images of things. But it is
expeſted the orator ſhould reaſon coolly,
tho ſtrongly and forceably; and not by
theatrical repreſentations ſo tranſport the
mind, as to take it off from refleſtion, unleſs perhaps on ſome particular occaſion.
And yet on the other hand, metaphors
ought not to ſink below the dignity of
what they are deſigned to expreſs; but the
idea they convey ſhould at leaſt be equal
to the proper word, in the place of which
they are ſubſtituted.

But there is a very great difference in
the choice of metaphors, as they are deſigned either to praiſe, or diſpraiſe. One
thing may be compared to another in a
great variety of reſpeſts. And the ſame
thing may be made to appear either noble
or baſe, virtuous or vicious, by conſidering
it in a different light. Such metaphors
therefore, as are choſen to commend, muſt
be taken from great and laudable things;

　　　　　　and

and on the contrary, thofe which are defigned to difcommend, from things vile and
contemptible. Ariftotle gives us a very
pleafant example of this in the poet Simonides. A certain perfon, who had carried
the prize at a race of mules, offered him a
reward to write a poem in honor of that
action. Simonides thought he did not bid
high enough, and therefore put him off
with faying, the fubject was too mean to
write in praife of mules, which were the
offspring of affes. But upon his being offered a larger fum he undertook the tafk,
and, as Ariftotle obferves, when he has occafion to fpeak of the mules in that poem,
he does not mention them by that name ;
but calls them, *the daughters of fleet and
generous horfes*; tho he might with as much
propriety have called them, *the daughters of*
De rhe-
*tor.Lib.*iii.
c. 2.
dull affes [1]. But it was the poet's bufinefs
in praifing to take the moft advantageous
part of the character. Where things are
capable of fuch different turns, metaphorical expreffions are generally moft beautiful.
And fometimes the fame metaphor may be
applied contrary ways, both in praife and
difpraife, as it will fuit different properties
of the thing, to which it refers. So a dove
in a metaphorical fenfe may reprefent, either

in-

innocence, or fear; and an iron heart may
denote, either courage, or cruelty, as an hard
head ſtrength, or weakneſs of thought. And
this ambiguity, in the application of metaphorical words, often affords occaſion for
jeſts, and conciſe wit. I obſerved before
that Cicero never calls ill men, *lights of
the ſtate.* But he once in this manner calls
Sextius Clodius, *the light of the ſenate* [1]. [1] *Pro Milon. c.* 12.
For, when his kinſman Publius Clodius had
been killed by Milo, and his corps was
brought to Rome, Sextius raiſed the mob,
and in a tumultuous manner carried it into
the ſenate houſe, where they burnt it, and
by that means ſet the building on fire. For
which ſeditious action Cicero paſſes that
joke upon him, under the metaphor of
light, which elſewhere he always uſes in a
good ſenſe.

BUT to procede, all forced and harſh
metaphors ſhould be avoided, the one being
no leſs diſagreable to the mind, than the
other to the ear. Nor ſhould they come
too thick in a diſcourſe. In a word, they
ought not to be uſed, but either where a
proper word is wanting, or they are more
ſignificant, or beautiful than the proper
word. But altho theſe cautions do more
eſpecially relate to metaphors, yet they are
alſo

LECT. XXVI. also to be attended to in some other tropes; for which reason I treated of them more largely in my last discourse.

GIVE me leave only to add, that from what has been hitherto discoursed concerning the nature, and properties of metaphors, it is very evident, that the Cynics, and such of the Stoics, who fell in with them, were guilty of a mistake in asserting, that there is no turpitude, or immodesty in words. The argument they went upon in defending their notion was this. If two words signify the same thing, they are both immodest, or neither of them. Not both, because there is nothing, which cannot some way or other be modestly expressed. Consequently, if one of the words be modest, the other must be so also: because they have both the same sense [1]. But this way of reasoning is false and sophistical. For a word is either modest or immodest, according to the different manner, in which it affects the mind, and the emotions it excites, when pronounced. But it is plain, that of the several words made use of to express the same thing, some may be heard without the least offence to the chastest ear, and others not without offering violence to the modesty of the auditors. And this difference

[1] See Cic. *Off.* *Lib.* i. *c.* 35. *Ad fam.* *Lib.* ix. *ep.* 22. *& Voss. Inst orat.* *Lib.* iv. *c.* 6. §. 14.

ference arifes from feveral caufes. For one word may only exprefs the thing in general, and fo convey but a confufed and imperfect idea; and another may be more proper and peculiar to that thing, and fo reprefent it more fully. Nay, even of thofe words, which are commonly efteemed fynonymous, or of an equivalent fignification, one either from its nature and origin, or from ufe, may have an immodeft idea affixed to it, which another has not. And from thence it happens in moft languages, that fome words, which at firft were modeft and innocent enough, have afterwards become obfcene and indecent. Befides, words may be rendered immodeft by conveying a more lively image of the thing to the fenfes, than others do. And this, as was faid before, is the property of fome metaphors.

L E C-

LECTURE XXVII.
Of a Metonymy.

THE moſt conſiderable *Trope* next to
a *Metaphor* is a *Metonymy*, whether
we conſider its force and elegancy, or the
frequent uſe of it both in ſpeaking and writing. Having therefore treated upon the
former in my laſt diſcourſe, I ſhall endeavour in this to give the beſt, and cleareſt account I can of the latter. And in doing
this I ſhall firſt explain the nature of a *Metonymy* in general, and then conſider the
ſeveral ſpecies contained under it.

Now a *Metonymy*, as defined by Quintilian, is, *the puting one word for another* [1].
But Voſſius deſcribes it more fully, when
he calls it: *A trope, which changes the names
of things, that are naturally united, but in
ſuch a manner, as that one is not of the eſ-
ſence of the other* [2]. That a *Metonymy* is
thus diſtinguiſhed from the other tropes, has
been ſufficiently ſhewn already in my two
laſt diſcourſes. When it is ſaid, *to put one
word for another*, or, *to change the names of
things*, the meaning is, that the word ſo
uſed changes its ſenſe, and denotes ſomething different from its proper ſignification.
Thus,

[1] *Inſt. orat.*
Lib. viii.
c. 6.

[2] *Inſt. orat.*
Lib. iv.
c. 7. §. 1.

Thus, when *Mars* is put for *war*, and *Ceres* for *corn*, they lofe their perfonal fenfe, and ftand for fuch effects, of which thofe deities were faid to be the caufe. So like-wife, when Virgil fais:

> *He drank the frothing bowl* [1].

the word *bowl* muſt neceffarily fignify the *liquor* in the bowl. And, when in another place defcribing the temple of Juno at Car-thage, in which the actions of the Trojan war were reprefented, and the images of the heroes, he makes Aeneas, upon difcove-ring that of Priam among the reft, cry out,

> *Lo here is Priam* [2],

it is plain the word *Priam* there muſt ſtand not for his perfon, but his *image* or *figure*. And this property of changing the fenfe of the word appears peculiar to a *Metonymy*. In treating upon a metaphor I obferved the miftake of thofe, who teach, that a word ufed metaphorically lofes its proper fignifi-cation; whereas it only changes its place, but not its fenfe; being applied to a thing, to which it does not naturally belong, by way of fimilitude. And as the not atten-ding to this has run fome perfons into very great abfurdities, in treating upon metapho-rical expreffions, and reafoning from them in the tropical fenfe; fo the like has hap-pened

[1] *Aeneid. Lib.* i. *c.* 739.

[2] *Ibid. v.* 440.

LECT.
XXVII. pened to others in fome inftances of a *Me-*
tonymy, where by mifapprehending their
true nature, they have reafoned from them
in the literal fenfe, as I fhall fhew prefently.
A *Metonymy* is not fo extenfive as a metaphor, nor altogether fo neceffary : becaufe
nothing is faid by a *Metonymy*, which cannot be expreffed in proper words ; whereas
metaphors are often ufed for want of proper
words to exprefs fome ideas. However,
Metonymies are very ufeful in language, for
they enrich a difcourfe with an agreable variety, and give both force and beauty to an
expreffion. And what I obferved with relation to a metaphor, is true alfo of this
trope ; that fome *Metonymies* even in common difcourfe are more frequently made ufe
of, than the proper words, in whofe room
they are put. So, *pale death, a blind way,*
and *a happy ftate*, are very common expreffions with us. And it is more ufual to fay,
This is fuch a perfon's hand, or, *I know his
hand*, than his writing, when we intend
this latter fenfe of the word.

I NOW procede to the divifion of *Meto-*
nymies, which are commonly diftinguifhed
into four kinds, from the different manner,
in which things are naturally, but externally
united to one another. Now things are
thus

thus united, or one thing depends upon another, either with refpect to its production, or in the manner of its exiftence, when produced. In the former way the effect depends upon its caufe, and in the latter the adjunct upon its fubject. And hence arife four forts of *Metonymies*, which receive their names from the *caufe* and *effect*, the *fubject* and the *adjunct*.

It is called a *Metonymy* of the *caufe*, when the external caufe is put for the effect. The external caufe is twofold, the agent and end, which are ufually called the efficient and final caufe. Of the former kind are fuch *Metonymies*, where the inventor or author is put for what was invented, or effected by him. Thus, as I faid before, *Ceres* is fometimes put for *corn*, the ufe of which fhe was faid firft to have introduced; and *Mars* for *war*, over which he was thought to prefide. And by this way of fpeaking, any artift or writer is put for his work. So Juvenal blaming the luxury, and profufenefs of the Romans, fais : *There are few tables without Mentor* [1], that is, which were not made by him, or after his manner. And our Saviour fais in the parable of the rich man, and Lazarus, *They have Mofes, and the prophets* [2], meaning the

[1] *Sat.* viii. *v.* 104.

[2] *Luke* xvi. 29.

books

books of Mofes, and the prophets. But under this fort of *Metonymy* is included not
only the agent, ftrictly fo called, but alfo
any means, or inftrument made ufe of in the
doing of a thing, when put for the thing
done.   Thus, *polite literature* is called *humanity*, becaufe it cultivates and improves
the human mind.   And in that expreffion
of Cicero : *Words move no body but him, who*
De Orat. *underftands the tongue* ¹ *:* the word *tongue,*
Lib. iii.
c. 59.   which is the inftrument of fpeech, is put
for *fpeech*, or *language*.   And in the like
fenfe *arms* are fometimes put for *war*, and
the *fword* for *flaughter*.   By the fame kind
of *Metonymy* likewife any affection, or quality is put for its effect.   As when it is faid,
the end of government is to maintain juftice,
that is, *fuch mutual offices among men, as are*
the effects of juftice. And fo likewife in that
of Cicero : *It is the bufinefs of magiftrates to*
² *Pro Mi-* *check the levity of the multitude* ² *:* by which
lon. c. 8. he means tumults occafioned by their levity. Moreover, as human affections are attributed to the deity in a metaphorical fenfe,
fo feveral parts of the human body are like-
³ *Ifaiah* l. wife afcribed to him by this kind of *Meto-*
2. liii. 1. *nymy.* Thus, his *hand* and his *arm* are ufed
⁴ *Pfalm* to exprefs his *power* ³; as his *ear* and *eye* his
xvii. 6.
xxxiii. 18 *care* and *providence* ⁴; thefe being the in-
ftruments

ſtruments of ſuch effects in mankind. *Me-*
tonymies of the final cauſe are ſuch, by
which the end in doing a thing is put for
the thing done. As when we ſay, *The
watch is ſet*, meaning the *watchmen*, who
are appointed for that purpoſe. And ſo
likewiſe that expreſſion, *to make an example*,
as it ſignifies to *puniſh*, in order to deter
others from the like crimes by ſuch an
example. As alſo that of Virgil,

 Phillis ſhould garlands crop [1],   [1] *Eclog.* x.
by which are meant *flowers* to make gar-   *v.* 41.
lands.

THE ſecond kind of *Metonymy* puts the
effect for the efficient cauſe, whether the
agent, or only the means and inſtrument.
So Virgil calls the two Scipios, *The deſtruc-*
tion of Lybia [2], becauſe they were the agents,   [2] *Aen.* vi.
who effected it. And Horace compliments   *v.* 844.
his patron Maecenas with the titles of being,
his guard and honor [3], that is, his guardian,   [3] *Carm.* i.
and the author of his honor. But when   [1, 2.]
Cicero tells the citizens of Rome, that *the*
death of Clodius was their ſafety [4], he means [4] *Pro Mi-*
the occaſion only of their ſafety. And elſe-   *lon. c.* 2.
where he calls that, *a dark hope, and blind*
expectation [5]; the effect of which was du- [5] *In Rull.*
bious and uncertain to thoſe, who enter-   ii. *c.* 25.
tained it. And in like manner the ſons of

     E e   the

LECT.
XXVII.

the prophets, when they were eating the pottage, which Eliſha had ordered to be ſet before them, cried out, *There is death in the*

pot ¹, that is, *ſome deadly thing*, as is preſently after explained. And thus ſweat, which is the effect of labor, is ſometimes put for labor. As in the threat denounced againſt Adam : *In the ſweat of thy face ſhalt*

² *Gen.* iii. 19.

thou eat bread ² *:* that is, by labor in cultivating the ground. And, in alluſion to this way of ſpeaking, Antony the orator tells Craſſus, *the improvement of the ſtile by conſtant exerciſe, as he preſcribed, was a thing*

³ Cic. *De orat. Lib.* i. c. 60.

of much ſweat ³. And, *virtue is ſaid to be gained by ſweat*, that is, continued care and exerciſe in ſubduing the paſſions, and bringing them to a proper regulation. But in theſe two expreſſions there is likewiſe a metaphor, the effect of bodily labor being applied to that of the mind. In all theſe inſtances the effect is put for the efficient cauſe.

THE third kind of *Metonymy* is, when the ſubject is put for the adjunct. By ſubject here in a large ſenſe of the word may be underſtood that, wherein ſome other thing is contained, or about which it is converſant, as likewiſe the poſſeſſor with reſpect to the thing he poſſeſſes, and the thing

ſig-

fignified, when put for the fign of it. Now
by the firft of thefe ways of fpeaking the
feat of any faculty, or affection, is ufed for
the faculty, or affection itfelf. So it is ufual
to fay, *a man of a clear head*, when we mean
a clear mind or underftanding; the feat of
the mind being in the head. And a perfon
is faid, *to have a warm heart*, becaufe the
heart has been thought the feat of the affections. In like manner the place, where
any actions are performed, is put for the
actions done in it. As when Cicero fais:
*Do not always think of the forum, the benches,
the roftra, and the fenate* [1]; meaning the
difcourfes, which were ufually made in thofe
places. So likewife the country, or place of
refidence, is put for the inhabitants, as in
that paffage of Cicero: *And to omit Greece,
which always claimed the preeminence for
eloquence, and Athens, the inventrefs of all
fciences, where the art of fpeaking was invented and perfected; in this city of ours,*
meaning Rome, *no ftudies have prevailed
more, than that of eloquence* [2]. Where the
words Greece and Athens ftand to denote
the inhabitants of thofe places. And hither may alfo be refered fuch expreffions,
in which the time is put for the perfons
living in it, as, *the degeneracy of the prefent*

*[1] De Orat.
Lib. i.
c. 8.*

[2] Ibid. c. 4.

E e 2 *age,*

age, the virtue of former times. In the fecond way above mentioned, the object is ufed
for the perfon, or thing imployed about it.
As when Cicero fais: *In time of battle the*
laws are filent [1]. Where by *laws* he intends
the *judges*, who pronounce fentence according to law. By the third of thefe ways,
in which the poffeffor is put for the thing
he poffeffes, we fay, *to devour, deftroy,* or
ruin a man, meaning not his *perfon*, but his
eftate. And mythologifts explain the fable
of Acteon by this trope, who is faid to have
been devoured by his dogs. For by dogs
they underftand flatterers and parafites, who
confumed his eftate, and brought him to
beggary. By the laft way before recited,
which puts the thing fignified for the fign,
ftatues and pictures are called by the names
of the perfons, which they reprefent. As in
that jeft of Cicero upon his brother Quintus, when, as Macrobius relates, *being in the*
province, which his brother had governed, and
feeing a large portrait of part of his body,
holding a fheild, tho Quintus was but a little
man, he faid: My half brother is biger than
my whole brother [2]. The popifh doctrine of
tranfubftantiation is founded upon an abufe
of this trope. For when our Saviour, fpeaking of the bread and wine at that time
before

[1] *Pro Mi-
lon. c. 4.*

[2] *Saturn.
Lib.* ii.
c. 3.

before him, fais : *This is my body, and this*
is my blood [1] *:* his plain meaning is, they
were the figns of his body and blood, the
thing fignified being put for the fign by this
fort of *Metonymy*. But the papifts take the
expreffion literally, which muft doubtlefs be
very abfurd; fince the words relate to the
time then prefent, while Chrift was yet living, and fpoke them; when it was impoffible for the bread and wine to be converted into his body and blood, it being
evident to all, who were prefent, that thofe
elements, and his body exifted feparately at
the fame time. But if the words are explained by this trope, the fenfe is plain and
eafy, and the way of fpeaking familiar to
all writers. Whereas they, who plead for
the literal fenfe, might with equal reafon
affert, that thofe expreffions above mentioned are to be taken literally, in which
feveral parts of the human body, as the
hand, the arm, the ear, and the eye, are
afcribed to the deity: or that, when our
Saviour in a metaphorical fenfe calls himfelf, *a vine*, and *a door* [2], thefe words
were defigned to be applied to him ftrictly and properly, and not by way of fimilitude only, as is the cafe in all metaphors.

THE

LECT.
XXVII.

THE fourth kind of *Metonymies* is that, wherein the adjunct is put for the subject, which is done in the same variety of ways as the former. It is therefore a *Metonymy* of the adjunct, when the thing contained is put for that, which contains it. As when Virgil sais, *They lie down upon purple* [1], that is, couches died with purple. And again, *They crown the wine* [2], meaning the bowl, which contained the wine; it being the custom of the antients to deck their bowls with garlands at their entertainments. By this trope likewise virtues and vices are put for the persons, in whom they are found. As in that beautiful passage of Cicero, where comparing the profligate army of Catiline with the forces of the state, he sais: *On this side modesty is ingaged, on that impudence; on this chastity, on that lewdness; on this integrity, on that deceit; on this piety, on that profaneness; on this constancy, on that fury; on this honor, on that baseness; on this moderation, on that unbridled passion: in a word, equity, temperance, fortitude, prudence, and all virtues ingage with injustice, luxury, cowardice, rashness, and all vices* [3]. And to this trope those expressions are to be refered, in which any thing is put for the object, about which it is conversant. As in that saying

of

[1] *Aen.* i. *v.* 704.

[2] *Ibid. v.* 724.

[3] *In Catil.* ii. *c.* 11.

of the wife man: *Hope defered makes the heart fick:* where hope is put for the thing hoped for. And thus Suetonius calls the emperor Titus, *the love and delight of mankind* [1], whofe mild, and obliging temper rendered him the object of thofe agreable affections to all perfons under his government. A third ufe of this trope is by puting a thing for the time, in which it was done. Thus we fay of a perfon, *He has ferved fo many campains,* meaning fo many fummers, that being the ufual time, in which armies are drawn out into the feild. Laftly, by this *Metonymy,* the fign is put for the thing it fignifies. As, *the fcepter* for *the regal dignity,* and *the fword* for *the authority of the magiftrate.*

THESE are the four kinds or fpecies, into which a *Metonymy* is ufually divided. But Voffius adds two others, namely of the *antecedent* and *confequent* [2], which bear fome analogy to the caufe and effect, as the one does at leaft give occafion to the other. Both of them are often called *Metalepfis;* but fince that name is likewife applied to another different trope, as will be fhewn afterwards; I would rather choofe with Voffius to bring thefe under a *Metonymy,* and confider them as two diftinct fpecies of it.

[1] *In Vit. init.*

[2] *Inft. orat. Lib.* iv. *c.* 10. §. 1.

LECT.
XXVII.

it. By the former, *to hear,* when spoken of a superior sometimes signifies to *grant,* or *comply with;* and of an inferior *to obey.* Thus the servant in Terence, sais: *shall I assist Pamphilus, or hearken to the old man* [1], that is, obey his orders, and forbear. By the latter, it is not unusual to say, *I subscribe,* or *set my hand to such a thing,* meaning, that we assent or agree to it, and as a consequence are ready to attest it under our hand. So when Cicero, speaking of the pirates, who had lately infested the seas, sais: *Shall I complain, that foreigners were taken in their passage hither, when the Roman legates have been redeemed* [2]; by which is intimated, that they were first taken, and afterwards purchased their redemption. And in that expression of Terence: *You will own that kindness well placed* [3]: the sense is, you will perceive or find it so, a consequence of which will be an acknowledgement of it.

As to any observations necessary in the choice of *Metonymies,* I think nothing need be added, to what has been said already, when I treated upon the use of tropes in general.

[1] *Andr. Act.* I. *Sc.* 3. *v.* 4.

[2] *Pro leg Manil. c.* 12.

[3] *Phorm. Act.* III *Sc.* 2. *v.* 9.

END *of the* FIRST VOLUME.